Interventions 2020

Interventions 2020

MICHEL HOUELLEBECQ

Translated by Andrew Brown

Polity

Originally published in French as *Interventions 2020*
© Michel Houellebecq and Flammarion, Paris, 2020

This English edition © Polity Press, 2022

Polity Press
65 Bridge Street
Cambridge CB2 1UR, UK

Polity Press
101 Station Landing
Suite 300
Medford, MA 02155, USA

ISBN-13: 978-1-5095-4995-5 (hardback)

A catalogue record for this book is available from the British Library.

Library of Congress Control Number: 2021945287

Typeset in 11 on 14pt Warnock Pro
by Cheshire Typesetting Ltd, Cuddington, Cheshire
Printed and bound in Great Britain by TJ Books Ltd, Padstow, Cornwall

The publisher has used its best endeavours to ensure that the URLs for external
websites referred to in this book are correct and active at the time of going to
press. However, the publisher has no responsibility for the websites and can
make no guarantee that a site will remain live or that the content is or will
remain appropriate.

Every effort has been made to trace all copyright holders, but if any have been
overlooked the publisher will be pleased to include any necessary credits in any
subsequent reprint or edition.

For further information on Polity, visit our website: politybooks.com

Contents

vi   Contents

1

Jacques Prévert is a jerk

Jacques Prévert is someone whose poems you learn at school. It turns out that he loved flowers, birds, the neighbourhoods of old Paris, etc. He felt that love blossomed in an atmosphere of freedom; more generally, he was *pretty much on the side of* freedom. He wore a cap and smoked Gauloises; he sometimes gets confused with Jean Gabin. Also, he was the one who wrote the screenplay for *Quai des brumes*, *Portes de la nuit*, etc. He also wrote the screenplay for *Les Enfants du paradis*, considered to be his masterpiece. All of these are so many good reasons for hating Jacques Prévert – especially if you read the scripts that Antonin Artaud was writing at the same time, which were never filmed. It's dismaying to note that this repulsive *poetic realism*, of which Prévert was the main architect, continues to wreak havoc – we think we're paying Leos Carax a compliment by identifying him with this style (just as people make out that Rohmer is undoubtedly a new Guitry, etc.). In fact, French cinema has never recovered from the advent of the talkies; one day these talkies will finally kill cinema. Too bad.[1]

After the war, around the same time as Jean-Paul Sartre, Jacques Prévert enjoyed enormous success; one can't help being struck by the optimism of that generation. These days, the most influential thinker is more likely to be Cioran.[2] At that time, people listened to Vian, Brassens . . .[3] Lovers smooched on public benches, there was a baby boom, and plenty of low-cost housing was built to accommodate all those people. Lots of optimism, faith in the future, and a certain amount of bullshit. Obviously, we've got a lot smarter since then.

With the intellectuals, Prévert was less fortunate. Yet his poems are full of those silly puns that are so entertaining in Boby Lapointe . . .[4] Still, it's true that the *chanson* is, as we say, a 'minor' genre, and even intellectuals need something to relax to. But when they focus on written texts, their real livelihood, they become harsh critics. And Prévert's 'textual work' remains embryonic: he writes with clarity and a real naturalness, sometimes even with emotion; he's not interested in writing as such, nor in the impossibility of writing; his main source of inspiration, it seems, is life. So on the whole he hasn't provided fodder for postgraduate theses. Today, however, he has entered the *Pléiade*, which constitutes a second death.[5] There his work lies, complete and frozen. This is an excellent opportunity to wonder why Jacques Prévert's poetry is so mediocre – so much so that one sometimes feels a sort of shame when reading it. The classic explanation (his writing 'lacks rigour') is quite wrong; through his puns, his light and limpid rhythms, Prévert actually expresses his conception of the world perfectly well. The form suits the content, which is the most that can be demanded of a form. Moreover, when a poet immerses himself so much in life, in the real life of his time, it would be an insult to judge him by purely stylistic criteria. If Jacques Prévert writes, it's because he has something to say; that's all to his credit. Unfortunately, what he has to say is boundlessly stupid; sometimes it makes you feel nauseous. There are pretty girls with no clothes on, and middle-class men who bleed like pigs when their throats are cut. The children are charmingly immoral, the thugs are alluring hunks, the pretty girls with no clothes on give their bodies to the thugs; the middle-class men are old, obese, impotent, and decorated with the Legion of Honour; their wives are frigid; the priests are disgusting old caterpillars who invented sin to stop us from living. It's all very familiar; one can be forgiven for thinking that Baudelaire does it better. Or even Karl Marx who, at least, doesn't miss his target when he writes that 'the bourgeoisie, wherever it has got the upper hand [. . .] has drowned the most heavenly ecstasies of religious fervour, of chivalrous enthusiasm, of philistine sentimentalism, in the icy water of egotistical calculation'.[6] Intelligence is of no help at all in writing good poems; it does however stop you writing bad ones. If Jacques Prévert is a bad poet, this is mainly because his vision of the world is commonplace, superficial and false. It was already false in his own time; today its inanity is so glaring that the entire work seems to be the expansion of one gigantic cliché. On the philosophical and political level, Jacques Prévert is above all a libertarian; in other words, basically, an idiot.

We've been splashing about in the 'icy water of egotistical calculation' since our earliest childhood. We can live with this situation, we can try to survive it; we can also just let ourselves sink. But what it's impossible to imagine is that freeing the powers of desire alone is likely to melt the ice. The story goes that it was Robespierre who insisted on adding the word 'fraternity' to the motto of the French Republic; we're now in a position to gauge the full irony of this anecdote. Prévert certainly saw himself as a supporter of fraternity; but Robespierre was not an opponent of virtue – far from it.

2

The Mirage by
Jean-Claude Guiguet

A cultivated middle-class family on the shores of Lake Geneva. Classical music, short sequences with a great deal of dialogue, cutaways to the lake; all of this might give one the impression of déjà vu. The fact that the girl is painting intensifies our worries. But no, this isn't the twenty-fifth Eric Rohmer clone. It's, oddly, much more than that.

When a film constantly juxtaposes the maddening and the magical, the magical rarely wins out; yet that's what happens here. The actors, somewhat hit-and-miss in their approach, have a hard time interpreting a script that seems overwritten and sometimes borders on the ridiculous. People will say they haven't found the right tone; this may not be entirely their fault. What's the right tone for a sentence such as 'The fine weather has come to join us'? Only the mother, Louise Marleau, is perfect from start to finish, and it's undoubtedly her magnificent love monologue (it's an amazing thing in films, the love monologue) that elicits our unreserved approval. We can soon forgive some of the dubious dialogues, some of the rather heavy-handed musical punctuations; in any case, none of this would get noticed in an ordinary film.

Starting with a theme of tragic simplicity (it's spring and

the weather is fine; a woman of about fifty aspires to experience one last carnal passion; but if nature is beautiful, it's also cruel), Jean-Claude Guiguet has taken the maximum risk: that of formal perfection. The film is as far removed from the TV advert effect as it is from sputtering realism and arbitrary experimentalism; here, the sole pursuit is that of pure beauty. The way it's cut into sequences, classic, refined, tenderly daring, corresponds exactly to the impeccable geometry of the framing. It's all precise, sober, and structured like the facets of a diamond: a rare work. It's also rare to see a film where the light so intelligently suits the emotional tone of the scenes. The lighting and decoration of the interior scenes are profoundly right, infinitely tactful; they remain in the background, like a discreet and dense orchestral accompaniment. It's only in the outdoor scenes, in the sunny meadows bordering the lake, that the light bursts out, playing a central role; and this too is perfectly in line with the film's purpose. There is a terrible carnal luminosity to the faces. Nature wears a shimmering mask, which, as we know, conceals a sordid swarming, but this mask can't be torn away (never, by the way, has the spirit of Thomas Mann been so profoundly captured). We can't expect anything good to come from the sun; but human beings can perhaps, to some extent, manage to love each other. I don't remember hearing a mother say 'I love you' to her daughter so convincingly; not in any film, ever.

With violence, with nostalgia, almost with pain, *Le Mirage* sets out to be a cultivated film, a *European* film; and oddly enough it succeeds, combining an authentically Germanic depth and sense of fracture with a profoundly French luminosity and classic clarity of exposition. Truly a rare film.

3

Approaches to distress

'I'm fighting ideas that I'm not even sure exist.'

Antoine Waechter

Contemporary architecture as a vector for speeding up movements

The general public, as everyone knows, doesn't like contemporary art. This trivial observation in fact covers two opposing attitudes. Ordinary passers-by who happen to walk through a place where contemporary pieces of painting or sculpture are being exhibited will stop in front of the works on display, if only to make fun of them. Their attitude will swing between ironic amusement and outright sneer; in any case, they will be sensitive to a certain dimension of *derision*; the very meaninglessness of what is presented to them will be a reassuring guarantee of harmlessness; they will certainly have *wasted their time*, but in a way that is basically not all that unpleasant.

Placed, this time, amid contemporary architecture, the same passers-by will feel much less like laughing. Under

favourable conditions (late at night, or against a background
of police sirens), a phenomenon clearly marked by *anxiety* will
be observed, and all their organic secretions will go into over-
drive. In each case, the functional unit comprising the organs
of vision and the locomotor limbs will experience a significant
intensification.

This is what happens when a coach full of tourists, thrown
off course by the web of exotic traffic signs, drops off its passen-
gers in the banking district of Segovia, or the business centre
of Barcelona. Immersed in their usual world of steel, glass and
signposts, visitors immediately rediscover the rapid stride, the
functional and oriented gaze that correspond to the environment offered to them. Progressing between pictograms and
written signs, they soon reach the cathedral district, the historic
heart of the city. Immediately their pace slows; the movement
of their eyes becomes somewhat random, almost erratic. A
certain dazed amazement can be read on their faces (their jaws
drop, a phenomenon typical of Americans). Obviously, they
feel they are in the presence of unusual, complex objects that
are difficult to decipher. Soon, however, messages appear on
the walls; thanks to the tourist office, historical and cultural
landmarks are set in context; our travellers can take out their
camcorders to record the memory of their travels in a *guided*
cultural tour.

Contemporary architecture is a *modest* architecture; it manifests its autonomous presence, its presence *as* architecture,
solely through discreet *winks* – generally these are advertising
micro-messages about the techniques behind its own fabrica-
tion (for example, it's customary to ensure very good visibility
for lift machinery, as well as for the firm responsible for its
design).

Contemporary architecture is a *functional* architecture;
indeed, any aesthetic questions concerning it have long
since been eradicated by the formula: 'What is functional is

necessarily beautiful.' This is a surprising bias, which the spectacle of nature constantly contradicts, as the latter incites us to see beauty as a way of *taking revenge on reason*. If the forms of nature appeal to the eye, this is often because they are useless, and do not meet any perceptible criterion of efficiency. They reproduce themselves in a rich, luxuriant way, apparently moved by an internal force that can be described as the pure desire to be, the simple desire to reproduce – a force that is not really understandable (just think of the burlesque and somewhat repulsive inventiveness of the animal world), a force that is nonetheless suffocatingly obvious. Admittedly, certain forms of inanimate nature (crystals, clouds, hydrographic networks) seem to obey a criterion of thermodynamic optimality; but these are precisely the most complex, the most ramified. They do not make one think of the functioning of a rational machine, but rather of the chaotic turmoil of a *process.*

Reaching its own optimum by creating places so functional that they become invisible, contemporary architecture is a *transparent* architecture. Since it has to allow for rapid movement of people and goods, it tends to reduce space to its purely geometric dimension. As it's meant to be crossed by an uninterrupted succession of textual, visual and iconic messages, it must ensure maximum readability for them (only a perfectly transparent place is likely to ensure a total conductivity of information). Subject to the harsh law of consensus, the only permanent messages this architecture can allow itself will be confined to objective information. Thus, the content of those huge signs that line motorway routes has been the subject of thorough preliminary studies. Numerous surveys have been carried out in order to avoid offending one or other category of users; social psychologists have been consulted, as well as road safety specialists; all of this just to end up with indications of the kind: 'Auxerre', or: 'The lakes'.

The Gare Montparnasse deploys a transparent and non-mysterious architecture, establishing a necessary and sufficient distance between video screens showing timetable information and electronic reservation terminals, organizing with adequate redundancy the signage of the departure and arrival platforms; this allows Western individuals of average or higher intelligence to achieve their goal of travel by minimizing friction, uncertainty, and wasted time. More generally, all contemporary architecture must be considered as an immense apparatus for the acceleration and rationalization of human movements; its ideal point, in this regard, would be the motorway interchange system that can be observed in the vicinity of Fontainebleau-Melun Sud.

This is also how the architectural ensemble known as 'La Défense'[1] can be read as a pure productivist arrangement, a device for increasing individual productivity. This paranoid vision may be locally accurate, but it fails to account for the uniformity of the architectural responses offered to cater for the diversity of social needs (hypermarkets, nightclubs, office buildings, cultural and sports centres). On the other hand, we will get a bit closer to the truth if we consider that we live not only in a market economy, but more generally in a *market society*, that is to say a space of civilization where all human relations, and similarly all human relationships with the world, are mediated through a simple numerical calculation involving attractiveness, novelty and value for money. In this logic, which covers erotic, romantic and professional relationships as well as purchasing behaviour as such, the point is to facilitate the establishment of many rapidly renewed relationships (between consumers and products, between employees and companies, between lovers), and thus to promote a consumerist fluidity based on an ethic of responsibility, transparency and free choice.

Building the shelves

Contemporary architecture implicitly adopts a simple program, which can be summed up as follows: *building the shelves
of the social hypermarket*. It achieves this on the one hand
by showing total fidelity to the aesthetics of the pigeonhole,
and on the other hand by favouring the use of materials that
show low granular resistance (metal, glass, plastics). The use of
reflective or transparent surfaces will also make it possible to
increase the number of displays. In all cases, the aim is to create
polymorphic, uniform, modular spaces. The same process, incidentally, is also at work in interior decoration: furnishing an
apartment these days is essentially a matter of knocking down
walls so to replace them with movable partitions – which will
actually hardly be moved at all, as there is no reason to move
them; but the main thing is that the possibility of movement
exists, that an additional degree of freedom has been created
– and the fixed decorations can be eliminated: the walls will
be white, the furniture translucent. Contemporary architecture is all about creating neutral spaces where the information
and advertising messages generated by social functioning can
be freely deployed, messages that in fact *constitute* that very
functioning. After all, what is produced by the employees and
executives gathered at La Défense? Strictly speaking, nothing;
indeed, the process of material production has become completely opaque to them. Digital information about objects in
the world is transmitted to them. This information is the raw
material for statistics and calculations; models are developed,
decision graphs are produced; at the end of the chain, decisions
are made, new information is reinjected into the social body.
Thus, the flesh of the world is replaced by its digitized image;
the being of things is supplanted by the graph of its variations.
Versatile, neutral and modular, modern places are adapted to
the infinite number of messages they are to transmit. They
cannot allow themselves to deliver an autonomous meaning,

to evoke a particular atmosphere; they can thus have neither beauty, nor poetry, nor more generally any character of their own. Stripped of all individual and permanent character, and on this condition, they will be ready to welcome the indefinite pulsation of the transient.

Mobile, open to transformation, always available, modern employees are undergoing a similar process of depersonalization. The techniques that teach adaptability, popularized by 'New Age' workshops, aim to create indefinitely mutable individuals, free from any intellectual or emotional rigidity. Freed from the shackles of belonging, loyalty, and rigid codes of behaviour, the modern individual is thus ready to take his place in a system of generalized transactions within which he or she can univocally and unambiguously be given an *exchange value*.

Simplifying the calculations

The gradual digitization of microsociological functioning, already well advanced in the United States, had lagged significantly behind in Western Europe, as the novels of Marcel Proust testify. It took several decades to completely filter out the symbolic meanings added onto the different professions, whether these meanings were laudatory (church, education) or deprecatory (advertising, prostitution). At the end of this decanting, it became possible to establish a precise hierarchy between different social statuses on the basis of two simple numerical criteria: annual income and number of hours worked.

In people's love lives, too, the parameters of sexual exchange had long been dependent on a lyrical, impressionistic, unreliable system of description. Once again, the first serious attempt to define standards came from the United States of America. Based on simple and objectively verifiable criteria (age – height – weight – hip-waist-chest sizes for women; age – height – weight – size of the erect penis for men), it was first popularized by the porn industry, soon followed by women's magazines. While the simplified economic hierarchy was sporadically the object of protest over a long period (with movements in favour of 'social justice'), it should be noted that the erotic hierarchy, perceived as more natural, was quickly internalized and immediately met with a broad consensus.

Now able to define themselves by a brief collection of numerical parameters, freed from the thoughts of Being that had long hampered the fluidity of their mental movements, Western human beings – at least the youngest – were thus able to adapt to the technological changes affecting their societies, changes that in turn led to extensive economic, psychological and social transformations.

A brief history of information

Towards the end of the Second World War, the simulation of medium and long-range missile trajectories, and the modelling of fissile reactions inside the atomic nucleus, created a need for more powerful algorithmic and numerical computations. Thanks in part to the theoretical work of John von Neumann, the first computers were born.

At that time, office work was characterized by a standardization and rationalization that were far less advanced than they were in industrial production. The application of the first computers to management tasks immediately resulted in the disappearance of all freedom and flexibility in the implementation of working procedures – in short, in a brutal proletarianization of the class of employees.

In the same years, with a comic belatedness, European literature found itself confronted with a new tool: the *typewriter*. Indefinite and varied work on the manuscript (with its additions, references and footnotes) disappeared in favour of a more linear and flatter writing; there was a de facto alignment with the standards of American detective novels and journalism (hence the appearance of the myth of the Underwood typewriter – Hemingway's success).[2] This degradation of the image of literature led many young people with a 'creative' temperament to move towards the more rewarding paths of cinema and song (ultimately dead ends; indeed, the American entertainment industry was soon to begin the process of destroying local entertainment industries – a process that is now coming to an end).

The sudden appearance of the microcomputer in the early 1980s may appear to be some sort of historical accident; it did not correspond to any economic necessity, and is in fact inexplicable unless we factor in such elements as advances in the regulation of low currents and the fine etching of silicon. Office workers and middle managers unexpectedly found themselves in possession of a powerful, easy-to-use tool that allowed them to regain control – de facto, if not de jure – over the core elements of their work. A silent and largely unrecognized struggle lasting several years took place between IT departments and 'basic' users, sometimes supported by teams of passionate micro-IT specialists. What is most surprising is that gradually, as they became aware of the high costs and low efficiency of heavy computing, while mass production allowed the emergence of reliable and cheap office automation hardware and software, general management switched to microcomputers.

For the writer, the microcomputer was an unexpected liberation: it was not really a return to the flexibility and user-friendliness of the manuscript, but it became possible, all the same, to engage in serious work on a text. During the same years, various indicators suggested that literature might regain some of its former prestige – albeit less on its own merits than through the self-effacement of rival activities. Rock music and cinema, subjected to the formidable levelling power of television, gradually lost their magic. The previous distinctions between films, music videos, news, advertising, human testimonies and reporting tended to fade in favour of the notion of a generalized spectacle.

The appearance of optical fibres and the industrial agreement on the TCP/IP protocol at the beginning of the 1990s made possible the emergence of networks within and then between companies. The microcomputer, now reduced yet again to being a simple workstation within reliable client-server systems, lost all its autonomous processing capacity. There was in fact a renormalization of procedures within more mobile, more transversal and more efficient information processing systems.

Microcomputers, though ubiquitous in business, had failed in the domestic market for reasons that have since been clearly analysed (they were still expensive, had little real use, and were difficult to work on when lying down). The late 1990s saw the emergence of the first passive Internet access terminals; in themselves they were devoid of intelligence or memory, so that unit production costs were very low, and they were designed to allow access to the gigantic databases built up by the American entertainment industry. Finally equipped with an at least officially secure electronic payment system, they were attractive and light, and soon established themselves as a standard, replacing both the mobile phone, Minitel and the remote control of conventional television sets.

Unexpectedly, the book was to constitute a perennial pole of resistance. Attempts were made to store works on an Internet server; their success remained restricted, limited to encyclopaedias and reference works. After a few years, the industry was forced to agree: the book – more practical, more attractive and more manageable – was still popular with the public. However, any book, once purchased, became a formidable instrument of disconnection. In the intimate chemistry of the brain, literature had often in the past been able to take precedence over the real universe; literature had nothing to fear from virtual universes. This was the beginning of a paradoxical period, which still lasts today, where the globalization of entertainment and exchange – in which articulate language was of little importance – went hand in hand with a strengthening of vernacular languages and local cultures.

The onset of weariness

Politically, opposition to globalist economic liberalism had actually started long before; it became apparent in France in 1992, with the campaign for the 'No' vote to the Maastricht referendum. This campaign drew its strength less from reference to a national identity or to republican patriotism – both of which disappeared in the slaughter of Verdun in 1916–1917 – than from a genuine widespread weariness, from a feeling of outright rejection. Like all historicisms before it, liberalism threw its weight around by presenting itself as an inescapable historical change. Like all historicisms before it, liberalism posed itself as the assumption and transcendence of *simple ethical sentiment* in the name of a long-term vision of the *historical future of humanity*. Like all historicisms before it, liberalism promised effort and suffering for the present, relegating the arrival of the general good to a generation or two away. This kind of argument had already caused enough damage, throughout the twentieth century.

The perversion of the concept of progress regularly wrought by various forms of historicism unfortunately favoured the emergence of *comical philosophies*, typical of times of disarray. Often inspired by Heraclitus or Nietzsche, well suited to middle and high incomes, with a sometimes amusing aesthetic, they seemed to find their confirmation in the proliferation, among the less privileged layers of the population, of many unpredictable and violent assertions of identity. Certain advances in the

mathematical theory of turbulence led, more and more frequently, to human history being depicted as a chaotic system
in which futurologists and media thinkers strove to detect
one or more 'strange attractors'. Though it was devoid of any
methodological basis, this analogy was to gain ground among
educated and semi-educated strata, thus durably preventing
the constitution of a new ontology.

The world as supermarket and derision

Arthur Schopenhauer did not believe in history. So he died
convinced that the revelation he brought, in which the world
existed on the one hand as *will* (as desire, as vital impetus), and
on the other hand as *representation* (in itself neutral, innocent,
purely objective and, as such, susceptible to aesthetic recon-
struction), would survive the passing of successive generations.
We can now see that he was partly wrong. The concepts he put
in place can still be seen in the fabric of our lives; but they have
undergone such metamorphoses that one wonders how much
validity remains in them.

The word 'will' seems to indicate a long-term tension, a con-
tinuous effort, conscious or not, but coherent, striving towards
a goal. Of course, birds still build nests, male deer still fight for
possession of the females; and in the sense of Schopenhauer
we can indeed say that it's the same deer that has been fighting, and the same larva that has been burrowing, ever since
the painful day of their first appearance on Earth. It's quite
different for men. The logic of the supermarket necessarily
induces a dispersion of desires; the shopper in the supermarket cannot organically be the person of a single will, a single
desire. Hence there is a certain depression of will in contemporary human beings: not that individuals desire less – on the
contrary, they desire more and more; but their desires have
become somewhat garish and screeching: without being pure

simulacra, they are to a large extent the product of external determinations – stemming from *advertising* in the broad sense. Nothing in them evokes the organic, total force, turned obstinately towards its accomplishment, which the word 'will' suggests. Hence a certain lack of personality, noticeable in everyone.

Deeply infected by meaning, the representation has lost all innocence. We can designate as *innocent* any representation that simply presents itself as such, which simply claims to be the image of an external world (real or imaginary, but external); in other words, one that does not include its own critical commentary within itself. The massive introduction into representations of *references*, derision, the '*meta*', and humour quickly undermined artistic and philosophical activity, turning it into generalized rhetoric. All art, like all science, is a means of communication between human beings. It's obvious that the effectiveness and intensity of communication decrease and tend to cancel each other out once a certain doubt settles on the veracity of what is said, on the sincerity of what is expressed (can anyone imagine, for example, an ironic or '*meta*' science?) The gradual crumbling of creativity in the arts is thus just another face of the very contemporary fact that *conversation* is now impossible. In everyday conversation, it's exactly as if the direct expression of a feeling, an emotion, or an idea had become impossible because it's too vulgar. Everything has to pass through the distorting filter of *humour*, a humour that of course ends up being empty and turning into tragic silence. Such is both the story of the all-too-familiar idea of 'incommunicability' (it should be noted that the repeated exploitation of this theme has in no way prevented incommunicability from spreading in practice, and that it remains more than ever topical, even if we have become a little weary of talking about it), and the tragic history of painting in the twentieth century. The course of painting thus clearly represents, admittedly more by an analogous atmosphere than by any direct approach, the course of human communication in the contemporary era. In both cases, we slip into an unhealthy, fake, profoundly derisive atmosphere – so derisive that it ends up being tragic. So average passers-by walking through an art gallery must not pause too long if they wish to maintain their attitude of ironic detachment. If they do so, after a few minutes they will be overcome, in spite of themselves, by a certain confusion; at the very least, they will feel numbness and discomfort; their capacity for humour will slow down to a worrying degree.

(The tragic occurs exactly at this moment when the derisive no longer manages to be perceived as 'fun'; this is a kind of brutal psychological inversion, which expresses the individual's irreducible desire for eternity. Advertising avoids this phenomenon, which flies in the face of its own objectives, only by an incessant renewal of its simulacra; but painting retains its vocation to create permanent objects endowed with a specific character; it's this nostalgia for authentic being that gives it its painful halo, and that willy-nilly make it a faithful reflection of the spiritual situation of Western humanity.)

In contrast, we can note the relatively good health of literature during the same period. This is very easy to explain. Literature is, profoundly, a conceptual art; it's even, strictly speaking, the only such art. Words are concepts; clichés are concepts. Nothing can be affirmed, denied, relativized, mocked without the help of concepts and words. Hence the astonishing robustness of literary activity, which can reject itself, destroy itself, declare itself impossible without ceasing to be itself – which resists every *mise en abyme*, every deconstruction, every accumulation of meta-levels, however subtle they may be, and which simply gets up, shakes itself down and gets back on its feet, like a dog coming out of a pond.

Unlike music, unlike painting, and also unlike cinema, literature can thus absorb and digest limitless amounts of derision and humour. The dangers that threaten it today have nothing to do with those that have threatened and sometimes destroyed the other arts; they are much more closely related to the acceleration of perceptions and sensations that characterize the logic of the hypermarket. A book can only be appreciated *slowly*; it involves reflection (not mainly in the sense of intellectual effort, but in that of *looking back*); there is no reading without pausing, without reverse movement, without re-reading. This is impossible and even absurd in a world where everything evolves, everything fluctuates, and nothing has permanent validity; neither rules, nor things, nor human beings. With all its strength (which was great), literature opposes the notion of permanent topicality, of the perpetual present. Books call for readers; but these readers must have an individual and stable existence: they cannot be pure consumers, pure phantoms; they must also be, in some way, *subjects.*

Undermined by the cowardly obsession with 'political correctness', dumbfounded by a flood of pseudo-information that gives them the illusion of a permanent modification in the categories of existence (we can *no longer think* what was thought ten, a hundred or a thousand years ago), contemporary Westerners no longer manage to be readers; they no longer manage to satisfy the humble demand of a book laid out in front of them: the demand that they simply be human beings, thinking and feeling for themselves.

Even more, they cannot play this role in front of another being. And yet they ought to be able to do so: for this dissolution of being is a tragic dissolution; and we all continue, moved by a painful nostalgia, to ask the other for what we ourselves can no longer be; to seek, like a blinded phantom, this weight of being that we no longer find within ourselves. This resistance, this permanence; this depth. Of course, everyone fails, and the loneliness is excruciating.

The death of God in the West was the prelude to a formidable metaphysical soap opera, which continues to this day. Any historian of mentalities would be able to reconstruct the details of the stages; let's just say that Christianity succeeded in this *masterstroke* of combining a fierce belief in the individual – compared to the epistles of Saint Paul, the whole of ancient culture seems to us today curiously civilized and monotone – with the promise of eternal participation in the Absolute Being. After the dream had faded, various attempts were made to promise individual humans a minimum of being – to reconcile the dream of being that they carried inside them with the haunting omnipresence of becoming. All of these attempts so far have failed, and unhappiness has continued to spread.

Advertising is the latest of these attempts. Although it aims to arouse desire, to provoke it and to *be* it, its methods are basically quite close to those that characterized the old morality. It sets up a harsh and terrifying Superego, much more ruthless than any imperative that has ever existed, one that sticks to the individual's skin and keeps repeating: 'You must desire. You must be desirable. You must participate in competition, in struggle, in the life of the world. If you stop, you no longer exist. If you fall behind, you're dead.' Denying any notion of eternity, defining itself as a process of permanent renewal, advertising aims to vaporize human subjects, to transform them into obedient phantoms of becoming. And this skin-deep, superficial participation in the life of the world is supposed to take the place of the desire for being.

Advertising fails, depression spreads, distress increases; however, advertising continues to build the infrastructures for the reception of its messages. It continues to perfect ways of getting around for people who have nowhere to go because they are nowhere at home; to develop means of communication for people who have nothing more to say; to facilitate the possibilities of interaction between people who no longer want to enter into a relationship with anyone.

The poetry of arrested movement

In May 1968, I was ten years old. I played marbles, I read *Pif le Chien*;[3] life was good. Of the 'events of '68' I have retained only one memory, albeit a quite vivid one. My cousin Jean-Pierre was then in his first year of high school in Le Raincy.[4] High school then appeared to me (my later experience of it was to confirm this first intuition, while adding a painful sexual dimension) as a large and frightening place where older boys knuckled down to study difficult subjects in order to secure their professional futures. One Friday afternoon, I don't know why, I went with my aunt to wait for my cousin after class. That same day, the high school in Le Raincy went on an indefinite strike. The schoolyard, which I expected to be filled with hundreds of teenagers dashing about, was deserted. A few teachers were standing around aimlessly between the handball posts. I remember, while my aunt was trying to gather some scraps of information, walking for long minutes across this yard. There was total peace, absolute silence. It was a wonderful moment.

In December 1986, I was at Avignon railway station, and the weather was mild. Following various sentimental complications too tedious to relate, I absolutely *had* – at least so I thought – to get the express train back to Paris. I was unaware that a strike movement had just started across the entire French railway network. Thus, the operational succession of sexual relations, adventure and weariness was suddenly shattered. I spent two hours, sitting on a bench, facing the deserted railway landscape. Express rail coaches stood immobile on the sidings. You'd have thought they'd been there for years, and had never even gone anywhere. They were just there, motionless. Information was passed in hushed tones from one traveller to the next; the mood was one of resignation, of uncertainty. It could have been war, or the end of the Western world.

Several more direct witnesses to the 'events of '68' later told me that it was a wonderful time, when people talked to each other in the streets, and anything seemed possible; I'm happy to believe them. Others simply point out that the trains stopped running, that there was a petrol shortage; I have no difficulty agreeing. In all these eye-witness accounts I detect a common feature: magically, for a few days, a gigantic and oppressive machine stopped spinning. There was a hesitation, an uncertainty; a suspension occurred, a certain calm spread across the country. Of course, later on, the social machine started spinning again, even faster, even more ruthless than before (and May '68 only served to break the few moral rules that still hampered the voracity of that machine's operation). Still, there was a moment of pause, hesitation; a moment of metaphysical uncertainty.

It's undoubtedly for the same reasons that, once the first moment of annoyance is overcome, the public's reaction to a sudden shutdown of the information transmission networks is far from being absolutely negative. We can observe the phenomenon each time a computer reservation system breaks down (this is quite common): once the inconvenience has been admitted, and especially as soon as the employees decide to use their phones, what manifests itself among users is actually a secret joy; it's as if fate were giving them an opportunity to take a sly revenge on technology. In the same way, if you want to realize what the public thinks, deep down, about the architecture in which it is made to live, you just have to observe its reactions when the decision is taken to blow up one of the residential low-rise blocks built in the suburbs in the sixties: it's a moment of very pure and very violent joy, analogous to the intoxicating feeling of unexpectedly being set free. The spirit that inhabits these places is evil, inhuman, hostile; it's that of an exhausting, cruel, constantly accelerating piece of machinery; basically, everyone feels this, and desires the machine's destruction.

Literature can cope with everything, it can accommodate everything, it rummages through the garbage, it licks the wounds of misfortune. A paradoxical poetry, of anguish and oppression, has thus arisen amid the hypermarkets and office buildings. This poetry isn't cheerful; it can't be. Modern poetry is no more meant to build a hypothetical 'house of Being' than modern architecture is intended to build habitable places; this would be a very different task from that of increasing the number of infrastructures for the circulation and processing of information. As a residual product of impermanence, information is as different from meaning as plasma is from crystal; a society that has reached a plateau of overheating doesn't necessarily implode, but it does turn out to be incapable of producing meaning, as all of its energy is monopolized by the description in terms of information of its random variations. We can all, however, produce in ourselves a kind of *cold revolution*, by stepping for a moment outside the flow of information and advertising. It's very easy to do so; indeed, it's never been as easy as it is today to adopt an *aesthetic position* in relation to the world: you just need to step aside. And this step itself, in the last instance, is unnecessary. You just need to take some time out; turn off the radio, unplug the television; stop buying stuff, stop wanting to buy stuff. You just need to stop participating, to stop knowing; to temporarily suspend all mental activity. You literally just need to stay still for a few seconds.

4

Staring into the distance: in praise of silent cinema

Human beings speak; sometimes they don't speak. When they are threatened, they contract, their gaze darts around in search of something; in despair, they withdraw, curl up into a centre of anguish. When they are happy, their breathing slows down; they exist at a more spacious rhythm. In the history of the world there have been two arts (painting, sculpture) that have attempted to synthesize human experience by means of frozen representations – of arrested movements. They have sometimes chosen to arrest the movement at its most gentle point of equilibrium (at its point of eternity): all those Virgins with Child. They have sometimes chosen to freeze the action at its point of greatest tension, its most intense expressiveness – as in the Baroque, of course; but so many of Caspar David Friedrich's paintings also evoke a frozen explosion. They have developed over several millennia; they have also sometimes been able to produce works that are *finished*, in the sense of their most secret ambition: that of stopping time.

In the history of the world there has been one art whose object was the study of movement. This art was able to develop over a period of about thirty years. Between 1925 and 1930 it produced a few shots, in a few films (I am thinking especially of Murnau, Eisenstein, Dreyer) which justified its existence as art; then it was gone, apparently forever.

Jackdaws emit signs of alert and mutual recognition; up to sixty of these signs have been listed. Jackdaws remain an exception: taken as a whole, the world operates in terrible silence; it expresses its essence through form and movement. The wind blows through the grass (Eisenstein); a tear trickles down a face (Dreyer). Silent cinema saw an immense space open before it: it was not just an investigation of human feelings; not just a survey of the movements of the world; its deepest ambition was to constitute an inquiry into the conditions of perception. The distinction between figure and ground constitutes the basis of our representations; but also, more mysteriously, between figure and movement, between form and its process of generation, our mind seeks its way in the world – hence this almost hypnotic sensation that overwhelms us when we are faced by a fixed form generated by a perpetual movement, like the stationary ripples on the surface of a pond.

What remained of it after 1930? Some traces, especially in the works of filmmakers who had started to work in the era of the silent film (the death of Kurosawa will be more than the death of a single man); a few moments in experimental films, scientific documentaries, even serial productions (*Australia*, released a few years ago, is one example). These moments are easy to recognize: all speech is impossible; music itself becomes a bit kitschy, a bit heavy, a bit vulgar. We become pure perception; the world appears, in its immanence. We are very happy, *oddly* happy. Falling in love can also have this kind of effect.

5

Interview with
Jean-Yves Jouannais and
Christophe Duchâtelet

J-YJ and CD: In what way do the several works of which you are the author, from the essay on Lovecraft to your latest novel *Whatever*, via *Rester vivant* [*Staying alive*] and the collection of poems *La Poursuite du bonheur* [*The Pursuit of Happiness*] constitute an oeuvre?[1] What is the unity or the main obsession that guides it?

MH: Above all, I think, the intuition that the universe is based on separation, suffering and evil; the decision to describe this state of affairs, and perhaps to move beyond it. The question of the means – literary or not – is second. The initial act is the radical rejection of the world as it is; it's also a loyalty to the notions of good and evil, the desire to dig into these notions, to map out their realm, including within myself. Then, literature must follow. The style can be varied; it's a question of internal rhythm, of my personal state. I'm not too worried about issues of consistency; it seems to me that consistency will come of its own accord.

J-YJ and CD: *Whatever* is your first novel. What motivated this choice, after a collection of poems?

MH: I wish there weren't any difference between them. A book of poems should be readable straight from start to finish. Likewise, you should be able to open a novel at any page and read it regardless of context. Context doesn't exist. It's right to be wary of the novel; you mustn't get caught up in the story; nor by the tone nor by the style. Likewise, in daily life, you should avoid being trapped by your own story – or, more insidiously, by the personality you imagine to be yours. You need to conquer a certain lyric freedom: an ideal novel ought to be able to include passages that are versified, or sung.

J-YJ and CD: It could also include scientific diagrams.

MH: Yes that would be perfect. You should be able to put everything in it. Novalis, and the German romantics in general, aimed to achieve total knowledge. It was a mistake to give up on this ambition. We wriggle about like swatted flies; and yet we have a vocation for total knowledge.

J-YJ and CD: Obviously, as it happens, all of your writing is filled with a terrible pessimism. Could you give two or three reasons that you think may help stave off suicide?

MH: Kant clearly condemned suicide in 1785 in his *Groundwork of the Metaphysics of Morals*. Let me quote him: 'To annihilate the subject of morality in one's own person is to drive out morality from the world, insofar as that world depends on oneself.'[2] The argument seems naive and almost pathetic in its innocence, as often with Kant; I believe, however, that it's the *only* argument. It's only a sense of duty that can really keep us alive. Concretely, if you wish to endow yourself with a practical duty, you must make sure that the happiness of another being depends on your existence; you can for example try to raise a young child, or failing that, buy a poodle.

J-YJ and CD: Can you tell us about the sociological theory according to which the fight for social success specific to capitalism comes with a more treacherous and brutal struggle, this time sexual in nature?

MH: It's very simple. Animal and human societies set up different systems of hierarchical differentiation, which can be based on birth (the aristocratic system), wealth, beauty, physical strength, intelligence, talent, and so on. Actually, all these systems seem to me to be almost equally contemptible; I reject them; the only superiority I recognize is kindness. Currently, we move about in a two-dimensional system: erotic attractiveness and money. The rest, people's happiness and unhappiness, flows from these. In my view, this is by no means a theory; we do live in a simple society, which these few sentences describe completely.

J-YJ and CD: One of the most violent scenes in the novel is set in a nightclub on the Vendée coast. There are abortive scenes of seduction, flabby bellies that cause resentment and bitterness, purely sexual encounters. However, this place appears in your texts as the equivalent of the supermarket. Are people consumers in both places in the same way?

MH: No. A parallel could be drawn between special offers on chicken on the one hand, and miniskirts on the other; but the analogy ends there – with the enhancement of the supply. The supermarket is a true modern paradise; struggle ends at its threshold. The poor, for example, don't go inside. People have made their money elsewhere; now they're going to spend it, in the presence of an innovative and varied supply, often reliable in terms of taste and well documented from a nutritional point of view. Nightclubs present a very different picture. Many frustrated people continue – against all hope – to frequent them. They thus have the opportunity to verify, minute after minute, their own humiliation; here, we are much closer to hell. That being said, there are sex supermarkets, which produce a fairly comprehensive catalogue of porn on offer; but they lack the essential. For most people, the goal of the sexual quest is not pleasure, but narcissistic gratification, the homage paid by desirable partners to one's own erotic excellence. That's why AIDS hasn't brought about much of a change; condoms diminish the pleasure, but the desired goal is not, unlike in the case of food products, pleasure: it's the narcissistic intoxication of conquest. Not only do consumers of porn not experience this intoxication, they often feel the opposite. Finally, we can add, for the sake of completeness, that some people who embody deviant values continue to see a connection between sexuality and love.

J-YJ and CD: Can you tell us about that computer engineer, the one you call 'the network man'? What does this type of character refer to in our contemporary reality?

MH: We must realize that the manufactured objects of the world – reinforced concrete, electric lights, metro trains, handkerchiefs – are currently designed and manufactured by a small class of engineers and technicians, capable of imagining, then deploying the appropriate equipment; they alone are really productive. They represent maybe five per cent of the workforce – and that percentage is steadily declining. Other company staff – salespeople, advertisers, office workers, administrative executives, designers – have a much less obvious social utility; they could disappear without really affecting the production process. Their apparent role is to produce and manipulate different classes of information, that is to say different copies of a reality that escapes their understanding. It's in this context that we can situate the current explosion of networks of information transmission. A handful of technicians – at most five thousand people in France – are in charge of defining the protocols and producing the equipment that will allow, in the coming decades, the instantaneous worldwide transport of any category of information – text, sound, image, possibly tactile and electrochemical stimuli. Among them, some are creating a positive discourse on their own practice, according to which the human being, conceived as a centre for producing and transforming information, will find his or her full dimension only through interconnection with a maximum of similar centres. Most, however, do not produce any discourse; they just do their job. They thus fully realize the ideal of the technician, which has guided the historical movement of Western societies since the end of the Middle Ages, and which can be summed up in one sentence: 'If it's technically doable, it will be technically done.'

J-YJ and CD: Your story can be given an initial psychological reading, but it's its sociological character that creates the most lasting impression. Could this be a work of less literary than scientific ambition?

MH: Maybe, but that might be going too far. As a teenager, I was indeed fascinated by science – in particular by new concepts developed in quantum mechanics; but I haven't really addressed these questions in my writing yet; the real conditions for surviving in the world have undoubtedly occupied me too much. I am still a little surprised when I am told that I create successful psychological portraits of individuals, of characters: this may be true, but on the other hand I often have the impression that the individuals are almost identical, that what they call their self doesn't really exist, and that it would in a sense be easier to define a historical movement. Perhaps we here have the beginnings of a complementarity à la Niels Bohr: wave and particle, position and velocity, individual and history. On a more literary level, I strongly feel the need for two complementary approaches: the affective and the clinical.

On the one hand, dissection, cold analysis, humour; on the other, emotional and lyrical participation, where the lyricism is immediate.

J-YJ and CD: Despite the choice of the novel as a genre, you seem to think naturally in terms of poetry.

MH: Poetry is the most natural way to translate the pure intuition of an instant. There really is a core of pure intuition, which can be directly translated into pictures, or words. As long as we remain in poetry, we also remain in truth. Then the problems begin: when it comes to organizing these fragments, establishing a continuity that is both meaningful and musical. There, the experience of montage probably helped me a lot.

J-YJ and CD: Yes – before you started writing, you made some short films. What were your influences? And what's the connection between these images and your literature?

MH: I really liked Murnau and Dreyer; I also liked what has been called German expressionism – although the major pictorial influence on these films is arguably romanticism, more than expressionism. There's a study of fascinated stillness, which I tried to transcribe into pictures, then into words. There's also something else, deep inside me, a kind of oceanic feeling. I failed to transcribe it into films; I didn't even really get a chance to try. In words I may have succeeded sometimes, in a few poems. But one day or another, I'll surely have to come back to pictures.

J-YJ and CD: For example, would it be possible to adapt your novel for the cinema?

MH: Yes, absolutely. The scenario is basically quite similar to *Taxi Driver*; but the whole visual side would need changing.

Quite different from New York: the setting of the film would mainly consist of glass, steel, reflective surfaces. Landscaped offices, screens; the world of a new city, crossed by efficient and successful traffic. At the same time, the sexuality in this book is a succession of failures. Above all, any erotic magnification should be avoided – it's the exhaustion, masturbation, and vomiting that should be filmed. But all as part of a transparent, colourful and cheerful world. Diagrams and graphical representations could be introduced, too – the rate of sex hormones in the blood, salary in thousands of francs . . . We mustn't hesitate to be theoretical; we must attack on all fronts. The over-injection of theory produces a strange dynamism.

J-YJ and CD: You often describe your pessimism as just a passing stage. What might come next?

MH: I'd like to escape the obsessive presence of the modern world; move to a *Mary Poppins*-type world, where everything's fine. I don't know if I will. As for the general development of things, it's also difficult to comment. Given the current socio-economic system, especially taking into account our philosophical presuppositions, humans are clearly rushing towards imminent disaster, under atrocious conditions; we're there already. The logical consequences of individualism are murder and unhappiness. The enthusiasm that's driving us to this destruction is remarkable; really very curious. It's, for example, astonishing to see the cheerful shrug with which people have jettisoned psychoanalysis – which admittedly deserved it – and replaced it with a reductionist reading of the human being, based on hormones and neurotransmitters. The gradual dissolution over the centuries of social and family structures, the growing tendency of individuals to perceive themselves as isolated particles, subject to the law of shocks, as provisional aggregates of smaller particles . . . all this, of course, makes any political solution inapplicable. So it's legitimate to begin by clearing away the sources of hollow optimism. Returning to a more philosophical analysis of things, we realize that the situation is even stranger than we thought. We're moving towards disaster, guided by a false image of the world; and no one realizes. Even neurochemists don't seem to realize that their discipline is advancing across a minefield. Sooner or later they'll tackle the molecular bases of consciousness; then they'll collide head-on with the ways of thinking resulting from quantum physics. We'll be forced to redefine the conditions of knowledge, of the very notion of reality; we should start to become aware of it on an emotional level, right now. In any case, as long as we're stuck in a mechanistic and individualistic view of the world, we will die. I don't think it's wise to stay in a state of suffering and evil any longer. The idea of the self has been centre stage for five centuries; it's time to take off in a new direction.

6

Art as peeling

onday, the art school in Caen. I've been asked to explain why kindness seemed to me more important than intelligence, or talent. I did my best, I struggled; but I know it was true. Then I visited Rachel Poignant's studio, which uses casts of different parts of her body. I came to a halt in front of long thongs covered with the cast of one of her tits (the right one? the left one? I can't remember). In their rubbery consistency, and general appearance, they definitely looked like octopus tentacles. Still, I slept pretty well.

Wednesday, the art school in Avignon, for a 'day of failure' organized by Arnaud Labelle-Rojoux. I was supposed to be talking about sexual failure. Things got off to an almost cheerful start, with a screening of short films brought together under the title of *Films Without Qualities*: some hilarious, others strange, sometimes both (I think the tape is currently running in different art centres; it would be shame to miss it). Then I saw a video by Jacques Lizène. It's haunted by sexual misery. His penis protruded from a hole made in a plywood sheet; it was encircled in a noose by a string used to activate it. He moved it slowly about, jerkily, like a soft puppet. I was very uncomfortable. This atmosphere of decomposition, the sad fuck-up of contemporary art, ends up by suffocating you; sometimes you miss Joseph Beuys and his generous-minded propositions. Nonetheless, this witness to our age has a relentless precision about it. All evening I thought about it, and was forced to accept this observation: contemporary art depresses me; but I realize that it's by far the best recent commentary on the state of affairs. I dreamed of a rubbish bin overflowing with coffee filters, peelings, meat smothered in gravy. I thought of art as a kind of peeling, of the bits of flesh that stick to the peels.

Saturday, a literary gathering in the north of the Vendée. A few 'right-wing regionalist' writers (it's easy to see they're right-wingers: when they talk about their origins, they like to point out a Jewish ancestor four generations back, so that everyone can see how broadminded they are). Otherwise, as everywhere, a very diverse audience: the only thing they have in common is that they like reading. These people live in an area where the number of shades of green is endless; but, under a perfectly grey sky, all the shades of green fade away. So what we have here is a faded infinity. I thought of the orbits of the planets after the end of all life, in an increasingly colder universe, marked by the gradual fading of the stars; and the words 'human warmth' almost made me cry.

On Sunday, I took the TGV back to Paris; my holidays were over.

7

Creative absurdity

*L*a *Structure du langage poétique* meets the academic criteria of seriousness – not that this is necessarily a criticism.[1] Jean Cohen observes that, compared to prosaic, ordinary language, the sort that is used to transmit information, poetry allows itself considerable deviations. It constantly uses irrelevant epithets ('white twilights', in Mallarmé; 'black perfumes', in Rimbaud). It does not resist the pleasure of the obvious ('Don't tear it up with your two white hands', in Verlaine; the prosaic mind sneers – could she have three hands?) It doesn't shrink from a certain inconsistency ('Ruth was musing and Booz dreaming; the grass was black', in Hugo; two juxtaposed notations, underlines Cohen, whose logical unity is difficult to see). It delights in redundancy, proscribed in prose under the name of repetition; a borderline case would be García Lorca's poem, *Llanto por Ignacio Sanchez Mejias*, in which the words '*cinco de la tarde*' ['five o'clock in the afternoon'] occur thirty times in the first fifty-two lines.

To establish his thesis, the author undertakes a comparative statistical analysis of poetic texts and prose texts (the height of prosaic being for him – and this is highly significant – the writings of the great scientists of the end of the nineteenth century: Louis Pasteur, Claude Bernard, Marcelin Berthelot). The same method allows him to observe that the poetic gap is much wider among the Romantics than among the classical writers, and increases even more among the Symbolists. Intuitively, we probably suspected as much; still, it's nice to see it established so clearly. Once we've finished reading the book, we're certain of one thing: the author has indeed spotted certain deviations characteristic of poetry; but what do all these deviations lead to? What is their purpose, if they have one?

After a few weeks of crossing, Christopher Columbus was informed that half of the provisions were exhausted; there was no sign of approaching land. It was at this precise moment that his adventure turned heroic: when he decided to continue west while knowing that there was no human possibility that he would get back home. From the introduction to *Le Haut Langage*, Jean Cohen plays his cards: on the question of the nature of poetry, he will be deviating from all existing theories. What makes poetry, he tells us, is not the addition of a certain music to prose (as was long believed when every poem had to be in verse); nor is it the addition of an underlying meaning to the explicit meaning (Marxist, Freudian interpretations, etc.). It isn't even the multiplication of secret meanings hidden under the primary meaning (the theory of polysemia). In short, poetry isn't prose plus something else: it's not *more* than prose, it's something *other* than prose. *La Structure du langage poétique* ended with the observation that poetry moves away from ordinary language, and moves away from it more and more. A theory then naturally comes to mind: the goal of poetry is to establish a maximum deviation, to break or deconstruct all existing codes of communication. Jean Cohen also rejects this theory; all language, he assures us, accepts the function of intersubjectivity, and poetic language is no exception to this rule: poetry speaks differently of the world, but it does indeed

speak of the world, as human beings perceive it. It's exactly at
this point that he takes a considerable risk: for if the deviant
strategies of poetry are not in themselves their own goal, if
poetry is really more than a piece of linguistic research or a
game with language, if it really aims to establish a different way
of speaking of the same reality, then we are dealing with two
irreducible visions of the world.

The marquise went out at five seventeen; she could have gone
out at half past six; she could have been a duchess and gone
out at the same time.[2] The water molecule is made up of two
hydrogen atoms and one oxygen atom. The volume of financial
transactions increased dramatically in 1995. To free itself from
Earth's pull, a rocket must develop a lift-off thrust directly pro-
portional to its mass. Prosaic language organizes reflections,
arguments, facts; basically, it mainly organizes facts. Events that
are arbitrary, albeit described with great precision, intersect in
neutral space and time. Any qualitative or emotional aspect
disappears from our view of the world. This is the perfect realization of Democritus' sentence: 'Sweet and bitter, hot and cold,
colour are only opinions; there is nothing true except atoms
and the void.' This is a text of real but limited beauty, which
irresistibly evokes the famous *Minuit* style,[3] whose influence
has persisted for forty years, precisely because it corresponds to
a democratic metaphysics that is still largely the majority view;
so clearly a majority view that it's sometimes confused with
the scientific program as a whole, although science has made
merely a circumstantial pact with it, in its fight against religious
thought (though this pact has now lasted for several centuries).

'When the low, heavy sky weighs down like a lid . . .' This
terribly *loaded* line, like so many lines by Baudelaire, aims at
something quite different from transmitting information. It's
not only the sky, it's the whole world, the being of the speaker,
the soul of the listener that are imbued with a tone of anguish
and oppression. Poetry occurs; the affective meaning pervades
the world.

Poetry, according to Jean Cohen, aims to produce a funda-mentally alogical discourse, in which all possibility of negation is suspended. For the kind of language that informs, what is might not be, or might be quite different, elsewhere, or in another time. Poetic deviations, on the contrary, aim to create an 'effect of limitlessness' where the field of affirmation invades the whole world, without letting the contradiction subsist as an outside. This brings the poem closer to more primitive manifestations, such as lamentation or howling. The register is admittedly considerably wider; but the words are fundamen-tally of the same nature as the cry. In poetry, words start to vibrate, they find their original vibration; but this vibration is not only musical. Through words, it's the reality they designate that regains its power of horror or enchantment, its primary pathos. Azure is an immediate experience. Likewise, when daylight declines, objects lose their colours and contours, slowly blend into a darkening grey, and human beings feel alone in the world. This was true from their earliest days on earth, this was true even before there were human beings; it's much older than language. These overwhelming perceptions are what poetry seeks to rediscover; of course it uses language, the 'signifier'; but, for poetry, language is only a means. Jean Cohen sums up his theory with this formula: 'Poetry is the song of the signified.'

It's therefore understandable that he came up with another idea: certain modes of perception of the world are in them-selves poetic. Anything that contributes to dissolving limits, to making the world a homogeneous and poorly differentiated whole will be imbued with poetic power (this is the case with mist, or twilight). Certain objects have a poetic impact, not as objects, but because, insofar as they crack open the limits of space and time by their mere presence, they induce a particular psychological state (and it must be recognized that his analyses of the ocean, ruins, and ships are disturbing). Poetry is not just another language; it's another gaze. A way of seeing the world, all the objects in the world (highways as much as snakes, parking lots as much as flowers). At this point in the book, Jean Cohen's poetics no longer belongs to linguistics at all; it relates directly to philosophy.

All perception is organized around a twofold difference: between the object and the subject, between the object and the world. The sharpness with which these distinctions are envisaged has profound philosophical implications, and the existing metaphysics can be distributed along these two axes without being forced. Poetry, according to Jean Cohen, leads to a general dissolution of reference points: object, subject, world merge into the same affective and lyrical atmosphere. The metaphysics of Democritus, on the other hand, brings these two distinctions to their maximum clarity (a blinding clarity, the dazzle of the sun on white stones, on an August afternoon: 'It's nothing but atoms and the void').

In principle the matter seems cut and dried, and poetry condemned – as the attractive residue of a prelogical mentality, that of the primitive or the child. The problem is, Democritus' metaphysics is wrong. More precisely: it's no longer compatible with twentieth-century advances in physics. Indeed, quantum mechanics invalidates any possibility of a materialist metaphysics, and leads to a fundamental re-examination of the distinctions between object, subject and world.

As early as 1927, Niels Bohr was led to propose what has been called 'the Copenhagen interpretation'. The product of a laborious and sometimes tragic compromise, the Copenhagen interpretation emphasizes the instruments and protocols of measurement. Giving full meaning to Heisenberg's uncertainty principle, it establishes the act of knowledge on new bases: if it's impossible to simultaneously measure all the parameters of a physical system with precision, this is not simply because they are 'disturbed by the measurement'; more profoundly, they don't exist outside of it. It makes no sense to talk about their previous state. The Copenhagen interpretation frees the scientific act by setting the couple of observer and observed in the place of a hypothetical real world; it allows science to be overhauled in all its generality as a means of communication between human beings about 'what we have observed, what we have learned' – to use Bohr's words.

Overall, the physicists of the present century have stuck with the Copenhagen interpretation; which is not a very comfortable position. Of course, in the daily practice of research, the best way to progress is to stick to a hard positivist approach, which can be summed up as follows: 'We are content to bring together observations, human observations, and to correlate them by laws. The idea of reality isn't scientific, it doesn't interest us.' But it must still be unpleasant, sometimes, to realize that the theory you're producing absolutely cannot be formulated in plain language.

It's at this point that we start to glimpse strange parallels. For a long time I have been struck by the way that, whenever people put questions to the theorists of physics, the latter – once they have left behind spectral decompositions, Hilbert spaces, Hermitian operators, etc., namely the usual fare of their publications – pay a powerful tribute to poetic language. Not to detective novels, nor to serial music: no, what interests and troubles them is, quite specifically, poetry. Before reading Jean Cohen, I had no idea why; upon discovering his poetics, I realized that something was definitely happening, and that this something was not unrelated to Niels Bohr's proposals.

In the mood of conceptual catastrophe produced by early quantum discoveries, it was sometimes suggested that it would be appropriate to create a new language, a new logic, or both. Clearly, ancient language and logic did not lend themselves to the representation of the quantum universe. Still, Bohr was reluctant. Poetry, he pointed out, proves that the subtle and partly contradictory use of everyday language allows its limitations to be overcome. The principle of complementarity introduced by Bohr is a kind of *fine-tuned management* of contradiction: complementary points of view on the world are simultaneously introduced; each of them, taken in isolation, can be expressed unambiguously in plain language; each of them, taken in isolation, is false. Their joint presence creates a new situation, one that is uncomfortable for reason; but it's only through this conceptual malaise that we can access a correct representation of the world. At the same time, Jean Cohen argues that poetry's absurd use of language is not its own goal. Poetry breaks the causal chain and constantly plays with the explosive power of the absurd; but it's not absurdity. It is absurdity made creative; creator of a different meaning, strange but immediate, limitless, emotional.

8

The party

The purpose of the party is to make us forget that we are lonely, miserable and doomed to death; in other words, to transform us into animals. This is why primitive human beings have a very highly developed sense of the party. A nice dose of hallucinogenic plants, three tambourines, and they're off: it doesn't take much to keep them amused. In contrast, Westerners generally only end up in an inadequate state of ecstasy after endless raves from which they emerge deaf and drugged: they have no sense of the party at all. Profoundly self-conscious, radically alien to others, terrorized by the idea of death, they're quite incapable of achieving any exaltation. However, they persist. The loss of their animal condition saddens them, they're ashamed and resentful; they'd like to be party animals, or at least pass for such. They're in a really lousy situation.

What the hell am I doing with these jerks?

'For where two or three are gathered together in my name, there am I in the midst of them' (Matthew 18: 20). But that's the whole point: gathered together in the name of what? What could possibly justify gathering together?

Gathering together to have fun

This is the worst possible scenario. In such circumstances (nightclubs, dance sessions, parties), which are obviously no fun at all, there's only one solution: flirting. Thereupon, we leave the register of the party to enter that of a fierce narcissistic competition, with or without the *option of penetration.* (It's traditionally considered that a man needs penetration to obtain the desired narcissistic gratification; he then feels something analogous to the click of the 'free game' on old pinball machines. The woman, most often, is satisfied with the certainty that someone wants to penetrate her.) If these kinds of games disgust you, or you just don't feel able to put a good face on them, there's only one solution: make your getaway.

Gathering together to fight (student demonstrations, environmental gatherings, talk shows in the suburbs)

The idea, in principle, is ingenious: indeed, the benevolent glue of a common cause can entail a group effect, a feeling of belonging, even an authentic collective intoxication. Unfortunately, crowd psychology follows invariable laws: the stupidest and most aggressive elements always end up dominating the proceedings. So we find ourselves in the middle of a bunch of loud, even dangerous loudmouths. The choice is thus the same as in a nightclub: leave before things start kicking off, or else flirt (in a more favourable context in this case: the presence of common convictions, the feelings provoked by the progress of the protest may have slightly cracked the carapace of narcissism).

Gathering together to fuck
(sex clubs, private orgies, some New Age groups)

One of the simplest and oldest formulas: unite humanity in what, after all, it most has in common. Sexual acts do take place, although there's not always the expected pleasure. There's that much to be said for it – not much else.

Gathering together to celebrate (masses, pilgrimages)

Religion proposes something very original: it boldly denies separation and death by asserting that, contrary to appearances, we are bathed in divine love while heading towards a blissful eternity. A religious ceremony in which the participants are imbued with faith would thus seem to be the sole example of a *successful party*. Some agnostic participants may even, for as long as the celebration lasts, feel overwhelmed by a sense of belief; but then they risk a terrible come-down (a bit like sex, but worse). One solution: to be touched by *grace*.

A pilgrimage, combining the advantages of the student demonstration and the Nouvelles Frontières trip,[1] all in an atmosphere of spirituality aggravated by fatigue, also offers ideal conditions for flirting, which becomes almost involuntary, and even sincere. A lofty hypothesis for the end of a pilgrimage: marriage plus conversion. On the other hand, the come-down can be terrible. Plan to follow up with a UCPA 'boardsports' stay,[2] which you'll always have time to cancel (find out beforehand about the cancellation conditions).

Partying without tears

In short, all you need do is plan to have fun; that way, you can be sure you'll get bored. The ideal would therefore be to forgo parties altogether. Unfortunately, the party animal is such a respected figure that this renunciation means your social image takes a real tumble. The following few tips should help you avoid the worst (namely remaining alone to the bitter end, in a state of boredom that turns into despair, under the mistaken impression that others are having fun).

– Be aware beforehand that the party will inevitably be a failure. Visualize examples of previous failures. You don't really have to adopt a cynical and jaded attitude. On the contrary, the humble and smiling acceptance of the common disaster makes it possible to achieve this success: to transform a failed party into a moment of pleasant banality.

– Always plan to come home alone, by taxi.

– Before the party: drink. Alcohol in moderate doses produces a socializing and euphoric effect that has no real competition.

– During the party: drink, but reduce the doses (the cocktail of alcohol plus ambient eroticism quickly leads to violence, suicide and murder). It's a smart idea to take half a Lexomil at the right time.[3] As alcohol multiplies the effect of tranquillizers, you'll soon find you're dozing off – now's the time to call a taxi. A good party is a brief party.

– After the party: call the hosts to thank them. Peacefully wait for the next party (leave it for a month, or just a week during the holiday period).

Finally, a consoling perspective: with age, the obligation to go to parties decreases, the inclination towards solitude increases; real life takes over.

9

Time out

What are you looking for here?

After 'the phenomenal success of the first edition', the second *Salon de la vidéo hot* is being held at the Porte de Champerret exhibition centre.[1] No sooner have I come out onto the esplanade when a young woman, of whom I can't remember a thing, hands me a leaflet. I try to talk to her, but she's already joined a small group of activists who are stamping their feet to warm up, each holding a bundle of leaflets. A question is printed across the leaflet she's given me: 'What are you looking for here?' I approach the entrance; the exhibition centre is in the basement. Two escalators purr faintly in the middle of a huge space. Men enter, alone or in small groups. Rather than an underground temple of lust, the place is vaguely reminiscent of a Darty.[2] I go down a few steps, then I pick up an abandoned catalogue. It's from Cargo VPC, a mail order company specializing in X-rated videos. Yes indeed, what am I doing here?

Back in the metro, I start reading the leaflet. Under the title: 'Pornography rots your mind', it sets out the following argument. All sex offenders, rapists, paedophiles, etc., have been found to possess numerous porn videos. The repeated viewing of these causes, 'according to all studies', a blurring of the borders between fantasy and reality, making it easy to act out one's fantasies, at the same time as depriving 'conventional sexual practices' of any pleasure.

'What do you think?' – I hear the question before I see the questioner. Young, with short hair, he seems intelligent and a little anxious as he stands in front of me. The metro train arrives, which gives me time to recover from my surprise. For years, I have walked the streets wondering if the day would come when someone would speak to me – for any reason other than a request for money. Well, here it is, that day has come. What it needed was the second *Salon de la vidéo hot*.

Contrary to what I thought, he's not an anti-pornography activist. In fact, he's just been to the Salon. He went in. And what he saw made him rather uneasy. 'All those men . . . there was something violent in their eyes.' I object that, yes, desire often gives the features a tense, violent mask. But no, he knows that, he doesn't want to talk about the violence of desire, but about *really violent violence*. 'I found myself in the midst of groups of men . . .' (the memory seems to oppress him slightly), 'lots of videos of rape, torture sessions . . . they were aroused, their looks, the atmosphere . . . It was . . .' I listen, I wait. 'I reckon it's going to end badly', he concludes abruptly before getting off at Opéra.

Much later, at home, I look at the Cargo VPC catalogue. The script for *Sodos d'ados* [*Teens taking it in the ass*] prom- ises us 'Frankfurters in their little holes, ravioli in their cunts, fucking in tomato sauce.' That of *Frères Éjac no. 6* [*Frères Jacques ejaculate no. 6*] features this scenario: 'Rocco ploughs those asses: shaved blondes, wet brunettes, Rocco transforms their rectums into volcanoes and disgorges his boiling lava into them.' Finally, the plot tag of *Salopes violées no. 2* [*Raped Sluts No. 2*] deserves to be quoted in full: 'Five superb sluts are assaulted, sodomized, and beaten up by sadists. No matter how hard they struggle and lash out with their claws, they're going to end up getting thrashed, transformed into human balls-drainers.' There are sixty pages in this style. I admit that I wasn't expecting this. For the first time in my life, I begin to feel a vague sympathy for American feminists. In recent years I'd heard of the emergence of a fashion for 'trash', which I stupidly blamed on yet another market segment being opened up. This was a naively economistic view, my friend Angèle, the author of a doctoral thesis on mimetic behaviour in reptiles, told me the next day. The phenomenon goes much deeper. 'To reassert himself in his virile power,' she launches in, play-fully, 'the man is no longer satisfied with mere penetration. He feels constantly evaluated, judged, compared to other males. To get rid of this discomfort, to achieve pleasure, he now needs to hit, humiliate, debase his partner; to feel she is completely at his mercy. And this phenomenon,' she con-cludes with a smile, 'is starting to be observed in women as well.'

'So we're screwed', I said after a pause. Well, yes, in her view. Yes, we probably are.

The German

This is how the life of the German goes. During his youth, during his middle age, the German *works* (usually in Germany). He is sometimes unemployed, but less often than a French person. As the years pass, however, the German reaches retire-ment age; he now has the choice of his place of residence. Does he then settle in a farmhouse in Swabia? In a house in the residential suburbs of Munich? Sometimes, but in reality less and less. A profound change is taking place in the German between the ages of fifty-five and sixty. Like the stork in winter, like the hippie of bygone ages, like the Israeli enthusiast for Goa trance, the sixty-year-old German *heads south*. He can be found in Spain, often on the coast between Cartagena and Valencia. Some specimens – generally from a more affluent socio-cultural background – have been reported from the Canaries or Madeira.

This profound, existential, definitive mutation does not surprise those around him; the way to it was paved by many vacation stays, made almost inevitable by the purchase of an apartment. This is how the German lives: he enjoys his last good years. This phenomenon was revealed to me for the first time in November 1992. Driving along, just north of Alicante, I had the strange idea of stopping in a mini-city, which could by analogy be described as a village – the sea was extremely close. This village didn't have a name; probably there hadn't been time; it was evident that no house dated back to before 1980. It was about five o'clock. Walking through the deserted streets, I first noticed a curious phenomenon: the signs of shops and cafes, of restaurant menus, were all written in German. I bought some groceries and soon found the place starting to come alive. An increasingly dense population thronged the streets, the squares, the sea front; they seemed to have a keen appetite for consumption. Housewives came out of their residences. Men with moustaches greeted each other warmly, and seemed to be finalizing the details for meeting up that evening. The homogeneity of this population, which had immediately struck me, gradually started to nag at me, and around seven o'clock I had to face the facts: THE CITY WAS ENTIRELY PEOPLED BY RETIRED GERMANS.

Structurally, therefore, the life of a German quite closely resembles the life of the immigrant worker. Imagine a country A, and a country B. Country A is conceived as a country of work; everything is functional, boring and precise. As for country B, people spend their leisure time there; their vacations, their retirement. They don't like leaving it, they aspire to return to it. It's in country B that they make real friendships, deep friendships; it's in country B that they acquire a residence, a residence they wish to bequeath to their children. Country B is generally located further south.

Can we conclude that Germany has become a region of the world where the Germans no longer wish to live, and from which they escape as soon as possible? I think we can. Thus, the Germans' opinion of their native country matches that of the Turks. There is no real difference; there remain, however, a few details that separate them.

In general, a German has a *family*, consisting of one or two children. Like their parents at their age, these children *work*. Here is an opportunity for our retiree to embark on a micro-migration – a very seasonal one, as it takes place during the holiday season, between Christmas and New Year's Day. (PLEASE NOTE: the phenomenon described below does not apply to the immigrant worker as such; the details were communicated to me by Bertrand, a waiter at the brasserie *Le Méditerranée*, in Narbonne.)

It's a long way from Cartagena to Wuppertal, even in a powerful car. And so, in the evening, it's not uncommon for the German to feel the need for a stopover; the Languedoc-Roussillon region, endowed with modern hotel possibilities, offers a satisfactory option. At this point, the hardest part is done – the French motorway network remains, whatever one may say, superior to its Spanish counterpart.

Feeling pretty relaxed after the meal (Bouzigues oysters, baby cuttlefish Provençal-style, a small bouillabaisse for two people when in season), the German starts to chat. He talks about his daughter, who works in an art gallery in Düsseldorf; about his son-in-law, who's in IT; about their relationship problems, and possible solutions. He talks.

Wer reitet so spät durch Nacht und Wind?
Es ist der Vater mit seinem Kind.[3]

What the German says, at this time of day and at this stage of his journey, doesn't matter much anymore. In any case, he's in an intermediate country, and can give free rein to his profound thoughts; and profound thoughts he has aplenty.

Later, he sleeps; that's probably the best thing he can do.

The brief for our column read as follows: 'Parity between the franc and the mark: the German economic model.' Good night, everyone.

Lowering the retirement age

In the past, we were activity leaders in holiday villages; we were paid to give people a fun time, or to try to do so. Later on, having got married (and most often divorced), we returned to the holiday village, this time as clients. Young people, other young people tried to give us a fun time. For our part, we tried to establish sexual relations with various members of the holiday village (sometimes they too had once been activity leaders, sometimes not). We sometimes succeeded; more often than not, we failed. We didn't have much fun. Today, concludes the former activity leader, our life really has no meaning left in it.

Built in 1995, the Holiday Inn Resort in Safaga, on the coast of the Red Sea, offers 327 spacious and pleasant rooms and six suites. Facilities include the lobby, coffee shop, restaurant, beach restaurant, nightclub and entertainment terrace. The commercial arcade has various shops, a bank, a hairdresser. Entertainment is provided by a friendly Franco-Italian team (dances in the evenings, various games). In short, and to use the expression of the tour operator, 'we're all a great team'.

Lowering the retirement age to fifty-five, continued the former activity leader, would be a measure that tour operators would warmly welcome. It's difficult to make a structure of this size profitable on the basis of a short and discontinuous season, mainly limited to the summer period – to a lesser extent to the winter holidays. The solution obviously involves setting up charter flights for young retirees, benefiting from preferential rates, so as to harmonize traffic flows. After his spouse's death, a retiree finds himself somewhat in the same situation as a child: he travels in groups, he has to make friends. But while boys play with boys, and girls chat with girls, retirees are happy to meet up regardless of gender. In fact, we see that they are continually coming out with allusions and innuendo of a sexual nature; their verbal lubricity is truly astounding. As painful as it may be at the time, it's obvious that sexuality seems to be something we miss later on in life, a theme on which we like to embroider nostalgic variations. So friendships are formed, in groups of two or three. They get together to discover the exchange rates, to plan an excursion in a 4 x 4. Retirees, a bit shrunk with age, their hair kept short, look like gnomes – cranky or nice, depending on their own personality. Their robustness is often astonishing, concludes the former activity leader.

'I tell everyone their religion, and all religions are to be respected', the masseur somewhat irrelevantly remarked. Annoyed by this interruption, the former activity leader took refuge in a pained silence. He was fifty-two years old – one of the youngest clients there, as January drew to a close. Besides, he hadn't retired, just taken early retirement, or was working part-time, something of the kind. Pointing out to everyone his qualifications as an expert in tourism, he'd managed to create a character for himself with the activities team. 'I opened the first Club Med in Senegal', he liked to remind them. Then he would hum, sketching out a dance step: 'I'm going to have a blast in Sééé-negal / And in my saddle I've got a lovely gaaaal.' Well, he was a very nice guy. But I can't say I was at all surprised when, the next morning, his body was found floating just below the surface in the lagoon pool.

Calais, Pas-de-Calais

Since I can see that everyone's awake,[4] I will take this opportunity to note a little petition that in my opinion has been
insufficiently publicized: the one launched by Robert Hue
and Jean-Pierre Chevènement to call for a referendum on the
single currency.[5] It's true that the Communist Party isn't what
it used to be, that Jean-Pierre Chevènement only represents
himself (or not . . .); the fact remains that their wishes chime
with those of the majority, and that Jacques Chirac promised
this referendum. Which, technically and at the time of writing,
makes him a liar.

I don't feel I'm showing any particularly subtle powers
of analysis when I diagnose that we live in a country whose
population is becoming impoverished, senses that it's going to
become more and more impoverished, and is also convinced
that all its misfortunes come from international economic
competition (simply because it's losing this very same 'international economic competition'). Europe? Until a few years
ago, nobody gave a damn about it; it was a project that hadn't
aroused the slightest opposition, nor triggered the slightest
enthusiasm; today, let's just say that a few drawbacks have
become apparent, and if anything there's a feeling of growing
hostility. Which, after all, would already be an argument for
a referendum. Remember that the Maastricht Referendum in
1992 almost didn't take place (the historical prize for contempt
undoubtedly went to Valéry Giscard d'Estaing, who considered
the project 'too complex to be put to the vote'), and that once it
was over it almost ended in a NO, while all the politicians and
the responsible media of France had called for a YES vote.

This deep-rooted, almost unbelievable stubbornness on the
part of the 'government' political parties to pursue a project
that doesn't interest anyone, and is even starting to disgust
everyone, in itself explains many things. Personally, when I
am told about our 'democratic values', I find it hard to feel

the required emotion; my first reaction would be to laugh out loud. If there is one thing of which I am sure, when I am asked to choose between Chirac and Jospin (!) and the government refuses to consult me about the single currency, it just shows we're *not* in a democracy. Well, democracy may not be the best regime, it may, as people claim, open the door to 'dangerous populist excesses'; but in that case I'd prefer to be told so frankly: the main lines have been followed for a long time, they're wise and fair; true, you can't exactly understand them, but you can, depending on your sensitivity, add a particular political hue to the composition of the next government.

In *Le Figaro* of 25 February, I noted some interesting statistics concerning the Pas-de-Calais. Forty per cent of the population lives under the poverty line (figures from INSEE);[6] six out of ten households are exempt from paying income tax. Contrary to what one might think, the National Front has only middling electoral support there; it's true that the immigrant population is constantly decreasing (on the other hand the fertility rate is very good, distinctly higher than the national average). In fact the deputy mayor of Calais is a Communist, who has the interesting peculiarity of being the only person to have voted at the last congress against the abandonment of the dictatorship of the proletariat.

Calais is a haunting city. Usually, in a provincial town of this size, there is a historic centre, busy pedestrian streets on Saturday afternoons, etc. In Calais, nothing of the kind. The city was ninety-five per cent razed to the ground during the Second World War; and in the streets, on a Saturday afternoon, there's nobody about. We walk past abandoned buildings, huge deserted car parks (this is certainly the city in France where it's easiest to park). Saturday evening is a little more cheerful, but its cheerfulness is of a peculiar kind: almost everyone is drunk. Among the various watering holes there's a casino, with rows of slot machines where people from Calais come and fritter away their jobseeker's allowance. The Sunday afternoon walk follows the route to the Channel Tunnel entrance. People stroll along the fences, usually with their families, sometimes pushing a pram, and watch the Eurostar pass by. They wave at the driver, who honks his horn in response before plunging under the sea.

Metropolitan comedy

The woman talked about hanging herself; the man was wearing a comfortable, elegant suit. Women rarely hang themselves, in fact; they remain faithful to barbiturates. 'Top level': it was top level. 'We must move on': why? Between you and me, the cushions of the metro seat were spilling their guts out. The couple got out at Maisons-Alfort. A creative type of about twenty-seven came to sit beside me. I disliked him from the start (maybe his ponytail, or his *quirky* little moustache; maybe also a vague resemblance to Maupassant). He unfolded a letter several pages long, began to read; the train was approaching the Liberté station. The letter was written in English, and was probably addressed to him by a Swedish woman (I checked the same evening in my illustrated Larousse; yes, Uppsala is in Sweden, it's a city of one hundred and fifty-three thousand inhabitants, and has a very old university; there doesn't seem to be much else to say about it). The creative type was reading slowly; his English was poor, I had no trouble reconstructing the details of the affair (fleetingly I realized that my morality was perhaps a little dubious; but after all, the metro is a public space, right?). Obviously, they'd met the previous winter in Chamrousse (but ... what an idea, a Swedish woman going skiing in the Alps?). This meeting had changed her life. She couldn't stop thinking about him, and besides she wasn't even trying (at that moment he gave an unbearable smirk of vanity, leaned back expansively in his seat, stroked his moustache). Through the words she was using, you could tell she was starting to be afraid. She was desperate to find him, she was considering looking for a job in

France, maybe someone could accommodate her, there were possibilities as an au pair. My neighbour frowned in annoyance: indeed, one day or another she'd just turn up, you could tell she was quite ready for something of the kind. She knew he was very busy, that he had a lot going on (I doubted this; after all, it was three in the afternoon and the guy didn't seem to be in much of a hurry). At that moment he looked around him with a glazed expression, but we were still only at Daumesnil station. The letter concluded with this line: 'I love you and I don't want to lose you.' I thought this was very beautiful; there are days when I'd really like to write like that. She signed her name 'Yours, Ann-Katrin', her signature surrounded by little hearts. It was Friday 14 February, Valentine's Day (this commercial custom, of Anglo-Saxon origin, seems to have taken root in Nordic countries). I thought to myself: women are really brave, sometimes.

The creative type was getting out at Bastille, and so was I. I was tempted to follow him for a moment (was he going to a tapas bar, or somewhere else?), but I had an appointment with Bertrand Leclair at *La Quinzaine littéraire*.[7] As part of this column, I was considering starting a controversy with Bertrand Leclair over Balzac. First of all, because I have difficulty understanding how the adjective 'Balzacian' – an adjective that, from time to time, he pins on this or that novelist – has anything pejorative about it whatsoever; secondly, because I'm a little fed up with all the polemics over Céline, an overrated author. But basically, Bertrand isn't all that interested in criticizing Balzac anymore; on the contrary, he's impressed by Balzac's incredible freedom; he seems to think that if we had *Balzacian* novelists today, it wouldn't necessarily be such a bad thing. We agree that such a powerful novelist is necessarily a huge producer of clichés; whether or not those stereotypes are still true today is another question that needs to be carefully considered on a case-by-case basis. End of the controversy. I think back to poor Ann-Katrin, whom I imagine with the pathetic

features of Eugénie Grandet (there's a sense of abnormal vital-
ity emanating from all of Balzac's characters, whether they're
heartrending or hateful).[8] There are those who can't be killed
off, and come back from one book to the next (too bad he
didn't know Bernard Tapie).[9] There are also the sublime characters, who write themselves into our memories straightaway
– precisely because they're sublime, and yet real. Is Balzac a
realist? We could just as well call him 'romantic'. Anyway,
I don't think he would feel out of place these days. After all,
there are still real elements of melodrama in life. Especially, it
has to be said, in the lives of others.

Just take it in your stride

On the Saturday afternoon, on the occasion of the Book Fair,
the Chambéry *Festival du premier roman* [*Festival of the first
novel*] organized a debate on the theme: 'Has the first novel
become a commercial product?' The debate was scheduled to
last for an hour and a half, but unfortunately Bernard Simeone
immediately gave the correct answer, which is YES. He even
explained the reasons clearly: in literature, as everywhere else,
the public needs new faces (I think he used the more brutal
expression 'new flesh'). It was no great merit on his part to
have seen things clearly, he apologized; he spent half his life in
Italy, a country that in many ways seemed to him to be *in the
avant-garde of the worst*. The debate then turned to the role of
literary criticism, a more confused subject.

In concrete terms, things kick off at the end of August, with
teasers of the style 'The new novelist has arrived' (group photo
on the Pont des Arts, or in a garage in Maisons-Alfort), and
ends in November with the awards ceremony. Then there's the
Beaujolais Nouveau, and Christmas beer, all of which keeps
you going until the holidays. Life isn't that hard, just take it
in your stride. Let's highlight, in passing, the tribute that the

industry pays to literature, since it associates literary joys with the darkest period, the Monday of the year, when we all go into the tunnel. The French Open, on the other hand, is organized in June. In any case, I'd be the last person to criticize my colleagues, who'll do anything without ever understanding exactly what's being asked of them. Personally, I've been very lucky, there was just a little slip-up with *Capital*, the magazine of the Ganz group (which, by the way, I confused with the show of the same name on the M6 channel on TV). The girl hadn't come with a TV camera, which should have alerted me; still, I was surprised when she admitted to me that she hadn't read a line of my book. I didn't catch on until later, when I read the special issue: 'AN EXECUTIVE BY DAY, A WRITER BY NIGHT: IT'S NOT EASY TO EQUAL PROUST OR SULITZER'[10] (in which, by the way, my words were not included). In fact, she would have liked me to tell her *my wonderful story*. I should have been warned; I could have done something, with Maurice Nadeau[11] as a gruff old magus and Valérie Taillefer as little Tinker Bell.[12] 'Go see Nadd-hô, son. He's the talisman, the memory, the guardian of our most sacred traditions.' Or maybe a bit more *Rocky*, in a more intellectual version: 'Armed with his spreadsheet, during the day, he struggles with just-in-time production; but it's with his word processor at night that he hammers out his fine sentences. His only strength is his faith in himself.' Instead, I was stupidly outspoken, even aggressive; miracles can't be expected if the concept isn't explained to us. It's true that I should have picked up a copy of the magazine, but I didn't have time (note that *Capital* is mostly read by unemployed people, which doesn't really make me laugh).

There's another disturbing misunderstanding, later, in one of the municipal libraries in Grenoble. Against all expectations, the policy of promoting reading among young people is proving to be a local success. Lots of people speak out, saying things like: 'Hey, Mr Writer, you're sending me a message, you're giving me hope!' – to the amazement of the writers on the podium. They don't reject the principle, by the way; they remember, little by little, yes indeed, one of the writer's potential missions, in very ancient times ... but like that, orally, in two minutes? 'No mention of Bruel',[13] grumbles someone whose name I've forgotten. Well, at least this lot seem to have read some books.

Fortunately, at the end, there's a precise, luminous, honest intervention by Jacques Charmetz, the creator of the Chambéry Festival (in the not so distant times when the first novel was more than a *concept*): 'That's not what they're for. Ask them, if you want, for some form of truth, whether allegorical or real. Ask them, if you want, to open wounds, and if possible to rub salt into those wounds.' I'm quoting from memory, but still: thank you.

What use are men?

'He doesn't exist. Get it? He doesn't exist.'

'Yes, I get it.'

'I exist. You exist. He doesn't exist.'

Having established Bruno's non-existence, the forty-year-old woman gently stroked the hand of her much younger partner. She looked like a feminist; she was wearing a feminist sweater. The other woman seemed to be a variety singer, at one point she talked about galas (or maybe galleys, I didn't quite catch it). Sucking on a strand of her hair, she slowly got used to Bruno's disappearance. Unfortunately, at the end of the meal, she tried to establish Serge's existence. Ms Pullover twitched violently.

'Can I tell you a bit more?' the other asked timidly.

'Yes, but keep it short.'

After they left, I pulled out a voluminous file of press clippings. For the twentieth time in two weeks, I tried to be terrified by the prospects offered by human cloning. It has to be said it got off to a bad start, with the photo of that fine Scottish sheep (which, as we could see from the TF1 news, bleats with astonishing normality). If the goal was to scare us, it would have been easier to clone spiders. I'm trying to imagine twenty or so individuals scattered across the planet, carrying the same genetic code as mine. I'm disturbed, true (even Bill Clinton is disturbed, which is saying a lot); but terrified, no, not exactly. Do I find my genetic code a bit comical? Not that either. Decidedly, 'disturbed' is the word. A few articles later, I realize that this isn't the problem. Contrary to what is foolishly repeated, it's wrong to claim that 'the two sexes will be able to reproduce separately'. For now, women remain, as *Le Figaro* aptly emphasizes, 'essential'. Man, on the other hand, is now admittedly more or less useless (what's annoying about the story is the way the spermatozoon is replaced by a 'slight electric shock'; this is lowering the bar somewhat). But then, more generally, what use are men? One can imagine that in earlier times, when bears were numerous, virility might have played a specific and irreplaceable role; today, one wonders.

The last time I heard about Valerie Solanas, it was in a book by Michel Bulteau, *Flowers*; he'd met her in New York in 1976.[14] The book was written thirteen years later; the encounter visibly shook him. He describes a girl 'with greenish skin, dirty hair, dressed in blue jeans and filthy fatigues'. She had no regrets about shooting Warhol, the father of artistic cloning: 'If I see that bastard again, I'm doing the same thing.' She had even fewer regrets about founding S.C.U.M. (the Society for Cutting Up Men), and was preparing to follow up on its manifesto. Since then, there's been radio silence; perhaps she's dead? What's even stranger, this famous manifesto has disappeared from bookstores; to get a fragmentary idea of it you have to watch *Arte* until late at night, and put up with Delphine Seyrig's diction. Despite all these drawbacks, it's worth it: the extracts I've heard are truly impressive. And for the first time today, thanks to Dolly the Sheep of the Future, the technical conditions are in place for the realization of Valerie Solanas' dream: a world made up exclusively of women. (The ebullient Valerie set our her ideas on a wide variety of subjects; I noted in passing that she demands we 'eliminate the money system' straightaway. Definitely, now is the time to re-publish this text.)

(*Meanwhile, the cunning Andy sleeps in liquid nitrogen, awaiting a very hypothetical resurrection.*)

The experiment could be tried soon enough, for those women interested, perhaps on a reduced scale; I hope that the men will know how to quietly fade away. One last tip, all the same, to ensure we get off to a good start: avoid cloning Valerie Solanas.

The skin of the bear

Last summer, around mid July, on the 8 p.m. news, Bruno Masure announced that an American probe had discovered traces of fossil life on Mars. There was no doubt that the molecules, dating back hundreds of millions of years, whose presence had just been detected, were biological molecules; they had never been encountered outside of living organisms. These organisms were bacteria, presumably methane-based archaeobacteria. Once Masure had established this, he moved on; obviously, the subject interested him less than Bosnia. This minimal media coverage seems, in theory, to stem from the fact that bacterial life is hardly very spectacular. A bacterium, in fact, leads a peaceful existence. Taking simple, unvaried nutrients from the environment, it grows; then it reproduces, rather boringly, by a process of successive divisions. The torments and delights of sexuality remain forever unknown to it. As long as the conditions remain favourable, it continues to reproduce (*it finds favour in the sight of the Lord, and its generations are countless*); then it dies. No thoughtless ambition tarnishes its limited and perfect course; the bacterium is not a Balzacian character. Of course, it sometimes leads this peaceful existence within a host organism (that of a dachshund, for example), and then the organism in question suffers, or even is completely destroyed; but the bacterium is unaware of this, and the disease of which it's the active agent develops without affecting its serenity. In itself, the bacterium is irreproachable; it's also completely uninteresting.

But the event itself remained. Thus, on a planet close to Earth, biological macromolecules had been able to organize themselves, to develop vague self-reproducing structures composed of a primitive nucleus and a poorly understood membrane; then everything had stopped, probably due to climatic variations; reproduction had become more and more difficult, before stopping altogether. The story of life on Mars came across as a rather modest story. However (and Bruno Masure did not seem to be fully aware of the fact), this ministory of a somewhat flaccid failure violently contradicted all the mythical and religious constructions that humanity classically delights in. There was no single, great creative act; there were no chosen people, nor even a chosen species or planet. There were, almost throughout the universe, only uncertain and generally unconvincing attempts. And the whole thing was crushingly monotonous. The DNA of bacteria found on Mars was exactly the same as the DNA of terrestrial bacteria; this observation in particular overwhelmed me with a diffuse sadness, as this radical genetic identity seemed to foretell exhausting historical convergences. Under the bacterium, in short, we could already get a whiff of Tutsis and Serbians – all those people who spread out in conflicts as tedious as they are interminable.

Life on Mars, however, had had one extremely good idea: it stopped before it had done too much damage. Encouraged by the Martian example, I began to write a quick plea for the extermination of bears. At the time, a new pair of bears had

just been introduced to the Pyrenees, which was causing dis-
content among sheep producers. There was indeed something
unhealthy, perverse about this obstinate attempt to pull these
plantigrades back from extinction; naturally, the measure was
supported by environmentalists. The female was released, then
the male, a few kilometres away. Those people were really
ridiculous. No dignity.

As I opened up about my exterminating project to the deputy
director of an art gallery, she countered with an original, more
culturalist argument. The bear, she said, should be preserved
because it was part of the very ancient cultural memory of
mankind. In fact, the two oldest known artistic representations
were of a bear and a female sex. From the most recent dating,
the bear even seemed to have come a bit earlier. Depictions
of mammoths, of the phallus? These were more recent, much
more – they didn't stand a chance of being older. Faced with
this authoritative argument, I bowed my head. Well, let's go
with the bears. For summer holidays I recommend Lanzarote,
which looks a lot like the planet Mars.

10

Opera Bianca

4"

M: What is the smallest element in a human society?[1]

36"

W: We associate the wave with the woman,
The corpuscle with the masculine
We compose small dramas
In the desire of an evil God.

M: In the absence of any conflict, a world appears, develops. The network of interactions envelopes space, creates space by its instantaneous development. By observing the interactions, we know the world. Defining space through observables, in the absence of any contradiction, we set forth a world we can talk about. We call this world: reality.

43"

M: They floated in the night near an innocent star,
      Watching the birth of the world,
      The development of plants
      And the impure abundance of bacteria;
      They came from far away, they had plenty of time.

      They didn't really have
      An idea of the future,
      They saw the torment
      The lack and desire.

      Settling on Earth
      Among the living,
      They knew war,
      They rode the wind.

W: They gathered at the edge of the pond;
      The fog rose and revived the sky;
      Remember, friends, the essential forms,
      Remember human beings; remember them for long.

50"

M: I would like to announce good news, to offer consoling
      words; I cannot. I can only witness the gulf between
      our approaches and our attitudes widening. We
      roam through space, the rhythm of our footsteps
      cuts through space with the precision of a
      razor;
      We travel through space and space grows darker and
      darker.
      There was a precise moment of withdrawal.

I cannot remember it, but it must have happened at a
   certain altitude.

W: There must have been a time of communion where we had
    no objection to the world; how is it then that our loneli-
    ness is so profound?
    Something must have happened, but the roots of the
       explosion remain impenetrable to us;
    We look around, but nothing seems concrete, nothing
       seems stable.

                              56"

W: We walk through the city, we encounter gazes
    And this defines our human presence;
    In the absolute calm of the weekend,
    We walk slowly around the station.

    Our oversized clothes shelter grey flesh,
    Almost motionless at the end of the day;
    Our tiny, half-doomed soul
    Stirs between the folds, and then becomes still.

M: We have existed, such is our legend;
    Some of our desires have built this city.
    We fought hostile powers,
    Then our emaciated arms let go of the controls
    And we floated away from all possibilities;
    Life has grown cold, life has left us
    We contemplate our half-effaced bodies,
    In the silence, some sensitive data emerge.

59"

M: The perfectly limpid sky
     Penetrated into our crystalline lenses
     We no longer took thought for tomorrow,
     The night was almost empty.

     We were prisoners among the instruments
     And the measures seemed perfectly futile,
     We had tried to do some useful work
     And the ants danced under an oppressive sun.

     There was something crazy in the air
     An electricity, a slipping of chains,
     Passers-by exchanged looks full of hatred
     And seemed to be mulling over marvellous torments.

W: You will know the three directions of space
     And you will realize the nature of time,
     You will see the sun set over the pond;
     In the night you will think you have found your place.

M: Dawn returns, the sand shifts between the bodies;
     Spirit of clairvoyance, head north equitably;
     Spirit of intransigence, support our struggles and efforts;
     This world expects from us a drive toward death.

1'00"

W: There comes a time when the words exchanged
     Instead of turning into shards of light
     Twist around you, choke your thoughts,
     Words have a matter
     (A viscous matter

When they are very heavy;
Thus, the words of love,
Amorous matter.)

M: Life is perpetuated by a crisscross of lightning bolts,
Information circulates;
Deep in the night destinies interconnect;
The cards are fixed.

W: We go through our days with still faces,
There is no more love in our barren gazes
Childhood is over, the games are sorted,
We make our way to the endgame.

M: The last particles
Drift in silence
And the void articulates
In the night, its presence.

W: Dust swirls across the grey, shifting ground;
A gust of wind rises and purifies space.
We wanted to live, traces of this remain;
Our slow motion bodies are frozen in expectation.

1'04"

M: In the solitude, the silence, the light, man is charged with a
mental energy which he then dissipates in his relationships
with others. Indifferent, perfect and round, the world has
kept the memory of its common origin. Portions of the
world appear, then disappear; they appear again.

W: At the end of the whiteness, there is death
And bodies separate in motion

Between raw particles,
I complete my journey of emotion.

M: Life is perfect, life is round;
This is a new history of the world.

W: There is no more topology
In the sub-atomic universe
And the spirit finds a home
At the bottom of the quantum crack,

The spirit coils and huddles down
In a pathetic universe
In a breaking of symmetry,
In the splendour of the identical.

M: Everything appears, everything shines in an unbearable
light; we have become like gods.

1'06"

W: A meeting takes place
At some time or another,
The night fills our eyes
And of course we are wrong.

M: The world is dissociated; it's made up of individuals.
Individuals are made up of organs; the organs of molecules. Time is running out; it separates into seconds. The
world is dissociated.

W: The process of seduction
Is a measured process,
Alone in the night of interaction
Between the light and the cess.

M: Neurons evoke the night. In the starry network of neurons, representations are formed; their course is random
and brief.

W: We would need to cross a lyrical universe
As we cross through a body that we have loved greatly
The oppressed powers should be awakened,
The thirst for eternity, dubious, filled with pathos.

M: The cerebral night is deep,
It created the world
And the whole set of instruments.

We are still descending towards the whiteness.

1'10"

W: In the contradiction that fills our mornings
We breathe, it's true, and the sky is peaceful
But we no longer believe that life is possible,
We no longer really feel that we are human beings.

M: The movement of indifference
On an axis that's cold and morbid
Is a metaphor for absence,
A semi-transition to the void.

The signals of the veiled reality,
In their half-luminescence
Hideous as a starry sky,
Semi-transitions to absence.

The shocks of neural machines
In a field of fictitious desires

Define a liberal world
Where nothing is final.

W: Nature must conform to the human sphere
And the human sphere must end and become rigid,
I've always been scared of falling into the void,
I was alone in the void and my hands were sore.

M: In death, the unmeated bodies
Of those we thought we knew
Have the rather stilted pose
Of those who will not be reborn.

They are there, simple and without wounds,
All their desires are appeased,
They are no more than a skeleton
That time will eventually have erased.

1'17"

M: We assume the existence of an observer.

W: You are here
Or elsewhere
And you sit cross-legged like a tailor
On the tiles of your kitchen
And your existence is in ruins,
Lift up your voice to the Lord.

Look! There are molecules
That exist in a half-connection
There are half-betrayals,
There are ridiculous moments.

M: We do not live; we perform movements that we believe to
be voluntary. Death will not reach us; we are already dead.

W: You are thinking of Schrödinger's cat,
Half-dead or half-alive
Of the nature of light
And the ambiguity of whiteness.

M: Language is like doing the dishes in a mountain chalet, said
Niels Bohr. Our water is dirty, our tea towels are soiled; yet
at the end of the day we still manage to clean the plates.

W: You stand on the footbridge,
And you think about washing-up liquid.

M: Two beings are reunited, each in their cerebral night.
However, at the exact midpoint of their consciousness of
the world, at a time fixed by the unfolding of the instru-
mental protocol, at a precise, non-random time, at a
necessary time, a performance takes place.

2'15"

M: Charged with energy, particles circulate in an enclosed
space, in a limited time. Let us call this space the city; let us
equate energy with desire; we obtain a metaphor for life.

W: You think you are shaping individual beings,
At each moment your eye takes their measure
There are exceptions, residual cases
But you are sure of yourself, you know nature.

M: Obeying the theory of shocks, the particles bristle in
reaction, with carapaces, thorns, defensive or offensive
weapons; we obtain a metaphor for animal evolution.

W: In the middle of the night you see the trajectories
    Of objects which circulate, clear as at noon,
    For you freedom is the meaning of history
    And action at a distance is an imprecise dream.

M: Just as the rock needs the water
    That erodes it,
    We need new metaphors.

W: You have an agenda and an address,
    Human beings are mobile and often vulnerable
    They clash with human beings for a few years,
    Then they break down into unstable aggregates.

    Two particles come together
    And their wave function is shared
    Then they separate in the night,
    They go their separate ways.

    Let us subject particle B to the action of an electric field,
    Particle A will react identically
    Whatever the distance
    There will be an action, an influence.

M: The separation of the world into objects is a mental pro-
    jection. Phenomena take place; an experimental set-up
    is fixed. Regarding the result of the measurements, an
    agreement can be reached in the community of observers.
    With a certain approximation, we can define values. These
    values are the result of an interaction between the world,
    consciousness and the instrument. So, through a reason-
    able intersubjectivity, we can bear witness to what we have
    observed, what we have seen, what we have learned.

11

Letter to Lakis Proguidis

My dear Lakis,[1]
Ever since we've known each other, I've sensed that you were disturbed by this bizarre (compulsive? masochistic?) attachment that I regularly show for poetry. You naturally sense the drawbacks: the anxiety of the publishers, the bewilderment of the critics; and let's add, for the sake of completeness, that ever since I've become a successful novelist, I've irritated the poets. Faced with a mania pursued with such obstinacy, you legitimately start to ponder; this pondering eventually gave rise to an article that appeared in issue 9 of *L'Atelier du roman*. Let's say it straight out: I was struck by the seriousness and depth of this article. After reading it, I felt it was getting hard to evade the issue any longer; I, in turn, had to try to explain myself and answer your questions.

The idea of a literary history separate from human history as a whole seems to me quite invalid (and I would add that the democratization of knowledge is making it more and more artificial). It's therefore neither out of provocation nor whimsy that I will be appealing, in what follows, to extra-literary fields of knowledge. Without a doubt, the twentieth century will remain as the age when, in the minds of the general public, a scientific explanation of the world triumphed, an explanation that they associated with a materialist ontology and the principle of local determinism. For example, the explanation of human behaviour by a short list of numerical parameters (essentially, concentrations of hormones and neurotransmitters) is gaining ground every day. In these matters, the novelist is obviously part of the general public. The construction of a character in a novel should therefore, if he is honest, appear to him as a somewhat formal and futile exercise; all in all, a technical specifications sheet would be sufficient. It's painful to say it, but the notion of a character in a novel seems to me to presuppose the existence, perhaps not of a soul, but at least of a certain *psychological depth*. At the very least, we must agree that the gradual exploration of a certain psychology was long considered to be one of the novelist's specialties, and that this radical reduction of his or her powers can only lead to a certain hesitation as to the merits of such practices.

Perhaps there's an even more serious problem: as the examples of Dostoyevsky and Thomas Mann eloquently show, the novel is a natural place for the expression of debates or fraught philosophical controversies. It's an understatement to say that the triumph of scientism dangerously limits the space for these debates and the magnitude of these controversies. When they seek clarification on the nature of the world, our contemporaries no longer turn to philosophers or thinkers from the 'human sciences', whom they consider (most often rightly) to be trivial glove puppets; they immerse themselves in Stephen Hawking, in Jean-Didier Vincent or in Trịnh Xuân Thuận.[2] The recent vogue for café discussions, the more general mass success of astrology and clairvoyance seem to me at best to be compensatory reactions, of a vaguely schizophrenic kind, to what is perceived as the inevitable extension of the scientific worldview.

Under these conditions, the novel, the prisoner of a stifling behaviourism, eventually turns to its sole, its ultimate lifeline:

'writing' (by now, the word 'style' is hardly used any more: it's not impressive enough, it lacks mystery). In short, on the one hand there's science, seriousness, knowledge, reality. On the other hand, literature, its gratuitousness, its elegance, its formal games; the production of 'texts', playful little objects that can be commented on by adding prefixes (para, meta, inter). What's the content of these texts? It's not healthy, it's not allowed, in fact it's unwise to talk about it.

This spectacle has its depressing side. For my part, I've never been able to witness without a pang the orgy of techniques implemented by this or that '*Minuit* formalist' for such a slender final result. To keep my grip, I often repeated to myself this phrase from Schopenhauer: 'The first – and practically the only – condition of good style is having something to say.' With its characteristic brutality, this phrase can be helpful. For example, during a literary conversation, when the word 'writing' is spoken, you know it's time to relax a bit. To look around, to order a new beer.

What's the connection with poetry? Apparently none. On the contrary, at first glance, poetry seems even more seriously contaminated by this stupid idea that literature is a work on language with the aim of producing writing. One aggravating circumstance is that it's particularly sensitive to the formal conditions of its exercise (for example, Georges Perec managed to become a great writer despite Oulipo; I don't know of any poet who resisted *lettrisme*).[3] It should be noted, however, that the erasure of the character (as in a novel) doesn't concern poetry at all; philosophical debate has never been its natural place – nor any debate, for that matter. So poetry retains many of its powers intact – provided, of course, that it agrees to use them.

I find it interesting that you mention Christian Bobin in connection with me, if only to underline what separates me from this amiable idolater (what annoys me about him is not so much the way he marvels at the 'humble objects of the world created by God' but rather the fact that he constantly gives the impression of marvelling at his own marvel).[4] Going down a few rungs on the ladder of horror, you could have mentioned the uncertain Coelho.[5] I have no intention of dodging the confrontation with these unpleasant corollaries of my decision to awaken the dormant powers of poetic expression. If, the minute it tries to speak of the world, poetry sees itself so easily accused of metaphysical or mystical tendencies, this is for one simple reason: between mechanistic reductionism and New Age silliness, there's nothing left. Nothing. A terrifying intellectual nothingness, a total desert.

The twentieth century will (also) remain as that paradoxical period when physicists refuted materialism, renounced local determinism, in short completely abandoned the same ontology of objects and properties that was at the same time spreading among the general public as constitutive of a scientific vision of the world. In this (most excellent) no. 9 of *L'Atelier du roman*, mention is made of the endearing figure of Michel Lacroix. I have carefully read and re-read his latest book, *L'Idéologie du New Age* [*The New Age Ideology*].[6] I've come to the definite conclusion that he has no chance of emerging victorious in the fight he's picked. The New Age finds its source in the unbearable suffering engendered by social dislocation; it has from the outset favoured the new means of communication; and it offers effective technologies for well-being. So he is right to say that it's infinitely more powerful than people might think. New Age thought – and here, too, he is right – is much more than a remix of old kinds of quackery: it was the first to consider annexing, for its own benefit, the recent changes in scientific thought (the study of overall systems as irreducible to the sum of their elements; the demonstration of quantum non-separability). Instead of attacking this field (where New Age thought is ultimately fragile – after all, the changes that have occurred would fit a completely positivist philosophy as much as an ontology à la Bohm), Michel Lacroix merely utters touching and varied lamentations, testimonies of a childish fidelity to the thought of otherness, to the legacies of Greek or Judeo-Christian civilizations. It's not with arguments of this type that he has any chance of resisting the holistic bulldozer.

Having said that, I myself couldn't have done any better. This is what bothers me: intellectually, I feel incapable of going any further. However, I have a hunch that poetry has a role to play; maybe as a sort of chemical precursor. Poetry did not just precede the novel; it also preceded, more directly, philosophy. If Plato excluded the poets from that city he devised, it was because he no longer needed them (and, having become useless, they would soon become dangerous). Basically, if I write poems, this is perhaps mainly to emphasize a monstrous general lack (a lack that can be seen as emotional, social, religious, or metaphysical; and each of these approaches will be equally true). It's perhaps also because poetry is the only way to express this lack in its pure state, its native state; to simultaneously express each of its complementary aspects. Perhaps it's to leave the following minimal message: 'Someone, in the mid-1990s, felt keenly the emergence of a monstrous general lack; unable to give a clear account of the phenomenon, he did, however, as a testimony to his incompetence, leave us a few poems.'

12

The question of paedophilia

Through the wording of your questions, I feel I am subtly being asked to say something politically incorrect – probably by highlighting the sexual urges supposed to run through childhood; this is a path I will not take.[1] The sexual urges of childhood, in reality, don't exist; they're an outright invention. In all the cases so complacently reported by the media, the child is absolutely, totally a victim. Still, there's something too comfortable about this emphasis on paedophilia and incest; the paedophile seems to me the ideal scapegoat for a society that organizes the exacerbation of desire without providing the means to satisfy it. In one sense, this is what you'd expect (advertising, and the economy in general are based on desire, not on its satisfaction); I still believe it's useful to point out this obvious truth: under the current conditions of the sexual economy, the mature man wants to fuck, but he no longer has the possibility of doing so; he doesn't even really have the right to do so anymore. So we mustn't be too surprised if he takes it out on the one person unable to resist him: the child.

The ideal paedophile is fifty-two years old, bald, with a potbelly. A sales engineer in a struggling company, he often lives in a semi-residential suburb, in the middle of some dingy region or other; he has no sense of rhythm at all. Married for twenty-seven years to a woman of his age, he's a practising Catholic – and well known to his neighbours as a good chap. His sex life is far from being a fireworks display.

At first, the paedophile discovers pornography, he becomes a fervent consumer of it; in this way, he considerably intensifies his torments – while decreasing the purchasing power of the household. Prostitution gives him only limited relief; inadequate and brief, his erections are a stumbling block for him: no matter how much he pays, the prostitute's contempt scares him a little. More generally, he's not wrong to be afraid of women; he does know, however, that he has nothing to fear from the child. He'd like to be a child himself.

The child is innocent, really innocent, he lives in an ideal world, the world before sexuality (and besides that, the world before money). Not for very long (just a few years), but he doesn't know that yet. Loved by his parents, he is indeed lovable. He considers adults to be wise and benevolent beings. He's wrong.

The meeting between these two people, the paedophile and the child (one of them the happiest person in the world, since he as yet knows no desire; the other the unhappiest person in the world, since he knows desire without knowing satisfaction), will provide the conditions for a perfect melodrama. At the end of the confrontation, the child will be permanently defiled. Those few years of innocence, of the world before sex, will have been stolen from him. The paedophile will have plunged much lower down the spiral of self-loathing. He will gladly welcome his capture, as it confirms what he already knew: he is the most monstrous and ridiculous person in the world. He's old, he's dirty, his soul is ugly – plus he's not even a writer. He is the first to request his own castration. He has finally understood what everyone around him knew already: when you are no longer desirable, you no longer have the right to desire. The wrong he has committed is one for which he will pay dearly. For several years he will be buggered, beaten and humiliated by the other inmates. Even in prison, he will be the lowest of the low (the killer, a dangerous beast, is as such respected; but you have to be very miserable and very cowardly – his fellow inmates think, quite correctly – to attack a child).

Basically, being neither a paedophile nor the victim of a paedophile, I do not feel directly concerned by these questions. I personally discovered sexual desire at a normal age (if memory serves aright, around thirteen). I'm glad that the initiation did not take place earlier, that the phenomenon somehow befell me like a natural biological disaster – so that I can't blame anyone. Of course, I'd have preferred a few years' respite; still, I feel it's a bit silly to talk about 'paedophilia' when dealing with girls of sixteen or seventeen (I've observed this abuse of language several times on the TF1 news). The questionnaire also maintains this ambiguity by alternately using the terms minor and child; between childhood and the status of adult there's a crucial stage, which is *adolescence*. Adolescence in our contemporary societies is not a secondary, transient state; on the contrary, it's the state in which, as we gradually age in our physical being, we are today condemned to live, practically until the day we die.

13

Humanity, the second stage

For my part, I've always considered feminists to be amiable dimwits, harmless in principle, but unfortunately made dangerous by their disarming lack of lucidity. So, in the 1970s, you could see them fighting for contraception, abortion, sexual freedom, etc., just as if the 'patriarchal system' was an invention of wicked males, when the historical aim of men had obviously been to fuck as many girls as possible without having to face the burden of a family. The poor ladies were even naive enough to imagine that lesbian love, an erotic condiment enjoyed by almost all active heterosexuals, was a dangerous challenge to male power. Finally, they displayed – and this was the saddest thing about it – an incomprehensible appetite for the professional world and for business life; men, who had long known what to expect when it came to the 'freedom' and 'fulfilment' offered by work, chuckled softly.

Thirty years after the beginnings of 'mainstream' feminism, the results are appalling. Not only have women entered the corporate world on a massive scale, but they perform most of the tasks in it (anyone who has actually worked knows what to expect in this respect: male employees are stupid, lazy, quarrelsome, undisciplined, and generally incapable of devoting themselves to any collective task). The market of desire has considerably extended its empire, so women must at the same time, and sometimes for several decades, dedicate themselves to the maintenance of their 'seduction capital', devoting crazy amounts of money and energy to achieve a not very convincing overall result (the effects of aging remain roughly inescapable). Having by no means renounced motherhood, they must ultimately raise alone the child or children they have succeeded in extracting from the men who have crossed their lives – the said men having in the meantime left them for a younger woman; and they're pretty lucky if they manage to get payment of child support. In short, the immense process of domestication accomplished by women over the previous millennia in order to suppress a man's primitive inclinations (violence, fucking, drunkenness, play) and to make him a creature more or less able to lead a social life has been reduced to nothing, in the space of a generation.

The goal of feminists (to enter male society as 'free and equal' members, even if this means sacrificing certain female values) has in any case been achieved, in the West at least. Valerie Solanas' goal (destroying male society, replacing it with a society based on opposing values) was, to say the least, of a different nature.[1] From the first pages of the *S.C.U.M. Manifesto*, we feel that we are dealing with a text of a different calibre. The amiable babble of someone like Simone de Beauvoir (the famous formula 'One is not born, but rather becomes, a woman' testifies merely to a crass ignorance of the most elementary biological data) is succeeded by a realistic position tinged with common sense: the differences between men and women are mainly genetic, secondarily cultural. Moreover, the question is of only moderate interest to Valerie Solanas: for her, indeed, women are not only different, they are *superior*. Man is a biological accident, a failed woman – an emotional cripple, incapable of caring for others, compassion or love. Profoundly selfish, definitively trapped within himself, he is 'trapped in a twilight zone halfway between humans and apes'.[2] An unhappy ape, aware of his disgrace, he has no other interest in existence than frantically showing off his sex (by fucking as many women as possible; by entering into sterile and harmful competitions with other males, his companions in misery). In short, man is an ape armed with a machine gun. In keeping with his selfish and violent nature, he has thus succeeded in transforming the world, in the expression of the incisive Valerie, into a 'shitpile'.

It's tempting to dismiss this rapid explanation of history and consign it to one of the categories of delirium; however, compared to heavier theories (Marxism, etc.), it largely holds up. An amusing confirmation of this can be found in the 'false friend' of the English title: reading the words 'cutting up', almost all men immediately understand this to mean 'castrating' them, and are curiously reassured when they learn that 'cut up' actually means 'to tear to pieces, to cut to pieces'; this just shows the pathetic depth of male anguish when it comes to their touted virility. It should also be noted that those who currently devote their energy to stupid fights (sports competitions, gang fights, ethnic conflicts, civil or religious wars), quite wrongly monopolizing the attention of the media to the detriment of more valid subjects, are different in every respect (religious beliefs, racial affiliation, political beliefs, etc.); their only attested common point is, precisely, the one put forward by Valerie Solanas: they are men. You won't find a single woman among those obscure morons who play around with their machetes, rocket launchers or Kalashnikovs. Likewise, and despite thirty years of uninterrupted feminist propaganda, a woman still does not seem altogether at home in a business meeting or a cabinet meeting. This failing, Valerie Solanas would say, is the proof of her fundamental superiority. Woman didn't invent power, or competition, or war; it's kind of obvious.

Though its first pages are dazzling, the *S.C.U.M. Manifesto* then slips, it unfortunately has to be admitted, into Stirner-style hogwash, or even worse. From the start, to tell the truth, one feels a vague concern at the way Valerie Solanas understands male psychology *so well*; this anxiety gradually takes on a certain consistency, and we observe with sadness, in this daring pamphleteer, the way typically masculine traits start to multiply. First, these include megalomania, senseless vanity, delusional overestimation of oneself (traits that end up making her almost as ridiculous as Nietzsche in his terminal phase). Second, the unhealthy attraction to violence, assassination, conspiracy, 'revolutionary' action; the seeds can be found right from the start when, starting from the indisputable natural inferiority of man, she concludes that this deprived portion of humanity needs to be liquidated; we end up with a rather despicable text, with openly Nazi fantasies (these begin with the mention of 'degenerate art', continue with the proposal to use gas chambers, and lead to the image of something akin to a Night of the Long Knives). Finally, typical of her time and her country, Valerie Solanas seems bogged down in an unthinking respect for the 'individual' and 'freedom', even in the absence of any conclusive definition of the concept; her unattractive description of the 'free woman' – that is to say of the S.C.U.M. woman – thus brings us back to the darkest hours of the 1960s. All of this is especially regrettable as Valerie seems on several occasions to have been close to an authentic concept of individual nonexistence; unaffected by the reactionary gossip so common in her time concerning the 'right to be different', she continues to energetically advocate the scientific improvement of mankind; unlike that culturalist nonsense about ambiguity and 'uncertain identities', she remains convinced that the solution to the problems she is raising lies in genetic engineering.

As it is, the *S.C.U.M. Manifesto* is certainly not, contrary to what Valerie Solanas claimed in 1977, the 'best text in all history'; but one cannot fail to be struck by the depth of the biological intuitions that run through it. On the one hand, embryogenetic research has clearly confirmed the secondary and optional role of the male sex in animal reproduction. On the other hand, the progress made in cloning techniques gives hope for the advent of reliable reproduction, while opening up the possibility of new, strange human relations, based both on difference and on identity (identical twins are a possible current example of such relations). Finally, in the longer term, direct intervention on the genetic code should make it possible to overcome certain limitations currently considered to be inseparable from the human condition (the most spectacular, of course, being aging and death).

While it's understandable that such prospects sow terror among the devotees of revealed religions (the creation of life being considered by them as the exclusive domain of the divine), it's however difficult to understand the reluctance expressed by various thinkers who in principle define themselves as 'progressive'. Is this a limitation of Western political thought that, from Hobbes to Rousseau, has been unable to think of society other than as a collection of individuals and has found its apogee in the classical conception of 'human rights' and 'democracy'? Is it an obscure and infantile nostalgia for the tragic stage, for the 'philosophy of the absurd', even for randomness as a regressive divinity? Is it a new kind of jealousy, an anticipatory jealousy of the possibilities open to future generations? Either way, it's certain that Valerie Solanas (an incomplete, tortured, contradictory, fascinating and infuriating person, as prophets always are) is to be found on the side of the progressives. Her contempt for nature is infinite, absolute, without limits. Here, by way of example, is the paragraph where she synthesizes – magnificently – the ideal of hippie life: 'He would like to return to Nature, to wild life, to find the lair of the furry animals of which he is a part, far from the city where at least one finds some traces, a vague beginning of civilization, to live at the primary level of the species and to occupy himself with simple, non-intellectual jobs: raising pigs, fucking, threading pearls.'

Thus, in the mid-1970s, bogged down in an unprecedented ideological morass, and despite slipping into occasional Nazi tropes, Valerie Solanas was practically alone in her generation to have the courage to maintain a progressive and rational attitude, in accordance with the noblest aspirations of the Western project: to establish man's absolute technological control over nature, including his own biological nature, and its evolution. And this was with the long-term purpose of rebuilding a new nature on a foundation conforming to moral law, that is, to establish the universal kingdom of love. End of story.

14

Empty heavens

In the film he was planning to make about the life of Saint Paul, Pasolini intended to transpose the apostle's mission to our contemporary world; to imagine what form it might take in the midst of commercial modernity, but without changing the text of the epistles. But he intended to replace Rome with New York, and he gave an immediate reason for this: like Rome in Saint Paul's day, New York is now the centre of the world, the seat of the powers that dominate the world (in the same spirit he proposed replacing Athens by Paris, and Antioch by London). After a few hours in New York, I realized that there was probably another, more secret reason, one that only the film could ever have revealed. In New York as in Rome, despite the apparent dynamism, one feels a curious atmosphere of decrepitude, death, the end of the world. I know very well that 'the city is fizzing, it's a melting pot, a crazy energy swirls around it', etc. Strangely, though, I wanted to stay in my hotel room instead; to watch the seagulls flying across the abandoned port facilities on the banks of the Hudson. The rain was falling gently on brick warehouses; it was very calming. I could well imagine myself remaining cloistered in a huge apartment, under a dirty brown sky, while on the horizon the last red glow of sporadic fighting would gradually spread. Later on, I'd be able to head out, go for a walk through its finally deserted streets. Rather as layers of vegetation overlap in a thick undergrowth, heights and styles come together in New York in an unpredictable jumble. One sometimes has the impression of walking less down a street than in a canyon, between rocky fortresses. It's somewhat similar to Prague (but New York is more limited; its buildings still cover only a century of architecture), – you sometimes feel you're circulating in an organism, subject to the laws of natural growth. (In contrast, the Buren columns, in the gardens of the Palais-Royal, remain frozen in a stupid opposition to their architectural environment; we clearly feel the presence of a human will, and even of a rather petty human will, intent on producing a kind of sight gag.) It's possible that human architecture attains its greatest beauty only when, bubbling up in varied juxtapositions, it starts to evoke some natural formation; just as nature only attains its greatest beauty when, through the play of light and the abstraction of forms, it allows the suspicion of a *voluntary* origin to hover over it.

15

I have a dream

Let's get things clear: life, as it is, isn't bad. We've made some of our dreams come true. We can fly, we can breathe underwater, we've invented household appliances and computers. The problem begins with the human body. The brain, for example, is an organ of great richness and people die without having exploited all of its possibilities. Not because our head is too big, but because life is too short. We age quickly and die. Why? We don't know, and if we did, we'd still be dissatisfied. It's very simple: human beings want to live and yet they have to die. Thus, our first desire is to be immortal. Of course, no one knows what eternal life looks like, but we can imagine it.

In my dream of eternal life, not much is happening. Maybe I live in a cave. Yes, I like caves, it's dark and cool and I feel safe inside. Often, I wonder if there's been any real progress since life in the caves. As I sit there, calmly listening to the sound of the sea, surrounded by friendly creatures, I think about what I would like to remove from this world: fleas, birds of prey, money and work. Probably also porn movies and belief in God. Every now and then I decide to quit smoking. Instead of cigarettes, I prefer to take pills that have a similar stimulating effect on my brain. In addition, I have a wide variety of synthetic drugs at my disposal; each of these drugs develops my sensitivity. I'm then able to hear ultrasound, see ultraviolet rays – and other things that I have a hard time understanding.

I'm a bit different now, not just younger, my body is transformed, I've got four legs, that's good, I can stand much better, solidly grounded. Even when I drink too much, I'm not afraid of falling. Unlike primitive humans, kangaroos, and penguins, nothing really disturbs me. What's more, I no longer need clothes. Clothes are impractical, whatever their shape, they interfere with the breathing of the skin. Naked, I feel freer. Most importantly, I'm neither male nor female – I'm a hermaphrodite. Before I could only imagine the feeling of penetration, as I'm not homosexual. Now I have some idea, it's a fundamental experience that I've been waiting for a long time. I have nothing more to hope for. Some readers will wonder if life, in the most beautiful cave with the most adorable of creatures, doesn't end up being boring after thousands of years (or even hundreds of thousands of years, in my case). No, I don't think so, at least not for me. I don't find it boring to repeat endlessly what I like doing – I'd even go further: true happiness is in repetition, in the perpetual restarting of the same, as in dance and music, for example. *Autobahn* by Kraftwerk. The same goes for sex: when it's over, we'd like to do it again. Happiness is an addiction, an addiction that can be found in chemicals or in human beings; when I have my pills or my friends I don't need anything anymore. Boredom is the alternative to happiness, everyday routines, new products, information – even presented in an attractive way. I've found happiness in my cave, I have nothing more to hope for, I can take a bath whenever I want. Outside it's warm and clear, I think a bit about Germany where people lived together in small spaces and I'm happy that Heaven isn't overcrowded.

People are free to choose their tombs, they wander around as much as they want.

I open my eyes and find that my dream is rather superficial. I light a new cigarette, chew on the filter, in reality there's no harmony with the universe. In moments of happiness, by example when contemplating a beautiful landscape, I instantly know that I'm not part of it, the world appears to me as something strange, I don't know of any place where I can feel at home. God himself can't solve this problem, and besides, I don't believe in God, he's not necessary, either here or in paradise. I believe in love, it's the only good thing we have, better than a fitness program, better than sport. Maybe one day my dream of eternity will come true, then I'll be a creature with legs, wings or tentacles, maybe somewhere else. Unlike most people I don't fear death, as I get older I rediscover my long-forgotten youth, and once in a while, when the going gets tough, I bury myself comfortably in my work. My books already guarantee me a form of immortality.

16

Neil Young

In his thirty years (to date) of a nearly perfectly erratic career, Neil Young may have accidentally coincided with certain fashions. In the mid-1970s all the hippies liked 'Harvest', and in the 1980s he paid a heavy price for this success, until the grunge generation realized that he was also producing tortured, violent records, with strange complaints coming from his electric guitar; for a few years, once more, Neil Young was in fashion, hailed as a precursor. It's strange that none of this succeeded in deflecting him; but, to tell the truth, in order to be deflected, one must have an initial direction. 'The goal of any style,' writes Nietzsche at the end of *Ecce Homo*, 'is to communicate by signs, including the rhythm of these signs, a psychological state, a tension of feelings; I have a wide multiplicity of psychological states within me, and so I have a very large number of possible styles.' We could compare the musical journey of Neil Young (incoherent, uncontrollable, but always overwhelmingly sincere) to the biography of a manic depressive; or to the course of an atmospheric disturbance crossing an area of valleys and mountains. It really feels like he's grabbing the closest musical instrument and, simply and directly, expressing the emotions running through his soul. Most often, the instrument is a guitar; but there are other musicians who are great guitarists, while very few artists are as immediately present as he is, alive in each of their notes, in each tremor of their voice. 'Soldier', clumsily composed on the piano with a few fingers, is one of his most mysterious and beautiful songs; in 'Little Wing', the harmonica acquires a sad violence, a tone of desperation that breathes across the ages; and it's in a perfectly incongruous jazz context that 'Twilight' appears, one of his most poignant drifting songs. Perfection in Neil Young is fragile, it's born in the midst of chaos. None of his albums are perfectly successful; but I don't know of any that doesn't have at least one beautiful song.

His most beautiful records are undoubtedly those that oscillate between sadness, loneliness, daydreaming and peaceful happiness. We can imagine his ideal listener, his invisible double. Neil Young's songs are made for those who are often unhappy, lonely, approaching the gateways of despair – but who continue to believe that happiness is possible. They're for those who are not always happy in love, but keep falling in love again; those who know the temptation of cynicism, but can't give in to it for very long; those who can cry in rage at the death of a friend ('Tonight's the Night'); those who really wonder if Jesus Christ can come and save them; those who continue, in all good faith, to believe that we can live happily on Earth. You have to be a very great artist to have the courage to be sentimental, to take the risk of sentimentality. But it feels so good, sometimes, to hear a man humbly complain, in a sad little voice, about having been abandoned by a woman: 'A man needs a maid', 'What did you do to my life', for this reason, will last. It feels so good, too, to immerse yourself in those true hymns to love, scintillating and magical, that Neil Young has produced over the years in collaboration with Jack Nitzsche: 'Such a Woman', and especially the extraordinary 'We never danced.' But, like Schubert, Neil Young is perhaps even more overwhelming when he tries to describe happiness.

'Sugar Mountain', 'I Am a Child', are so pure, so naive, that they leave us heartbroken. Such happiness is not possible, not here, not with us. We would need to have preserved our childhood. Not only is there no other song that I know of, but no other artistic creation that tries, as 'My Boy' does, to express the dark and poignant feeling of the mature man who is saddened to see his son already starting to leave childhood behind him. You'll have had so little time, my son; we'll have had so little time together. 'Oh, you'd better take your time / My boy / I thought we had just begun.' Some texts by Neil Young evoke adolescence through the violence of the feeling of love; but this is common in rock, and I believe his most original and beautiful songs are the ones where he has managed to become a child again. Sometimes this man has seen strange things in the sky, in the ripples of water on the surface of a pond. 'After the Gold Rush' transports us directly to a dream: 'Here we are in the years', so familiar and so unsettling, evokes those scintillating afternoons in Clifford Simak's novels.

How does a person become Neil Young? He tells us in the very autobiographical 'Don't be denied': the disunited childhood, the beatings at school, the meeting with Stephen Stills, the desire to be a star. And, through it all, the will to hold out – not to let yourself get demolished by the world. 'Oh, friend of mine / Don't be denied.' Who's he singing for? For his friend, for the whole world? I admit it, I've often felt he was singing for me. When I listen to these immense unstructured, improbable drifts that punctuate his work ('Last Trip to Tulsa', 'Twilight', 'Inca Queen', 'Cortez the Killer', and so on), it's always the same image that comes to my mind: a man is moving forward along a difficult and rocky path. He keeps falling; his knees are bleeding; he gets up and continues to move forward. (It's almost the same picture as in *Winterreise*; except that, in Schubert, it's cold, the path is covered with snow, and the man is terribly tempted to curl up in the sweetness of death and the snow.) The electric guitar travels across strange, frightening and sublime landscapes; sometimes everything calms down, and the world beats to the rhythm of a hot swaying motion; sometimes violence and terror invade the world. The voice continues, stubborn and fragile. The voice guides us. It comes from far, far away in the soul; it refuses to give up. It's not a very manly voice; there's something of the woman, the old man and the child in it. It's the voice of a human being, who, furthermore, has something naive and important to tell us: the world can be as it is, that's the world's business; it's no reason for us to give up on making it better. This is the simple message of 'Lotta Love': 'It's gonna take a lotta love / To change the way things are.' It's the message of 'Heart of Gold', his most immediately immortal song: 'I'm still searching for a heart of gold / And I'm getting old.' I've been listening to Neil Young for almost twenty years now; he has often accompanied me, in times of suffering and doubt. I now know that time will not prevail against us.

17

Interview with Christian Authier

CA: How did you experience these controversies over your statements about Islam?

MH: In fact, I wasn't really expecting them. I know it may come as a surprise, but when I said, 'after all, Islam is the dumbest religion', I thought I was saying something obvious. I didn't think it would be criticized, or even contested. Most of the good authors of the past, from Spinoza to Lévi-Strauss, have come to the same conclusion; so I thought I could be satisfied with a brief summary. I hadn't understood that respect for identities had grown so strong. Respect has become obligatory, even for the most immoral and foolish cultures. In recent years, even the Catholic Church has taken to behaving like a minority demanding respect, although it remains far less virulent than Islam. What is curious is that no one had foreseen this reaction. Pierre Assouline certainly hates me, and he did a great deal to stir things up.[1] In fact, I reacted to the whole affair with surprise and a certain amount of dread.

CA: Do you have the feeling that, despite certain appearances, we're living in a Puritan era?

MH: Yes, I have the impression that centuries ago, and even at the beginning of the twentieth century, people spoke more freely about religions. Things hardened at a certain point. In this case, I have the impression that it wasn't the controversy that created the success, but the success that created the controversy. If the book had sold less, I'd have had more of a chance of it all going unnoticed; Assouline also admits, quite nastily, in his think-piece, that his relentlessness was linked to my predictable success.

CA: How do you feel when Guillaume Durand[2] asks you on a *Campus* interview whether you're wearing a Vichy shirt in reference to Pétain?

MH: I like Guillaume Durand, but that wasn't very funny. It was an attempt at a bit of humour, but it fell rather flat. I think the news had got on top of him.

CA: Beyond the passages in the novel and then your statements about Islam, you must have thought that *Platform* would provoke violent reactions. This book contains fierce attacks on the West. More specifically, you make fun of journalists by citing their names . . .

MH: It's never very clever to mock the press, but they're not the ones who react most violently, in general: they're used to criticism. I was more afraid of the big brands – Eldorador, the Accor/Aurore group . . . As for *Le Guide du routard*, I wasn't really expecting it, but I can't say that I was all that surprised.[3] Basically, I wasn't expecting much. This book seemed less dangerous to me than *The Elementary Particles*. I believe things have got worse in the meantime. In three years, the demand for normality has become greater. Everyone was wrong: me, the publisher, the press secretary . . . nobody had seen where the problems would come from. Really, no one was thinking of

Islam, which isn't the main subject of the book, but just part of the backdrop.

AC: Barely a few days after the polemics, this 'backdrop' burst into the news . . .

MH: The terrorists' profile surprised me. I'd heard that some radical Islamists had pretty good scientific educations, but I didn't really believe it. In fact, the terrorists' profile is much closer to cult members than to regular terrorists. It's pretty scary. People have started to say in certain newspapers what I had thought for a long time, which is that Islamic fundamentalism is not really a deviation from the Islam of the Qur'an. It's just an interpretation of the Qur'an, one that's perfectly consistent. What fascinates me is to see that a large majority of people in the media keep repeating that the underlying message of Islam is a message of tolerance, one that forbids murder, is full of respect for other believers . . . I have a theory in general about history: there's no point in calling on very distant eras to explain recent history. You just have to look back a generation or two, and you get the picture. It always annoys me when people talk about the splendours of the Andalusian Middle Ages or whatever, because none of that has any effect in practice these days.

CA: A figure in *Platform* thinks that Islam is doomed in the long run, that it will be absorbed into liberal globalization and that the masses dream of nothing but the Western model . . .

MH: Yes, I think that's true, but you might find the long run to be a bit *too* long. Yes, I think that the masses do dream of the Western model. It seems to me a lesser evil in this case. There's obviously a struggle between two evils going on here, one of which is worse than the other.

CA: Regarding sexuality in the West, Michel questions narcissism, the loss of the taste for exchange and for giving as well as the inability to experience sex as something natural. Does this culture of narcissism strike you as the real heart of the matter?

MH: Yes, that's the main point. We spend too much time evaluating ourselves, evaluating others. After all, you have to forget about your own value in order to make love. As soon as being attractive is a goal in itself, sexuality becomes impossible. The decline of sentimentalism also causes the decline of sexuality. The popularity of S/M is more than just a fashion. Of course, there's a desire to sell new 'looks', but more deeply it corresponds to the way we envisage human relationships. S/M isn't very carnal, people use accessories, there's no skin-to-skin contact. I think there's a real loathing for the flesh in our societies, and this isn't easy to interpret. At one point in the novel, Michel says that the wasting away of sexuality in the West may have psychological causes, but that it's mainly a sociological phenomenon. I like the idea that there's no point in explaining sociological facts psychologically – it's a very positivist point of view. If I ponder this question from a psychological point of view, I can certainly find explanations such as the presence of porn images that make reality a little bland . . . pornography that harms real sexuality . . . representation that kills reality . . . All that's credible, but it's mainly the sociological aspect that strikes me. Human relations have generally declined.

CA: Michel and Valérie have a natural and instinctive sexuality.

MH: Sexuality is innocent in my work. It's never transgressive; in this, I feel quite close to Catherine Millet; but the general trend of pornography in modern art is more 'trashy'. I believe that fantasy kills sexuality, and that it's not very interesting. From a literary point of view, what is interesting, and difficult, are the sensations. Language isn't all that good at expressing sensations, whether they are pleasant or painful. Auguste Comte said something very true about the difficulty of describing painful symptoms to the doctor. You can locate pain, define it in terms of intensity, but it's hard to be more precise. It's the same problem with pleasure. And the difficulty becomes worse if you don't want to resort to metaphor. In *Platform*, Michel and Valérie love each other and the more they love each other, the more sexual it becomes between them. So, it's a mixture of sensations and emotions. I try to get close to reality. It's not the easiest thing to do.

CA: People have often forgotten that *Platform* was perhaps first and foremost a love story.

MH: Well yes, they've forgotten that. It's a shame because it's the first time I've created such a complex female character. Moreover, the shocking aspect of the book – love in the West – has been barely discussed at all. It's too dangerous, too complicated . . . Anyway, *Elle* pointed out that it's all a drama, which is true, but it means you refuse to believe in it.

CA: The love story is about to culminate in a happy ending . . .

MH: I'd love to write something completely idyllic. In this book, I wanted to have a lonely end in Pattaya. What struck me when I was there was seeing that, because everything is possible at the level of prostitution, it produces a kind of appeasement of desire. If you consider desire to be bad, as I do, it's a solution. To suppress desire, it must be satisfied – that's the easiest. For me, this is not a maximalist position.

CA: Michel no longer believes in collective projects or in politics. The solution for him and Valérie is a sort of individualistic escape . . .

MH: Valérie is the one in charge of this story. She is the one who tries to capture from society the money needed for their life together. She defines herself as a small predator with limited needs; I really like her. Like Dostoevsky, I believe that everyone who promotes generous and general ideas should be asked to make one particular person happy. It's true that my characters are all politically nihilistic. I'm forced to the realization that the society in which I live is moving towards goals that are not mine. The West isn't made for a human life. In fact, there's only one thing you can really do in the West, and that's to make money. So Valérie's attitude is quite common among young people: earn money quickly, then go and live somewhere else. It's a rational solution.

CA: Michel says that his ancestors had a project, believed in progress, in civilization and were attached to the idea of transmission. Your characters faithfully reflect the abandonment of all this.

MH: People are doing everything to bring the West to this position. For example, Berlusconi makes some remark and people immediately say that it's silly to classify civilizations on a scale of values . . . No, it's not silly. They want to discourage us from thinking that Western civilization may have been superior on certain points; suddenly, this civilization dissolves into cynicism. For a long time, there was this idea that the good of future generations was an important thing. People these days definitely project themselves less into some future. Life is reduced more and more to a matter of use values. Euthanasia is a phenomenon that reveals quite clearly this notion that there is nothing in life other than the interest and the pleasure that can be derived from it.

CA: There are some very savage scenes of urban violence in *Platform*. When there's no longer any possibility of identification with the other, you write, the only modality that remains is suffering and cruelty.

MH: I think a lot of this is because of the allure of consumption. And also, of course, because of the culture of the Left, which has tended to a large extent to promote Evil, to give it an aura, in particular through the figure of the 'bad boy', for example the Genet sanctified by Sartre. Sartre's motives could only be the propagation of immorality – he was obviously quite able to realize that Genet was a mediocre writer. All of this has contributed to the general devaluation of the concept of morality. But the situation is worse in the United States, even though the culture of the Left is much less present there. Basically, there's something stranger going on: people want to fight, they want violence. I have the impression that there are fewer and fewer compromises, even when it comes to quite subtle oppositions. For example, I know that my enemies will remain my enemies for good. Pure hedonistic individualism gives birth to the law of the jungle. But, in the jungle, animals minimize their personal risks. In modern Western man, there's also a real taste for violence. The recent special issue of *Technikart*, 'La vie *Fight Club*' ['Life *Fight Club* style'] was quite convincing from this point of view. This violence may be related to the difficulty in experiencing sensations in sexuality. The taste for normally pleasant things is lost. Then, the media that love a spectacle support the movement.

CA: *Platform* has a very strong comic element, especially in the first third of the novel. Did this follow from your desire to grab the reader from the start, so as to keep them reading?

MH: Yes I think so. I liked the characters of Robert and Josyane. I really like Robert. I like characters that piss people off. They exist in all groups. In the funny passages, apart from *Le Guide du routard*, I wanted to take off American bestsellers. More generally, I wanted to write a book that you could read without stopping. I sacrificed various things for the fluidity of the story and its speed. I also returned to a more traditional use of tenses, on the tried and tested basis of imperfect and preterite [*passé simple*], which makes the book clearer and gives it a more classic aspect.

CA: Why did you have silhouettes such as Chirac, Jospin, Jérôme Jaffré[4] or Julien Lepers[5] appearing in the background?

MH: With me, seeing bygone times come to life, even in their most minimal aspects, is one of the pleasures of reading novels of the past. So I allow myself to do that in my own books. After all, basically, everyone occasionally thinks about Chirac in their lives. They can't help thinking about him. Anyone living in France knows Chirac. It's in the same spirit that I cite real brands. Novels must be situated. It's in the logic of the novel. It needs the present.

CA: One sentence seems to encapsulate *Platform* both for Michel and for the West: 'People have lost heart.'

MH: I don't think the West really wants to live. This feeling was already present in the first scene of *Extension du domaine de la lutte* [*Extension of the Domain of Struggle*]. People have limited capacities for emotional engagement. You can't start life all over again. Only the Americans think you can.

CA: 'I'll be forgotten. I'll soon be forgotten.' These are Michel's last words. Do you think you will soon be forgotten?

MH: In fact, I wrote the entire ending with a lot of masochism. So maybe not. But I was very happy because it made me feel like it was my last book, a bit like a last will and testament. Vanity isn't such a powerful thing in me. I won't necessarily be forgotten very soon, but I will be forgotten.

CA: Beyond the recent controversies, you trigger passionate reactions from your readers. I've been present at certain scenes, and I feel that some people sometimes have a 'bone to pick' with you . . . How do you explain that?

MH: I don't know . . . maybe I make people anxious. So, ultimately, they want me to utter some reassuring words like, 'This was all for fun. In fact, everything is fine. Everything is getting better and better.' That's what I think I'm being asked: 'Everything will be fine. There is no conflict of civilizations. Jacques Chirac is there. Things seem to be going badly, but in fact they're going well . . .' There's something missing in my novels and people want me to say it for real: the final reassuring message. This reflects a form of general communication, such as: 'the situation is serious, but measures have been taken', or 'yes, she's dead, but I've embarked on the mourning process'. An expression of something purely negative is no longer acceptable.

CA: On a Canal+ programme, over a year ago, you said that you were afraid of being lynched one day. At present, are you afraid that you will not be forgiven for what you write or say?

MH: Yes, in France there will be more and more problems. I don't think things will calm down. So, yes, I'm a little scared. But you can also write without publishing.

CA: Part of the 'collateral damage' of these recent controversies was the way you vanished from the Goncourt prize list that many people had imagined you'd win. Did that hurt you?

MH: Not at all. The important point was that Nourissier[6] would support me all the way. Which he did. In fact, not being on the French Academy's prize list hurt me even more. I thought I had more support from the academicians. For the Goncourt, I knew it was basically Nourissier. So I didn't think I'd get it. But it was mostly the reactions of people, individually, that pained me. A few people rather gave up on me. Conversely, Alain Finkielkraut defended me fiercely.[7] The terrible thing is the extent to which you can't say anything anymore . . . Nietzsche, Schopenhauer and Spinoza wouldn't be accepted today. Political correctness, in its current form, makes almost all of Western philosophy unacceptable. More and more things are becoming impossible to think. It's scary.

CA: Isn't it simply the emergence of a smooth society that no longer tolerates the negativity you mentioned and that wants to eradicate Evil?

MH: I accept the idea that humanity can be born free of bad thoughts. I can argue with the overall project, but the problem is that humanity is born with bad thoughts. To take a simple example, I'm happy to be born genetically modified, so that the urge to smoke becomes non-existent in me. It's a consistent project: an undifferentiated, smooth humanity. Except that, in this case, they're trying to do it by castration, by constraint, and that won't work. I don't know what humanity might ulti- mately be like, but these days excessive standards have been imposed without bringing any real satisfaction in return. If I'm politically correct, what will I gain from it? They don't even promise me seventy-two virgins. They just promise they'll keep pissing me off, they promise I'll be able to buy Ralph Lauren polo shirts . . . That's why I think the only substance of the project is a desire to disappear. Deep down, I don't give a damn about the future of the West; but it can become difficult to fight self-censorship. We must mobilize a growing force. It's all maddening.

CA: What are your plans?

MH: I'm going to publish a book with Librio: *Lanzarote et autres textes* [*Lanzarote and Other Texts*]. Philippe Harel and I are going to adapt *The Elementary Particles*. But not everything is settled yet. We still don't have a producer.

18

Technical consolation

I don't love myself. I have little liking for myself, and even less self-esteem; besides, I'm not very interested in myself. I have known my main characteristics for a long time, and I have grown disgusted with them. As a teenager, or even a young man, I spoke about myself, I thought about myself, I was full of myself, as it were; this is no longer the case. I have removed myself from my thoughts, and the very prospect of having to tell a personal anecdote plunges me into a boredom bordering on catalepsy. When I absolutely have to do so, I lie.

Paradoxically, though, I have never regretted reproducing myself. You could even say that I love my son, and that I love him more each time I recognize in him traces of my own flaws. I see them manifesting themselves over time, with relentless determinism, and I rejoice in that. I shamelessly rejoice to see the repetition, and thus the eternalization, of personal characteristics that are in no way particularly commendable; that are even, quite often, contemptible; that have, in reality, no merit other than being mine. Besides, they're not even exactly mine; I realize that some have been copied exactly from the personality of my father, who was a total jerk; but, strangely enough, that doesn't detract from my joy. This joy is more than selfishness; it's deeper, more indisputable. Likewise, a volume is more than its projection on a flat surface; a living body is more than its shadow.

What saddens me on the contrary about my son is to see him display (thanks to the influence of his mother? the difference of the times? pure individuality?) the traits of an autonomous personality, in which I do not recognize myself at all, and that remains foreign to me. Far from marvelling at it, I realize that I will have left only an incomplete and weakened image of myself; for a few seconds, I can smell death more clearly. And, I can confirm it: death stinks.

Western philosophy hardly favours the expression of such feelings; these feelings leave no room for progress, for freedom, for individuation, for becoming; they aim at nothing other than the eternal, at the stupid repetition of the same. What's more, there is nothing original about them; they are shared by almost all of humanity, and even by most of the animal kingdom; they are nothing other than the ever-active memory of an overwhelming biological instinct. Western philosophy is a long, patient and cruel form of training that aims to persuade us that we are prone to certain misconceptions. The first is that we must respect others because they are different from us; the second is that we have something to gain from death.

Nowadays, as a result of Western technology, that veneer of propriety is quickly cracking. Of course, I'll get myself cloned as soon as possible; of course, everyone will be cloned as soon as possible. I'll go to the Bahamas, New Zealand or the Cayman Islands; I'll pay whatever price it takes (neither moral imperatives nor financial imperatives have ever weighed heavily against those of reproduction). I'll probably have two or three clones, as we have two or three children; between their births, I'll respect an adequate interval (they'll be neither too close together nor too far apart); as an already mature man, I will behave as a responsible father. I will give my clones a good education; thereafter, I will die. I will die without pleasure, because I do not wish to die. I am, however, until proven otherwise, obliged to do so. Through my clones, I will have achieved some form of survival – not quite sufficient, but greater than what children would have given me. This is the maximum, so far, that Western technology can offer me.

At the time of writing, it's impossible for me to predict whether my clones will be born outside a woman's womb. What seemed technically simple to the layman (nutrient exchanges through the placenta seem less mysterious in principle than the act of fertilization) turns out to be the most difficult to reproduce. If the technique has progressed sufficiently, my future children, my clones, will spend the beginning of their lives in a jar; that saddens me a bit. I love women's pussies, I'm happy to be inside them, in the elastic flexibility of their vagina. I understand the security reasons, the technical requirements; I understand the reasons that will gradually lead to in vitro gestation; I am just allowing myself, on this subject, a little display of nostalgia. Will my little ones, born so far away from the pussy, still have *any taste for pussy*? I hope so for them, I hope so with all my heart. There are many joys in this world, but there are few pleasures – and so few that do no harm. End of the humanist parenthesis.

If they are to grow in a jar, my clones will be born, obviously, without a belly button. I don't know who first used this term 'navel-gazing literature' in a deprecating sense; but I do know that I've never liked this facile cliché. What would be the point of a literature that claims to speak of humanity while excluding any personal consideration? Huh? Human beings are much more identical than they realize in their comic pretension; it's much easier than one might imagine to attain the universal by speaking of oneself. This is a second paradox: talking about oneself is a tedious and even repulsive activity; writing about oneself is, in literature, the only worthwhile thing, to such an extent that, traditionally, and quite accurately, we measure the value of books by their author's capacity for personal involvement. It's grotesque if you will, it's even insanely immodest, but that's how it is.

Writing these lines, I am actually, in practical terms, observing my navel. I rarely think about it, usually, and that's a good thing. This fold of flesh evidently carries with it the sign of a cut, of a hasty knot; it's the memory of the scissor cut by which I was, without further ado, thrown into the world; and ordered to make a shift in it by myself. You'll not escape this memory any more than I do; as an old man, even a very old man, you'll keep the mark of this cut intact in the middle of your stomach. Through this poorly closed hole, your most intimate organs will be able to escape at any moment and rot in the atmosphere. You can empty your guts at any time, under the sun; and die like a fish that you kill with a kick to the backbone. You will be neither the first nor the most illustrious. Remember the words of the poet:

The corpse of God
Squirms before our eyes
Like a dead fish
That we finish off with kicks.

You'll soon have got to that stage, you children of no consequence. You will be like gods – and it will not be quite enough. Your clones won't have navels, but they will have *navel-gazing* literature. You too will be navel gazers; you will be mortal. Your belly buttons will be covered in grime, and that will be the end of it. They'll throw earth on your face.

19

Sky, earth, sun

The successful writer enjoys certain luxuries, which society reserves for its distinguished or wealthy members; but, for a man, the most delicious gift of fame is what is called, using the Anglo-Saxon term, 'groupies'. These are young girls, sensual and pretty, who wish to give you their bodies in a spirit of love, simply because you wrote some pages that touched their souls. It seems possible today that I will tire of groupies, and glory; that would be sad, but it's possible. Even then, I believe I will continue to write.

Should we conclude that writing has become necessary for me? The expression of this thought pains me: I find it kitsch, conventional, vulgar; but the reality is even more so. Yet there must have been times, I told myself, when life was enough for me; life, full and whole. Life, normally, should be enough for the living. I don't know what happened, probably some disappointment, I've forgotten; but I don't find it normal that anyone should *need* to write. Not even that anyone should need to read. And yet.

From where I am, in Ireland, I have a view of the sea. It's is a mobile world, not entirely certain, and yet material. I hate the countryside, its overwhelming presence; it scares me. For the first time, I now live in a place where I can, through the window, contemplate the sea; and I wonder how I've ever been able to live until now.

Describing the world, inscribing blocks of reality, alive and irrefutable, I put them into perspective. Once transformed into written text, they take on a certain iridescent beauty, linked to their optional character. The countryside is never optional; the sea, sometimes, is.

Mist isn't enough, not nowadays; it's not material enough – you could compare it to poetry. The clouds, perhaps, if one lived among them, could be enough. Mist isn't enough; but nothing in this world is more beautiful than the mist rising over the sea.

20

Leaving the twentieth century

Literature is useless. If it had any use, the leftist scum who monopolized intellectual debate throughout the twentieth century couldn't even have existed. This century, thank God, has just ended; this is the moment to return one last time (let's hope so, at least) to the misdeeds of the 'left intellectuals', and the best thing to do is probably refer to *The Possessed*, published in 1872, where their ideology is already fully exposed, and their misdeeds and crimes already clearly announced through the scene of Shatov's murder. Now, how did Dostoyevsky's intuitions influence the historical movement? They absolutely did not. Marxists, existentialists, anarchists and leftists of all kinds have been able to prosper and infect the known world just as if Dostoevsky had never written a line. Did they at least contribute an idea, a new thought compared to their predecessors in the novel? Not the least. A crap century, one that invented nothing. At the same time, pompous in the extreme. A century that loved to gravely ask the silliest questions, such as: 'Can one write poetry after Auschwitz?'; continuing until its last breath to project itself into 'unsurpassable horizons' (after Marxism, the market) even though Comte, long before Popper, had already emphasized not only the stupidity of all historicisms, but their fundamental immorality.

In view of the extraordinary and shameful mediocrity of the 'human sciences' in the twentieth century, and in view of the progress made during the same period by the exact sciences and technology, one might expect that the most brilliant and most inventive literature of the period was science fiction; and this is indeed what we observe – with one qualification that needs to be explained. Remember, to begin with, that one can of course write poetry after Auschwitz, just as well as before, and under the same conditions; now let's ask a somewhat more serious question: can one write science fiction after Hiroshima? Looking at the publication dates, it seems that the answer is: yes, but not the same science fiction; and one can produce texts that are, it must be said, frankly better. A basic optimism, probably incompatible with the traditional novel, evaporated there, in the space of a few weeks. Hiroshima was undoubtedly the necessary condition for science fiction to truly attain the status of literature.

It's the duty of the authors of 'general literature' to point out to the populations the existence of their talented and unskilful colleagues who have committed the reckless act of working in 'genre literature', and thereby doomed themselves to radical critical obscurity. About ten years ago, I dedicated myself to Lovecraft; more recently, Emmanuel Carrère took charge of Philip K. Dick. The problem is that there are others, many more, even if we limit ourselves to the classics (those who began to publish around the Second World War, and whose work is essentially completed). If only for *City*, Clifford Simak deserves to go down in literary history. Remember that this book is made up of a succession of short tales featuring, in addition to dogs and other animals, robots, mutants and men. Each tale is preceded by a contradictory notice, in which the points of view of philologists and historians belonging to different canine universities are quoted, their debates usually revolving around this question: did man actually exist, or not – is he, as most specialists believe, a mythical deity invented by primitive dogs to explain the mystery of their origins? This fascinating meditation on the historical importance of the human species does not exhaust the intellectual riches of Simak's book, which is also presented as a reflection on the city, its role in the evolution of social relations, and the question of whether or not this role is finished. For most dogs, neither the city nor humans really existed; one of the canine experts has even demonstrated the following theorem: a creature with a nervous system complex enough to build an entity such as the city would have been unable to live there.

In its prime, science fiction could do this sort of thing: achieve an authentic perspective on humanity, its customs, its knowledge, its values, and its very existence; it was, in the truest sense of the word, a philosophical literature. It was also, deeply, a poetic literature; in his description of American landscapes and rural life, Simak, though with very different intentions, is almost equal to the way John Buchan used the Scottish moors to give cosmic breadth to the clashes he depicts between civilization and barbarism, Good and Evil. Style-wise, on the other hand, it's true that science fiction literature seldom reached the level of sophistication and elegance of the fantastic literature – especially that in English – of the turn of the century. Having reached maturity in the late 1950s, science fiction has only recently shown any real signs of exhaustion – much like fantasy literature to some extent did immediately before Lovecraft's appearance. Perhaps this is why no author so far has really felt the need to push the boundaries of the genre – boundaries that are quite flexible anyway. The only exception might be that weird, very weird writer R. A. Lafferty. More than science fiction, Lafferty sometimes gives the impression of writing a kind of *philosophy-fiction*, unique in the way that ontological speculation holds a more important place in it than sociological, psychological or moral questions. In *The World as*

Will and Wallpaper, with its nicely alliterative title, the narrator, wishing to explore the universe to its limits, after a certain time perceives repetitions, finds himself in similar situations as before, and ends up realizing that the world is made up of small entities, each born from an identical act of will, and repeated over and over again. The world is thus both unlimited and hopeless; I know few texts so poignant. In *Arrive at Easterwine: The Autobiography of a Ktistec Machine*, Lafferty goes even further in modifying the categories of ordinary representation; but the text unfortunately becomes almost illegible as a result.

Mention should also be made of Ballard, Disch, Kornbluth, Spinrad, Sturgeon, Vonnegut and so many others who, sometimes in a single novel, or even in a short story, have contributed more to literature than all the authors of the Nouveau Roman, and the overwhelming majority of crime fiction writers. Scientifically and technically, the twentieth century can be placed at the same level as the nineteenth. In terms of literature and thought, on the other hand, the collapse is almost unbelievable, especially since 1945, and the results appalling: you only need to remember the crass scientific ignorance of a Sartre and a Beauvoir, who were supposedly working within the field of philosophy, or the almost incredible fact that Malraux could – if only very briefly – be considered a 'great writer', you can gauge the degree of stupidity to which the notion of political commitment will have led us, and you are astonished that anyone can, even today, take an intellectual seriously. It's amazing, for example, that people like Bourdieu and Baudrillard still find newspapers willing to publish their rubbish. Indeed, I hardly think I'm exaggerating when I say that, intellectually speaking, nothing would be left of the second half of the century if it hadn't been for science fiction. This is something that will have to be taken into account when an attempt is made to write the literary history of this century, when people agree to look back on it and admit that we have finally left it. I'm writing these lines in December 2001; I believe the time is nigh.

21

Philippe Muray in 2002

'Progress is nothing but the development of order.'

Auguste Comte

The year 2002 will be marked by the long-awaited access of Philippe Muray's thought to a wider audience. Not that these thick grey-blue volumes, with their dissuasive titles, have really won the support of the crowds; but finally he has been quoted, and sometimes interviewed, by many widely distributed weeklies; from now on we can more or less follow Philippe Muray's positions just by checking out the *Relay* newsagents; this is considerable progress. If you really must talk about modernity (which I sometimes doubt), you may as well start with Philippe Muray's books; it will be more pleasant and more instructive than in the days when you had to wade through Bourdieu and Baudrillard (these examples, I agree, are a bit comical).

Let us view Philippe Muray as a machine, into which facts (sometimes real, often drawn from the mass media) are introduced, and from which interpretations emerge. These interpretations are guided by a coherent theory, about the rise of a new kind of soft terror, whose essence he has distilled into several brilliant and definitive formulas (the *'hyperfestif'*, the 'desire for the penal', and especially tolerance 'which no longer tolerates anything near it'). This theory is now classic, and must in my opinion be part of the baggage of every cultivated person.

The year 2002 will also be remembered as the year when the Muray machine encountered, for the first time, a few glitches. Its functioning, however, is beyond question; you might even say he has never been so brilliant. His magnificent description, for example, of the anti-Le Pen fortnight, which contributed to the merriment of France in April–May 2002, is undoubtedly one of his finest texts. All his qualities show themselves in full: a breadth of views, a historical sense, a precision in detail, and above all a prodigious glance, which allows him, among all the details, to choose the most significant, the one that goes right to the heart of things (in this case, the sign: 'No to the bad guys' brandished by the little girl). Actually, my theory is that it's not Philippe Muray who's going astray, but the world; the world around him is starting to produce some aberrant phenomena, which may conceivably be Muray-interpretable, but which are at least Muray-ambivalent; in short, the one good thought, and the soft terror that proceeds from it, is starting to emit faint creaks.

Let's start with the sinister *Rose Bonbon* affair.[1] Philippe Muray (interviewed, it's true, 'on the hoof' by *Le Figaro-Magazine*) saw it as a repetition of the tedious pantomime of the censor and the censored (which traditionally ends with the rout of the censor, covered in ridicule). The facts seem indeed to have proved him right this time; I would point out all the same that the affair was not cut and dried, and that it was concluded only by the intervention of Nicolas Sarkozy, who was aware of what a pain it could be to be associated with the 'return of moral order' when you're running for president. L'Enfant Bleu association lost, but in conditions that bode well for victory in the near future. The truth of this affair is that the anti-paedophile crusade, drunk on its successes, now refuses to accept any limits, not even respect for the presumption of innocence, and in any case certainly not that of the 'novelist's freedom of expression'. There have even been mind-boggling claims that Jones-Gorlin, as a novelist, was doubly guilty, since he could not even be credited with the *authenticity of testimony*. I'm not exaggerating: this was said, and written, by people with communal responsibilities.

However, those who think they possess the one sole truth here find themselves in a very painful position. For, while they love creative types who stir things up, they also love, with a love just as sincere, very small children. In other words, we are witnessing the development of a contradiction among those who think they possess the one sole truth – whom in the remainder of this text I will call, out of linguistic convention, the left).

My own trial, at first glance, seems less captivating; I'm a Western male, therefore a kind of hick, and in this sense my positions are simply very logical. The ingenious critic Pierre Assouline has even discovered that I've always been animated by an obsessive hatred of Arabs; that this was, contrary to appearances, the real subject of *Platform*, and perhaps of all my books. I really wonder what kept me from suing that loser; I probably need to work on my *penal desire*. Beyond my personal case, however, any keen observer will perceive that there are going to be problems, very soon – that, without ceasing to hound the Islamophobes, leftists will have to continue to support Taslima Nasrin (who for her part will cheerfully repeat that stupidity and cruelty are by no means monstrous excesses of Islam, but part of its intrinsic nature).[2] Bear in mind too that such examples will probably become more common, not to mention the suburban scum turning anti-Semitic, and all the other things we have to worry about. We should here mention the laboratory rats who are subjected by heartless ethologists to incessant contradictory stimuli. I don't remember exactly what happens to them; nothing very cheerful, at all events. In short, I can confirm that the leftists have got off to a bad start.

Perhaps the most significant episode of this new period has been the affair of the 'new reactionaries', already extensively reported in the gossip sheets. The book has met with a luke-warm welcome, to put it mildly. As chief cop, it was Edwy Plenel's duty to cover his subordinate;[3] he acquitted himself conscientiously, albeit without enthusiasm; perhaps he already sensed that the business wasn't worth getting too involved in. Most journalists, indeed, seem to have looked askance at this tedious name-dropping exercise; they found it very long, in spite of its ninety-six pages (compare this with the tangible delight with which they cite the smallest extract from Philippe Muray's fat tomes).

None of this was particularly alarming, at least not yet; a man of the left writes a tasteless book, there's nothing unusual about that, in fact it's perfectly in order; but what turned out to be more serious, clearly more serious, was the reaction of the defendants. The hapless Lindenberg probably imagined that they were going to scatter like little mice, swearing that *they* would never have done such a thing, the others maybe but not them, oh what a nasty trial! But what did we see? The complete opposite. Finkielkraut got downright angry, calling the book 'stupid' and 'despicable' in turn. Taguieff more mischievously hailed the appearance of the 'first soft pamphlet' from the ranks of the 'extreme centre'.[4] The two of them, plus a few others, promptly drew up a 'Manifesto for Free Thought'. So it wasn't especially shame, nor the terror of being unmasked, that could be seen in their guilty eyes; but rather a slight sparkle of satis-faction at the announcement of the resumption of hostilities.

Even more significantly, it was above all their opponents who denounced them as a whole, while they themselves seemed rather satisfied to be thus lumped together (personally, I can confirm this: belonging to a list that includes Finkielkraut,

Taguieff, Christopher Lasch, Muray and Dantec[5] makes me
feel very happy – I don't know the others so well, but it tends
to make me want to read them). Things got to such a point that
these same adversaries hastily absolved them of the odious
description, belatedly fearing that they might actually claim it
for themselves.

Alas, the damage was done, and the worm was in the fruit.
Hapless Lindenberg! The most decisive changes are sometimes
catalysed by the smallest incidents. After all, a few months ago
the 'new reactionaries' were so weak, so ghostly and above all
so badly organized that they hadn't even been able to muster
proper support for Jean-Pierre Chevènement's candidacy. This
slim booklet will have had the effect of tightening their ranks,
of making them aware that they had intelligence and talent
on their side, and of turning it, quite unwittingly, into the first
intellectual force in the country. Superbly played, Comrade
Rosanvallon! You'll be congratulated at the next Davos Forum.

Now that it's established that we're the best, we'll finally be
able to show the extent of our disunity in front of an audience
delighted by the quality of the exchange. In my personal diary,
I'm already planning a debate with Philippe Muray on the benefits of mass tourism; another with Dantec on the prospects
for human reproductive cloning; a sort of general colloquium
on monotheism, and perhaps another on prostitution (the
two subjects have at least this much in common: everyone
has something to say about them). I might as well tell you
right away: in 2003, there's going to be a serious buzz; it'll be a
change from the Saint-Simon Foundation.

We just need to find a sponsor, and it's with something of
a pang that I turn to you, lovable classic reactionaries, noble
guardians of the old heritage. This Christmas season, rejoice,
for the Lord has raised up to you abundant seed. You were
doubtless rather concerned to witness such a massive influx
onto your once peaceful shores – especially since the previous

occurrences of the new (the Nouveau Roman, the Nouveaux Philosophes) were enough to arouse legitimate suspicion about the quality of this immigration. Rest assured: they are smart, hardworking and up to date with your customs; they'll be able to adapt. We'll be able to preserve the best aspects of your tradition; we will maintain things. We will also be able to make the necessary adjustments as we enter the third millennium. Relax, kids, the matter's in hand; you can see the end of the tunnel. I don't need to brag to you about our intellectuals, you're already quite familiar with them. You know you have formidable recruits in Finkielkraut and Taguieff, capable of pulverizing any *second left*, should one arise. The case of novelists, I agree, is a thornier question. Let's pass quickly, if you don't mind, over the question of morals (drugs, orgies); you've already assimilated many others, and they weren't much better. But who can predict today what Maurice Dantec will think in five years' time? Right now he seems to be nourished by good authors (Revel, de Maistre);[6] but his basic project remains a synthesis between Catholicism and Nietzsche. An impossible project, and therefore a worrying one, for while it may entail interesting side-effects (the production of masterpieces), it offers no real guarantee of ideological reliability. My own case, I admit, and given the authors I like to quote (Schopenhauer, Auguste Comte, Wittgenstein when I'm in a good mood) is hardly less problematic. Well, how shall I put this? It's up to you to make an effort. You'll have to cover ideological deviations with a compassionate or sly veil; endeavour to focus only on the literary quality of the texts. You can do it; you've already done it, your glorious past testifies to it. Fear nothing; I feel you've almost reached your goal.

22

Towards a semi-rehabilitation of the hick

In a recent article in the *Nouvel Observateur* devoted to the sufferings of the man on the left, the excellent Laurent Joffrin, in my opinion, is wrong to say that my statement 'the dumbest religion is still Islam' brings me closer to the positions of your regular hick. In France, a country with a strong anticlerical tradition, the typical position of the regular hick would be something like: 'I reckon all religions are equal, they're all much of a muchness.' Pressed to say more, he'd probably add 'They're nothing but bullshit used to oppress people, to stop them from having fun and force them to kill each other, so they themselves can afford smart clothes when the poor plebs are starving.' This position, moreover, like everything the regular hick thinks, does have a certain immediate plausibility.

The regular hick is difficult to spot, and therefore to question, so let's turn for confirmation to some famous hicks such as Guy Bedos,[1] Siné[2] (and I will here remind the reader of the elegance of Siné's statements on Catherine Millet),[3] or better still Cabu, the inventor of the term.[4] First let's establish their hickery: of course, they don't belong to the category of the regular hick, and it seems preferable to reserve the name of top-class hick for more charismatic personalities, such as

Jean-Marie Le Pen; the term mid-rank hick would seem to suit them well enough, but I prefer, in my view more accurately, to describe them as incomplete hicks. Having in themselves the natural aptitudes of the hick, they've been unable to get them to bear fruit (because some trauma occurred, something diverted them from their path), and they were thus unable to achieve a pure hick-like serenity; thus there's something uptight and bad in them, which translates into an absolute lack of humour. The Zen Buddhist is sometimes very funny, the 'delicatessen' hick too; Cabu, never.

Now, what is Cabu's position on religions? More or less the one I quoted above. If, for Cabu, all religions are equal, it's because he's incapable of differentiating between them; at the most, he'll be able to distinguish between the way they dress.

Devoid of intelligence as of humour, the incomplete hick is, even more, devoid of moral sense – remember that a large part of Cabu's graphic work consisted in making fun of the disabled, and in slyly pleading in favour of their extermination (his bestial fierceness against 'Let them live', always associated with images of Down's syndrome people and paralytics, barely concealed an underlying 'Let them die.') Incapable of clearly grasping the different religions, he will be even less capable of judging them, and of saying for example: such and such a religion is noble, and excellent; another is mediocre, and of little profit; a third is frankly unacceptable. The intellectual examination of religions, and passing moral judgement on them, are, however, tasks incumbent upon every human being. Pleading a kind of animal innocence, the ordinary hick dispenses with such an examination; having wished by his denial to rise above his condition, the incomplete hick obliges us on the contrary to regard him with severity, and to conclude that here, as in many other respects, he has placed himself slightly below the normal level of humanity.

23

Conservatism, a source of progress

The paradox is only apparent: conservatism can be a source of progress, just as laziness is the mother of efficiency. This largely explains why the conservative attitude is so rarely understood.

Ever since the words 'new reactionary' first appeared in the astute Lindenberg's book, no one I know of has been able to give them any meaning. Undefined in its sense, the phrase is not even defined in its extension, as Jacques Braunstein finely noted in *Elle*. The first objective of the Deauville conference, it seems to me, is to emerge from this ambiguous situation, which, beyond the hapless Lindenberg, seriously calls into question the intellectual credibility of its sponsor, the cop Plenel, and the very consistency of a 'left-wing thought' of which it constitutes one of the last reverberations (like the dead fire of already extinct stars, etc.).

In order to avoid getting things wrong and prejudicing the future of any debate, I will try here to clear the terrain somewhat. Ontologically, reaction presupposes action; so if there are new reactionaries, there must be new progressives. How are we to define them? Using Taguieff's ingenious terminology, we can easily equate the new progressivism with *bougisme*.[1]

Unlike their predecessors, the new progressives do not identify progress by its intrinsic content, but by its novelty. In short,
they live in a sort of permanent epiphany, very Hegelian in its
silliness, where everything that appears is good by the simple
fact of its appearance. It would therefore be just as reactionary to oppose the thong as the Islamic veil, *Loft Story*[2] as the
sermons of Tariq Ramadan.[3] Everything that appears is good.

The new reactionaries, on the other hand, unenthusiastic
on principle about novelty, come across as a sort of grouch;
they would be, if the terms had their meaning, exactly what
one would call a conservative (royalist under the monarchy,
Stalinist under Stalin, etc.). The two attitudes at first glance
seem equally stupid, in their joint opposition to the common-
sense position of approving novelty if it's good, rejecting it if
it's bad. This symmetry, however, is only partially correct. At
this point, one could offer about fourteen remarks; for lack of
space, I will limit myself to two.

First, innovation is tiring. Any routine, good or bad, has the
advantage of being routine, so that it can be continued with
minimal effort. The first root of all conservatism is intellectual
laziness. But laziness, pushing one towards synthesis, and seeking common traits beyond surface differences, is intellectually
a powerful virtue. In mathematics, given two equally rigorous
demonstrations, we will always prefer the shorter one, the one
that will tire the memory less. The rather mysterious concept
of the 'elegance' of a demonstration is in fact almost equivalent
to its brevity (which is not surprising, considering that the
elegance of a movement can roughly be measured against its
economy).

Second, the scientific method as a whole (conventionally
conceived as an alternation between phases of theoretical
development and phases of experimental verification) has as
its first condition an essentially conservative disposition of
thought. A theory is a precious, hard-won thing, and a scientist
will not be resigned to abandoning it unless the experimental

facts definitely require it. A scientist will give up a theory only for serious reasons, and so will never be tempted to return to it.

This principled conservatism therefore has as a corollary the possibility of effective progress, or even, if circumstances require, of genuine revolutions (called 'paradigm shifts' since Kuhn). It's therefore by no means paradoxical to assert that conservatism is the source of progress, just as laziness is the mother of efficiency.

Such principles, I agree, do not immediately translate into political terms; that is why the conservative attitude, moderately sympathetic, with little ideological content to it, is so rarely understood. To use a metaphor, I would say that the conservative tends to idealize society in the form of a perfect machine, where the passage from one generation to the next takes place with minimal effort, where one seeks to minimize suffering and constraints in the same way that one seeks, in mechanics, to minimize friction (which for example results in a drastic limitation of population density). In all circumstances, the conservative will meditate on the principles, imbued with a Poitevin Taoism, of the late Senator Queuille[4] (such as: 'There's no political problem that can't be resolved by inaction'); the conservative won't forget old Goethe's saying that 'injustice is better than disorder' – cynical only in appearance, given the powerful ferment of injustice that is constituted by all disorder.

One of the last genuine conservatives was arguably that English lord, quoted by Aldous Huxley, who in 1940 wrote to the letters page of *The Times* proposing to end the war by compromise (*The Times* – which, said Huxley, had once been a conservative newspaper – declined to publish the letter).

Aware that men's life takes place in a biological, technical and sentimental environment (that is to say, only very incidentally political), and aware that its objective is the pursuit of private objectives, the conservative will instinctively reject any definite political conviction, and view the rebel, the resistance fighter, the patriot, the troublemaker as despicable individuals, driven by stupidity, vanity and the desire for violence. Unlike reactionaries, conservatives will have neither heroes nor martyrs; if they don't save anyone, they won't cause any casualties either; in short, there's nothing particularly heroic about conservatives; but they will be, and this is one of their charms, individuals who pose little danger.

24

Prolegomena to positivism

The disappearance of metaphysics

Everything in the political and moral thought of Auguste Comte seems designed to exasperate the contemporary reader. But before we come to that, which is the object of the volume under discussion, it's advisable to rule out, or at least to take into account, one preliminary difficulty: we have still not left the metaphysical state, the disappearance of which seemed imminent – indeed, we have less intention than ever of leaving it; in view of those magazines that regularly have headlines such as 'The Return of God', a satirist might even wonder if we don't risk leaving it *surreptitiously*; we might more seriously ask ourselves whether the metaphysical state, far from being, as Comte thought, a transitory phase in which previous theologies were dissolved, might not actually entail keeping them artificially alive by means of the uncertainty inherent in all metaphysics.

It's with Descartes, in fact, that the modern metaphysical period begins; the amazing scientific and technical progress of the Renaissance had taken place in a kind of philosophical innocence, in the absence of a way of thinking capable of structuring it. This was undoubtedly why the Catholic Church did not immediately perceive the danger, and reacted only too late, when the foundations of its spiritual authority had already been undermined. Walking alone across a field of ruins, Descartes made great innovations, separating physics from metaphysics with unprecedented clarity. By bringing the unnecessary categories of matter and mind face to face, he ipso facto created the conditions for most subsequent philosophical errors.

Conceived expressly to include all those problems without content (God, the human soul, etc.), the category of mind was to experience a tumultuous decline, marked by various attempts to give it a semblance of existence – some were grandiose, such as Kantianism; others were wretched, like the various forms of psychology.

Matter, for its part, seemed to fly from success to success. Demagogic and simplistic, Cartesian thought (positing on the one hand a machine-universe, made up of material cogs; on the other hand the mind, placed there as a precaution, for the use of sensitive souls or difficult problems) still weighs on us today. It's even sometimes confused with the scientific method, or with positivism; a cruel mistake, insofar as it merely hampered its progress. From the outset, it tried to oppose Newtonian physics, on the grounds that action propagated in a vacuum seemed inconceivable to a materialist; only experimental evidence finally made him listen to reason. Many years later, the debates waged throughout the twentieth century around the interpretation of quantum mechanics can only be explained by the attempt to safeguard, at all costs, a material and causal ontology. From a positivist point of view, in fact, neither Newtonian mechanics nor quantum mechanics pose any particular problem. Laws are produced that allow phenomena to be modelled and the results of experiments to be predicted; entities are not multiplied beyond what is necessary: anything else?

Pascal (who practised the sciences, before sinking into his mystical night) said: 'You have to say, roughly speaking: it's done by figure and movement, because it's true. But to say which ones, and to compose the machine, is ridiculous; for it's unnecessary, and uncertain, and painful.' With its characteristic insolence, this phrase, sharp as Occam's razor, is already positivist in inspiration. No more than God, in fact, does matter find favour in the eyes of positivist thought. Ontological modesty, submission to the experimental approach, a desire first of all to predict, and to explain if possible: this leads to a style that, though it has made possible all the scientific discoveries of the last five centuries, is slow to attract a wider audience.

For if the community of physicists has failed to completely chase away the ghosts of metaphysics, what can be said of the rest? After all, Comte did not even consider it useful to isolate a science called 'psychology' (for him this was a branch of animal physiology), and since his death we have seen theories that simply take for granted the existence of the 'subject', an irreplaceable noumenon whose phenomenon is undoubtedly something like the 'self'. On the political level, we need merely mention a trait that Comte considers to be one of the fundamental defects of the metaphysical state: the tendency to argue instead of observing; and to see, there too, where we are at. We need also simply note the persistent popularity of the theories of the 'social contract', based on the fiction of free individuals pre-existing the community and on the notion of 'human rights', independent of any duty that follows from it.

Comte took the transition of the material and life sciences to a positive state for granted, and proposed to extend positivism to the social sciences; in short, his whole philosophy was made possible only by a gigantic error of historical assessment. Its premises have not been realized, and are not in the process of being so; thus, its eventual action can lie only in an indefinite future.

His curious historical optimism was characteristic of the time; today we can hardly imagine the incredible élan, barely slowed down by the Napoleonic episode that swept through Europe following the French Revolution. This is true in the literary field: if we consider that in 1830, to limit ourselves to France and even to Paris, authors such as Balzac, Chateaubriand, Hugo were at the peak of their production (and these are just some of the most significant examples), we must imagine a powerful, shapeless creative urge bubbling up in all directions. Such an activity had its equivalent in the philosophical field; we know this was so in Germany, much less in France. It may seem surprising to compare Comte and Fourier, as their systems are so opposed. However, they have in common, in addition to a breadth of views bordering on megalomania and even madness (delusional in Fourier, manic in Comte), the certainty that society can be reorganized on entirely new bases in just a few generations – even just a few years, depending on the social formation involved.

Fourier's main subject, the one in which he excels, where he promises dazzling improvements in the course of a single human life, is what one might call *the motivation of producers*. On this Comte has little to say (but the same is true of Proudhon, Marx, and indeed all social reformers, except Fourier). His second innovation, which he envisioned in the longer term, revolves around the family, conjugality, sexual life in general; here too, Comte (if we except his strange final anticipation of the Virgin Mother) is content to reproduce the existing patterns.

Charles Fourier's omissions, however, are quite considerable. He does not deal with property, inheritance, or really with the political system; above all, he hardly deals with religion – at a time when the religious foundation of society was crumbling in France, he was content with vague proclamations against atheism. The two authors also have in common that they wrote much, too quickly, at the same time as having to survive in difficult material conditions; they both treated the most wide-spread stylistic conventions with contempt. Both, in fact, are these days viewed as illegible, except by certain perverse spirits who come to adore their quirks, to see in them the sign of genius – the burlesque deviation in Fourier, the obsessive repetition in Comte.

Fourier, so far, has had more commentators, arguably because the obsession with sex continued to grow throughout the twentieth century. The general public, it's said, is once again showing a thirst for the spiritual. This proclamation seems to me a little hasty; sexual needs seem to me far more urgent today than spiritual needs; but assuming that they are satisfied, and that spiritual needs arise in consequence, it will be in our interest, when the time comes, to dive back into Comte. Because his real subject, his major subject, is religion; and, here, the least we can say is that he is an innovative thinker.

The establishment of religion

Man belongs to a social species; this fact is the basis of Comtian thought, and it should never be lost sight of if we are to have a chance to grasp his ideas. Examining the social formations of the human species, their various organizations and their future, Comte's treatment is almost exhaustive: property, the family, the production system, education, science, art ... nothing escapes his elegant systematization. But of all the structures produced by a society, structures on which that society is in turn based, religion seemed to him to be simultaneously the most important, the most characteristic and the most threatened. Man, according to Comte, can roughly be defined as a social animal of a religious type.

Before him, religion was seen above all as a system for explaining the world; the rest, more or less, flowed from this. Comte was one of the first to feel that this system was

irreparably worn out; he was also one of the first to understand that the foundations of the social world, deprived of
their basis, would in turn crumble. He was one of the first to
understand that the rational explanation of the universe would
need to be confined to a more modest discourse; he was the
first, absolutely the first, to attempt to give the social world a
new religious basis.

The least that can be said is that he failed; positive religion
had a few, very few followers, and then died out. Such a failure,
in a philosopher who sought a place not only in the realm of
speculation, but also in that of short-term practical efficiency,
raises inevitable questions.

Comte understood that while religion continued to integrate
itself into a world system acceptable to reason, its mission was
to connect human beings and to regulate their acts (here the
best thing is to read his texts, and examine his terms); he had
foreseen its sacraments, and its calendar. Perhaps he had not
grasped the depth of the desire for immortality inherent in
human beings – those passages where, having approached this
question on his own terms, he turns the conversation towards
prayer, are captivating; probably not having had time to reread
himself, he allowed a kind of native doubt to persist in his philosophy. The abstract immortality inherent in human memory
nevertheless failed to convince the individuals of his time – let
alone of our own – hungry for a more material promise of
survival. Suppose that the prerequisites of Comte's system
have been fulfilled – which will take, perhaps, a few centuries.
Suppose that the theisms have been extinguished, materialism devalued, and positivism established as the only mode of
thought that works for a scientific age.

Suppose, further, that the 'irreplaceable and unique'
character of the human individual has been recognized as a
pompous fiction, its social character fully assessed and taken
into account. Suppose all of this is no longer the subject of
controversy and confrontation, but of an objective assessment,

as consensual as the results of genetics are at present. Will we have made any progress, however little, in establishing a common religion? Will the thought of humanity, or of the Great Being, be more desirable to individuals? And what will lead them, given their awareness that, as individuals, they are transient beings, to be satisfied with their participation in this fetish of a theory? Who, in the final analysis, can be interested in a religion that does not preserve them from death? To these questions Comte does not answer; there probably is no answer. The establishment of physical immortality, by technological means, is undoubtedly the necessary step that will make a religion possible again; but Comte makes us sense that this religion, a religion for immortals, will still be almost as necessary as it's possible.

25

I'm normal. A normal writer

It must have happened, I think, in the spring of 1992. My first collection of poems, *La Poursuite du bonheur* [*The Pursuit of Happiness*], had just been published. I was having lunch with Jean Ristat in a pizzeria in Ivry-sur-Seine.[1] He poured me some more wine, then, with a shy little smile, announced that he was on the jury for an award. A literary prize, yes, that was it. The Tristan-Tzara Prize, to be precise. Would I accept it, if the case should arise? Of course, nothing was definite; personally – why hide it? – 'you know what I think of your work . . .'. It was a nice ceremony, he said, in Aubigny-sur-Nère, in the Cher: there would be wine growers, municipal officials, a somewhat right-wing mayor . . . you know, real life. There would even be a senator, if he was free. But, if I refused, it would be embarrassing, very embarrassing; better not to talk about it. Either way, it wouldn't change our relationship, whatever decision I made.

But of course, Jean, of course. A literary prize? All in good time. Ultimately . . . yippee!

Four years later. My second collection of poems, *Le Sens du combat* [*The sense of struggle*] was published in April or March. The scene must have taken place in October, but I'm not sure (am I going senile?). One thing is certain: I was on the phone, and the role of Jean Ristat was this time played by Frédéric Beigbeder.[2] He was inclined to vote for me, I could sense it; and yet he was worried. Once I'd won the prize, wouldn't I just lose my mind, go stir crazy? End my literary career, burn my manuscripts, go to an ashram in Chile?

No, Frédéric, no. I'm in control, I have the situation well in hand; in any case, I'm being monitored by Lydie Salvayre, the author of *La Puissance des mouches* [*The Power of Flies*], and a psychiatrist by calling.[3] My mind is clear, coherent; my ideation is perfect, my responsibility barely diminished. Lydie can testify to this, under oath if required.

The Tristan-Tzara Prize comes with a cheque for five thousand francs (provided by Éditions Belin), fifty bottles of Sancerre (white and red variegated) and a white Sancerre jeroboam engraved with my name. The Prix de Flore comes with a cheque for forty thousand francs (provided by whom?) and three hundred and sixty-five glasses of Pouilly Fumé with a unit capacity of twenty-five centilitres (this time, it's the glass that is engraved with my name). Clearly, even without taking into account the *intangible benefits* (a trendy jury, photographers from *Gala* on the alert), the Prix de Flore is better. True, in the meantime I've published a novel, *Extension du domaine de la lute* [*Extension of the Domain of Struggle*], which has since become a *cult book* (nobody buys it, everyone reads it; fortunately, Maurice Nadeau always gets such things properly covered). Although I'm a recognized writer, I always cause anxiety. Invited to a conference in Grenoble (on the possibility of the existence or manifestation of a 'new generation of creators'; a conference, anyway), I chat with one of the organizers – one Sunday morning, at breakfast, just before my departure. Everything goes well; he confesses his relief to me. 'Houellebecq . . . a good idea . . .,' he'd been told, 'but you have to be careful . . . don't let him take his clothes off in public. Just try your best . . .' I don't know; I don't know what to say to him. There must be some false rumours going round.

So today, Thursday 7 November, I phone Flammarion. I get straight through to Valérie Taillefer. I've won the Prix de Flore. She seems happy. And (I point this out to show future generations that I wasn't altogether a bad person), what honestly gives me the most pleasure at this moment is to feel from her voice that Valérie Taillefer is happy. Relaxed. Still a little worried, towards the end: 'You'll come, won't you, Michel? You won't stand us up?'

Let's go back a bit. Let's clarify matters. Since the early nineties, my publications have been published at regular intervals. As a guest on TV shows, I've chatted, and made pertinent comments, with different presenters. I've turned up at book fairs and happily participated in the game of signatures and dedications. I've never insulted a photographer; on the contrary, I have excellent relations with some of them. I don't get it. What do people think is wrong with me? What do they suspect me of? I accept distinctions, honours, awards. I play the game. I'm normal. A normal writer.

Sometimes I get up at night, I look at myself in the mirror; I observe my face, I try to see what other people see, what it is that worries them. I'm not very handsome, that's for sure, but I'm not the only one. It must be something else. My gaze? Maybe my gaze. The only thing you don't see in the mirror is your own gaze.

In the taxi that takes us to Saint-Germain-des-Prés (we were together at a conference in Créteil), I chat pleasantly with Marc Weitzmann.[4] I try to keep the conversation playful; however, we're thinking about the Prix de Flore. He's glad I got it; a little surprised, too. He tries to interpret the event. No matter what, this boy can't believe things *just happen*; he's looking for signs. When it comes to a big fat literary prize, nice and corrupted, quite normal, one generally quickly finds a luminous and satisfactory explanation – of the style 'advance to Thingummy published by So-and-so'. For the Prix de Flore, it's more difficult. It's commonly known that the jury is bizarre, a mixture of socialites and little-known personalities. Difficult to bribe, unreliable. How is one to explain that I beat on the wire *Truismes*, by Marie Darrieussecq, the *novel-event* of the *rentrée*?[5] What's more, I won with a collection of poems.

Stimulated by the intellectual issues at stake, and also thinking I might use all this for a speech, I quickly make up a symbolic story. Like an ancient and powerful deity buried under the sands of the Tertiary sands, poetry has just emerged from its brutish slumber. *Iä Iä Cthulhu fhtagn!*[6] After decades of absence, it has seen fit to 'send a strong signal' to the second millennium and its putrefying liberalism (a tongue of flame darting from the index finger, as with Moses). I found myself caught in the tongue of fire (in the story, I'm the filament of the bulb that sizzles for a brief moment before it goes out). A few moths with ultra-sensitive antennae (Frédéric Beigbeder, Ariel Wizman)[7] noticed this flickering light. Filled with a new sense of mission, they took off in the Saint-Germain-des-Prés twilight to alert the intermediate populations. Not bad; a bit up his own backside, it has to be said; people will be worried. Would it be better to play the 'honest labourer of the text' card? No, that wouldn't work, I've always claimed the opposite.

I develop an intermediate strategy, and then we go in. Plenty of people around, but less than in Ravalec's short story[8] (BHL, absent;[9] his current squeeze, absent; Françoise Sagan isn't here either, but she may be dead, that would be an excuse). However, the little extra touch that makes you forget everything else: Charles-Henri Flammarion. It's such a hoot, this little dynastic aspect in French publishing. It seems to promise a world of unabridged editions, with a list of variants and a critical apparatus. 'Under the wise leadership of Charles-Henry, fourth of that name, the Flammarion house maintained its territories, wisely avoiding a dangerous border conflict with the book-seller Gallimard. The long reign of Charles-Henry, known as "Le Débonnaire", was somewhat troubled towards the end, like that of his predecessors, by problems of succession.'

I have fond memories of that award at Aubigny-sur-Nère. The whole village had turned up, gathered together in the village hall, for what was clearly the cultural event of the year. They seemed happy to see me, but mostly they seemed happy just to be there; another opportunity to meet up again, no more stupid than 14 July or 11 November. I was the necessary media-tor of their local festivities and I felt, as such, justified. Well, tonight, in the room at the Café de Flore, it's pretty much the same: the whole village has come along.

It was around eight o'clock that everything changed, probably definitively. I remember that moment very well. I was chat-ting, in a relaxed and somewhat languid manner, with Raphaël Sorin.[10] We were leaning on the balustrade on the first floor of the café. A photographer approached. Without interrupt-ing the conversation I turned my gaze slightly towards him, I smiled; he wasn't bothering me at all. I had long been looking for a way to live. Well here it was, I'd found it; I was going to be a star.

That being said, everything went smoothly. Philippe Vandel arrived, I was handed over the Prize.[11] Philippe is a friend and a great professional whom I respect.

Later, at Castel's, I try out my new status. All around me people are dancing or chatting. I'm sitting on a bench, my hands quietly resting on my knees. Anyone can approach me, touch me or talk to me; there's no problem. For each of them I'll have a kindly word, corresponding to their position. They'll find me very easy to get on with, knowing of course that things aren't going to go any further. In short, it's going to be rather like my life before, but calmer.

Soon after, very discreetly, I slip away – the party will be all the more fun in my absence. The air outside is calm, a little cold. I feel normal, fine. Everything's fine. Now, everything's fine.

26

I have read my whole life long

The first experience is hardly a memory, I can't quite find the words.[1] There was a veranda, in the shade, by the sunny courtyard (in my childhood memories it's always sunny). There's an armchair in the middle of the veranda, and the sensation of an endlessly repeated, delightful dive. The sensation also of something that would accompany me all my life. An impression of plenitude, because 'all my life' (perhaps eventually I'll manage to smile about it, but I say it today with a certain bitterness), 'all my life', at the time, seemed to me as if it would be very long.

I thought my life was going to be happy, and I didn't even exactly imagine unhappiness, life seemed to me to be a delight and a gift, and reading was one of the joys of this endlessly delightful life.

I was a child. I was happy, and happiness leaves few traces.

Little by little I learned what the life of men was really like; I learned it, too, through their books. Probably my grandparents never paid attention to the age difference that existed in principle between the works of the *Bibliothèque rose* [*Pink Library*] and those of the *Bibliothèque verte* [*Green Library*];[2] what other explanation can there be for the fact that I was able to find myself reading *Graziella* at the age of ten?[3]

This book contains the whole of nascent romanticism, in its budding youth and strength, and 'Le Premier Regret' ['The First Regret'], with which the book concludes, is a poem of incredible purity. Never before Lamartine and never after him (not even in Racine, or Victor Hugo) had a poet written, or will ever write, alexandrines with this naturalness, this spontaneity, this impulse straight from the heart.

How could Lamartine, who knew Graziella when he was eighteen and she was sixteen, ever have forgotten her? How could he still continue to live? And how could the reader of Lamartine devote his life to anything other than meeting a sixteen-year-old Graziella? What fascinating crap literature is, you have to admit it . . . So pernicious, so powerful, incredibly more powerful than cinema, and even more pernicious than music.

There were other things, too. There was the nauseating Jack London, whom Lenin loved so much (and it's undoubtedly Lenin's overt admiration for Jack London, his cynical acceptance of *the struggle for life*, poles apart from the supposed generosity that attaches to the word 'Communism', which opened my eyes and stopped me in advance, once and for all, from getting close to Marxism). There was the marvellous Dickens (never again will I laugh so loudly, so heartily, never again will I laugh until I cry, great gales of laughter, as I did when I was nine years old and discovered *The Pickwick Papers*. There was Jules Verne, there were Andersen's tales – 'The Little Match Girl' broke my heart, and continues, with ruthless regularity, to break it again every time I re-read it.

I also remember the *Rouge et Or* collection, with its naive illustrations (a bit more expensive probably, most likely a birthday or Christmas present) . . .[4] I have only good memories of that period. Still, they shouldn't have let me read *Graziella* when I was ten. Little girls were seeking my company at the time, and some, I realize today, already had ulterior motives, anyway, on the whole, things were off to a good start, but soon after that came puberty, just as the fashion for mini-skirts began, I struggled to reconcile that with reading *Graziella*, I started to reject what was reaching out to me – even though it inspired me with terrible longings – and to look for things in life that weren't there; in short things started to get pretty screwed up for me, and I still think a bit it's partly Lamartine's fault. It was around the same time that I gave up children's collections for paperbacks.

For me, there were two worthwhile collections: *Le Livre de Poche* and *J'ai lu*. I hated *Folio* and *Présence du Futur*: too expensive, with offputting covers – of the kind 'sober drawing on a white background' – and above all horribly poorly made; you only had to open these books a dozen times and the poorly glued pages would fall out and the book would go to shreds – while the books published by *Livre de Poche* and especially *J'ai lu* were indestructible, and this was essential because these were the books I opened more than a dozen times, I took them everywhere, to the cafe, to the high-school canteen, on the train – and soon I wasn't just taking commuter trains, but trains that crossed Europe, it was the time of the inter-rail card, I slept in dusty campsites, in the cellars of damp buildings, and my *J'ai lu* books are still around, I have them near me as I write, now I'm rich, I travel in business class, they have nothing to worry about, it's all okay.

Later, after my marriage and my professional life broke down, I took up writing. I started, more precisely, to write novels, which were published, which brought me fame and fortune, relatively speaking. Suddenly I started to read my contemporaries, I discovered *normal editions*. However, I have never stopped reading, or rereading, paperbacks, and it was a great joy for me to be published in *J'ai lu* – of course, I wouldn't have refused *Folio* or *Presses-Pocket* if my editor had wished it, but, all the same, the moment when I saw myself for the first time coming out as a *J'ai lu* remains one of the most beautiful moments of my life.

Today I read my contemporaries a little less, I reread more – that's normal, I'm getting old. I now know that I'll read until the end of my days – maybe I'll stop smoking, obviously I'll stop making love, and the conversation of men will gradually lose its interest for me; but I can't imagine myself without a book.

I have never felt any particular fetishism for original editions, for the book as object – I'm mainly interested in the content. And I'm gradually replacing my books in regular paperback editions with some of those wonderful objects, so practical when travelling – the *Pléiades*, the *Bouquins* or the *Omnibus*. There are still a few exceptions, for sentimental reasons, and it seems unlikely to me – even if things go wrong again, even if I end up in a furnished room with one or two big suitcases, and that's still possible, of course – that I will ever part with certain of my books; especially certain of my *J'ai lu* books.

27

Soil cutting

While the works of Alain Robbe-Grillet immediately filled me with deep, radical boredom, I spent hours, perhaps days, trying hard to read them. I proceeded as we usually do in such a case: I skipped about fifty pages to see if things improved later on, I read another of his books, I told myself that I would try my luck later, at another time of day, under more favourable circumstances. Nothing, however, tempered my boredom, nothing attenuated my certainty that none of it had any interest or meaning. I don't remember having taken such pains with any other author.

The best explanation is, I believe, of an extra-literary nature: the two of us had studied the same subject. Separated by some thirty years, we had completed our studies at the same school of agricultural engineers. Being former students of the same *grande école* creates, in the French education system, an unacknowledged complicity, especially in the case of Agro, no doubt – with its very special training, separated from other scientific studies from the preparatory classes onwards.[1] So, in the event of a meeting – which luckily never happened – we would have felt obliged to address each other as 'dear comrade'; and besides, I think we would have done so (matching it, of course, with a display of wry smiles; but we would have). If, throughout his life, he showed a great insolence towards institutions (going, in the case of the French Academy, as far as outright rudeness), Alain Robbe-Grillet demonstrated an unfailing submission and gratitude towards the first institution of his life: the National Agronomic Institute (Paris-Grignon). I'm exactly the same: neither of us has ever *reneged on Agro*.

I think he resented me because, before I came along, he was proud to be 'the agricultural engineer of French literature', and he was furious to have to share that title. Admittedly, he had other reasons to be furious, and certain press articles didn't help matters, especially abroad, which proclaimed that I was 'the only thing that had appeared in France since the Nouveau Roman'. He really wasn't keen on anything new appearing in France after the Nouveau Roman.

A muted, coded struggle thus unfolded between us, over several years. Did he keep repeating, against all the evidence, that Balzac corresponded to a period of sterility, of glaciation in French literature? I immediately praised Balzac to the skies, affirming that he was the second father of any novelist, and that no one could claim to have understood a single thing about the art of the novel unless he or she had sworn allegiance and love to Balzac. Did I keep asserting the pre-eminence, in my own writing, of sociology over psychology? He immediately lamented the contemporary renunciation of the formal ambitions of pure literature, of its reduction to a dimension of sociological exploration. All of this, right to the bitter end, was carried out in implicit terms; we always refrained from publicly referring to each other.

We were, I think, absolutely sincere: he in his detestation of Balzac, I in my love of him; he in his contempt for my literature, I in my contempt for his.

Now that Alain Robbe-Grillet has, in a rather mechanical way, predeceased me, I feel I can speak a little more freely, and without offence, of my *dear comrade*. Because there was something more, I came to realize, than just the fellowship of former students in my obstinate attempts to penetrate his indigestible literature. Alain Robbe-Grillet, yes, reminded me of Agro, and he even reminded me of something much more specific, which only former Agro students know: Alain Robbe-Grillet reminded me of *soil cutting*.

Pedology, or soil study, is obviously a fundamental discipline for the agronomist, but it would be even more so if it could draw on reproducible results, lead to definite forecasts, and lead the agronomist as a practitioner to well-supported diagnoses. Unfortunately, this is far from being the case. Soil science was still, at the time I studied it (let alone at the time of Alain Robbe-Grillet), at an embryonic stage. To call it a science would have done it too much credit; it was, at most, a *discipline of observation*.

The dominant method of pedology has been, since its inception, *soil cutting*. This consists of digging into the earth a trench with vertical walls, of varying height depending on the soil (the process generally continues until you reach the rocky layer). Once the trench is dug, what do you do? Well, you *observe*. That is, we draw, as precisely as possible, what we see (the implantation of the roots, the presence of pebbles, air pockets, animals and so on); this generally varies rapidly as one moves away from the surface. You can, if necessary, add notes to your drawing. In general, and it's interesting to note this, you take few photos (these are hardly used except to carry out the drawing later, in more convenient conditions, and if possible quite quickly; the intelligent gaze of a field observer is always considered superior to photographic reproduction). The chemical observations in situ remain rudimentary (they were limited in my time to a few pH measurements at various depths). It's of course possible to take soil samples in order to study them later; but here we are entering the realm of *soil analysis*, which is a whole different story.

Even if the aspiring agronomist is driven by the hope of finding, at the end of his observation, a known type of soil (and generally the observed soil is indeed what one would expect, taking into account the geological substrate and the climate), he should not, during his observation, take any account of this: such will be the very firm recommendation of his teachers. He may, being only human, expect to find podzol in Siberia, and laterite in Madagascar; but this should in no way affect the neutrality and objectivity of his sketches and comments.

Thus, through soil cuts, the agronomy student is trained in this austere discipline consisting in taking a neutral, purely objective look at the world: isn't this exactly what Alain Robbe-Grillet tried to do, later, in literature?

While this bias towards a-theoretical neutrality may reign supreme in the field of soil cuts, it is by no means unanimous in the philosophy of science. 'It's theory, and theory alone, that decides what should be observed', Einstein bluntly noted. Deploying more arguments, Auguste Comte concluded that without a preliminary theory, even a very approximate one, observation was condemned to being an empiricism without a project, and reduced to a tedious and meaningless compilation of experimental data.

'A tedious and meaningless compilation of experimental data': is this not, *exactly* how one might describe the literature of Alain Robbe-Grillet?

Having precisely defined what constitutes his limits, I would add that this is also what makes his strength – a quite negative strength, it has to be said. Refusing any theory prior to observation, Alain Robbe-Grillet thus protects himself from any *cliché* (because any cliché contains a succinct theory, and is only recognized as such when the theory is itself recognized as old, and considered obsolete). On the other hand, by opening my literature to theoretical conceptions that can be developed about the world, I constantly expose myself to the risk of the cliché – and even, to tell the truth, I condemn myself to it. My only chance of originality lies, to use Baudelaire's words, in *creating new clichés.*

28

The lost text

During my e-mail exchange with Amar Amirou (Rachid Amirou's brother, who kindly took care of collecting the scattered texts),[1] I mentioned several times an article of which I had forgotten almost everything, except that, in it, Rachid had drawn an audacious and unexpected parallel between the notion of the 'carrying capacity' of a landscape introduced by certain ecology specialists (such and such a natural landscape is capable of receiving a certain quantity – let's say per month – of human visitors; beyond that it would be desirable, so as to preserve its integrity, to prohibit access), and the more famous 'tolerance threshold' (applied this time to immigrant populations allowed in to reside in a territory).

We can certainly imagine that, just as an excess of human visitors (humans here being considered as a *nuisance*) can *spoil* a landscape, and reduce its value as a site visited, an excess of immigrant population, which fails to correspond to the ethnographic expectations of foreign visitors, may turn out to be counterproductive from the point of view of the tourist economy. But the tone used by Rachid in this article was one of insolence, of mild irony, by no means one of activism. Its purpose was to describe humanity and its behaviour, not to criticize or reform it; after all, he was a writer.

But he was also, and first of all, a sociologist, of indisputable originality even in the choice of his field of study, very little explored despite its richness (I still remember my surprise, on my first reading of *Imaginaire touristique et sociabilités du voyage* [*The Tourist Imaginary and the Sociabilities of Travel*], on seeing for the first time the activity of pilgrimage integrated into the framework of a general reflection on tourism). During this exchange of emails (in the end, we never found the text), his brother asked me for details of the article I was looking for: was it about theme parks (like 'Les sabotiers du Marquenterre?'),[2] amusement parks like the Smurfs parks, or simply natural parks? I then became aware of the incredible and almost comical diversity that our country (France) had been able to offer to tourists in recent years. And I said to myself that we would definitely miss a good sociologist of tourism. As for good writers, you can't have enough of them – at least, that's my opinion.

He had, admittedly, never written a novel – and, unlike Philippe Muray (whom he admired), he never even tried. I sometimes regretted this, though I knew that what he was doing was, in its own way, just as important. If he had ventured into the domain of fiction, he would certainly not have joined the Proust or Céline movements, or indeed any of the great tried and tested traditions. Rather, his taste led him to that little family – a rare and prestigious family – of ironic and benevolent spirits, luminous and strange, and above all endowed with a sparkling intelligence, which could count Borges or Perec among its members.

In *'Cantatrix sopranica L.' and Other Scientific Writings*, Georges Perec engages in a series of often hilarious parodies of scholarly communications.[3] It has often seemed to me that Rachid Amirou, in *Imaginaire touristique et sociabilités du voyage*, his only published book, sometimes engaged in an exercise of the same order, and that his choice of references and footnotes was often meant (by their position, their sonority, the slight break they induced) to wrest a slight smile from us – much more discreet, of course, than the burst of laughter provoked by some of the footnotes invented by Perec. And with this difference, too, that it was indeed originally a thesis, propounded in the most official of ways, and that the references obviously had to be exact, and verifiable. In short, he had to come forward wearing a mask, since any suspicion of a literary tone that he introduced might cast doubt on the scientificity of his contribution. So he was offering us both a scientific discourse – in itself interesting, and in places disturbingly innovative – and an ironic attitude towards this same discourse (not towards its content, but towards the very position of the sociologist producing 'scientific' discourses on the social state), an irony that, following the law of the genre he had chosen, had to remain undecidable from beginning to end.

As he was an academic, Rachid Amirou was unknown to the general public and often little appreciated by his colleagues. This is hardly surprising, given his obvious difference, and it must be said his striking superiority over those publications that commonly oscillate between a residual leftism (on the 'neo-colonialism' of tourists) and ecologizing pieties deploring the lost authenticity of indigenous populations (lying somewhere between Segalen and *Le Guide du Routard*). Unlike so many of his dreadful colleagues, he knew that the indigenous people had become so perverted that they were sometimes extremely happy to fit into a Western way of life to which they already aspired anyway – that they did not necessarily want to be, as he puts it, 'kept under the house arrest of their identity'. He did open up to me about this at times, but always without bitterness; he basically took this relative ostracism with good humour. He knew that while the prestige that came

with a successful academic and media career was likely to fall
to others, he remained, as a university professor, 'pretty much
unsackable'. That's true, I told myself, it's a status. There are
still statuses in France that allow relative freedom of thought
to be exercised. It's amazing, but it's a good thing.

I miss our conversations. Who now will tell me anecdotes
like the astonishing one about that village in the Var where the
inhabitants (retirees, mainly) are modestly paid by the municipality to emerge from their homes, drink their pastis, play their
game of pétanque at the hour when the tourist coaches start
pouring in? To lead, in short, exactly their usual way of life?

The texts gathered at the end of the volume establish with a
particular clarity (if only for the unusual character of the references used, such as Donald Winnicott and Philippe Muray) the
inability of previous sociological categories to grasp the new,
'postmodern' forms of the tourism industry. They obviously
suggest a work of greater scope. He was thinking about this
book – too much, I told myself; he would have done better to
focus just a bit on his cancer (it's infuriating to think that if
he'd caught it in time, he could easily have been cured). We
can only get a very vague idea of it through these texts, we can
only measure the magnitude of the task at hand. Since the publication of *Imaginaire touristique et sociabilités du voyage*, the
tourist industry has undergone astonishing changes, and more
than any other has helped reshape the face of many countries
– France in particular. Now that he's dead, who will be able to
tell us about it as well as he could?

29

Interview with Frédéric Beigbeder

Frédéric Beigbeder: So it's official, you're going to publish a novel next year?

Michel Houellebecq: Mmmm . . . yes, but I won't tell you the title. Teresa values exclusivity.

FB: Splendid: I deduce that you're staying with Flammarion! (Teresa Cremisi is their CEO.)

MH: I would like to start by talking about you, Frédéric. You've written a few books, some good, some not. But you've been the best literary critic for quite some time now, no two ways about it. That's why I'm afraid of you!

FB: Ha! Ha! Did you come to dinner to try to sweet talk me?

MH: Mmmm . . . I'm being perfectly serious: you're the critic I fear the most.

FB: [*Laughs.*] No, Michel, you decided to have dinner at my home because you can't smoke in restaurants anymore.

MH: Dominique Voynet[1] has said that the main danger for children is smoking indoors, at home. You'll see, soon we won't be allowed to smoke anywhere, not even at home! When I'm writing, my cigarette consumption increases dramatically. I'm on four packs a day right now. I don't think I could write without nicotine. That's why I can't slow down right now.

FB: Can we talk about your dental problem? It has transformed you a bit physically. The last time you came to dinner here, sorry to reveal your private life, but hey . . . you left your teeth behind on this table and then you did the whole Berlin Festival without your teeth! It changes your face in the photos . . . don't you mind?

MH: Well, uh . . . I do mind a bit, yes, to be honest. [*Laughs.*]

FB: But is your health okay?

MH: Uh . . . no. I think that when I finish this novel, maybe I will after all make an effort to cut down on smoking. Alcohol isn't a problem except with taxi drivers; half the time, the driver tells me 'Oh no, not you! You're going to throw up in my car!'

FB: So your physical evolution isn't a calculated attempt to give you a mug like Paul Léautaud?[2]

MH: No, I don't know what he looks like. I'm sometimes compared to Gainsbourg but that rather annoys me, because I prefer Polnareff or Joe Dassin.[3]

FB: 'To the top of her thighs / she's in boots / and it's a chalice / for her beauty.' Don't you like that?

MH: Ouf . . . I've written better things, you know. I want to make it clear: I'm someone who really likes song. I started listening to the charts when I was around eleven or twelve years old. The most violent aesthetic shock of my life will always be the discovery of rock.

FB: Is your god still Paul McCartney?

MH: Yes, but I can also be very moved by Schubert.

FB: I can testify that in Guéthary I saw you cry while listening to 'Let It Be'. You also cry when you listen to a lied by Schubert.

MH: Oh yes! 'The Shepherd on the Rock' is the only time in my life that I've burst into tears in the middle of a concert. It was very embarrassing for the singer because I make a noise when I cry. Well, maybe she was happy to have produced such an effect, but it was embarrassing. When the clarinet comes in it's one of the most beautiful things ever composed. When I want to imagine what a genius is like, I think of Beethoven more than Shakespeare. In more recent times it's McCartney and the older Hendrix. My encounter with Iggy Pop has been one of the greatest joys of my life. *1969*, by the Stooges, was the first record I ever bought.

FB: What's surprising is that you've been adapted into song by Iggy Pop, Carla Bruni and Jean-Louis Aubert. They have very different styles!

MH: Mmmm . . . The best artistes come to me quite naturally!

FB: You will soon be attending the inauguration of the calle Michel-Houellebecq in the Spanish city of Murcia. How does it feel to have a street named after you?

MH: Mmmm . . . it's a funny feeling. I think it impressed your daughter.

FB: Oh yes! She was blown away. I think you should live there. Then, we could write to you: 'To M. Michel Houellebecq, in the street of the same name.'

MH: Mmmm ... Practical, yes ... it looks a little bit aristocratic.

FB: Did you like playing your own role in *The Abduction of Michel Houellebecq*, directed by Guillaume Nicloux?

MH: It's funny because the kidnappers get fed up with their hostage. A sort of reverse Stockholm syndrome. Once again, I confirm my reputation as a jack of all trades! Well, as for Jean-Louis Aubert's recording, I have to point out that I did absolutely nothing. I was excited about the project but didn't do a thing.

FB: Simultaneously, your poetry is being published in the prestigious 'Poésie/Gallimard' collection. The preface, by Agathe Novak-Lechevalier, says that you're developing an art of 'telescoping'. You summarized it like this: 'Doing something religious that involves the existence of underground car parks.'

MH: That was a challenge! My problem was choosing the order of the poems in this anthology: whenever I found a great poem, biff baff, I swapped things round. It was like editing. *Non réconcilié* is really my 'best of'.

FB: I believe you wrote a novel in Cuba and Thailand. Do you write on purpose in countries that don't speak French?

MH: I need to be alone in my language. Throughout the day, I don't communicate in my language. French is reserved for writing, it allows you to stay focused.

FB: How do you start a novel? Do you choose a topic or do you wait for inspiration?

MH: Mmmm ... You have concerns that crop up and first pages that come along and you keep going. Bingo!

FB: You've often told me that you like long novels because they allow you to settle down, to feel comfortable developing and following characters ...

MH: I might be wrong but, this time more than the others, I'm trying to be perfect, so I correct all the time. And so the next one will be shorter than the others.

FB: Ah! That's good!

MH: What d'you mean, 'That's good!'?

FB: Uh ... I'm a bit lazy.

MH: You're insulting! Say it straight out if my big books piss you off!

FB: [*Laughs.*] Has the Goncourt Prize changed your life?

MH: No, not at all. My next novel isn't coming out in September, that's the only difference.

FB: *I* publish in September.

MH: You could still get the Goncourt prize.

FB: Impossible, I'm on the jury for the Renaudot prize.

MH: Ah! You're such an idiot! Why do you get into stuff like that? [*Laughs.*]

FB: It gives me an excuse for never getting the prize! After a few years of exile in Ireland, you came back to France a year ago in a tower block that looks like a New York skyscraper with a view of Chinese ideograms. You live like in *Blade Runner*, in the thirteenth arrondissement!

MH: There are two aspects here. On the one hand, I wanted to come back to France without feeling like I was in France. On the other hand, being close to the motorway, I can leave the country very quickly.

FB: Aren't you happy that you came back to your country?

MH: I feel extremely uncomfortable in France. There've been several more turns of the screw since I left. It's amazing how the government seems to want to increase the unhappiness of people, perhaps to unprecedented proportions. I'm sad about the state of my country. You want my opinion? I fear a civil war. Things are very tense right now. It might start kicking off any time.

FB: We knew about the 'social divide'; you're considered to be the novelist of the 'sexual divide'. What do you think of the law penalizing the clients of prostitutes?

MH: It's unadulterated bollocks. I know some prostitutes, as a friend and not even as a client. They still have a small sense of guilt because some of them have told me they buy a lot of bullshit, like designer clothes, to atone a bit, to spend their money faster. Other than that, they love their jobs, and preventing these girls from practising their trade is one first considerable piece of crap; not listening to prostitutes at all is tragic infantilization. As for slapping fines on clients, that's just disgusting, humanly speaking. I can't stand a government doing such things, it's just not possible.

FB: But how can the civil war you foresee be prevented?

MH: [*In a Gaullist tone*] I'm fine-tuning a project for a new Democratic Constitution. I spoke to Sarkozy, for whom I have a real affection. It's quite unusual to launch a political campaign in *Lui*, but I don't have a lot of serious channels for expressing my opinions, and then the old ways have to be changed.

FB: Tell us!

MH: Well, first of all, I want to establish a direct democracy, by abolishing Parliament. In my opinion, the President of the Republic must be elected for life but can be instantly deprived of office by a simple referendum, at the initiative of the people. The third important measure: the office of judge will become elective (of course only law graduates will be eligible, they won't be able to elect someone like you, for example).

FB: Let me tell you that I have a law degree from Assas!

MH: [*Smiling at his protests.*] The fourth measure is that the state budget will be decided by the citizens, who will have to fill in a sheet with boxes to tick every year. The people will thus decide which expenses they consider to be priorities. An average will be calculated and then budgets allocated to each ministry. We need more direct democracy if we want to move out of the crisis of political representation we're stuck in. If my measures aren't adopted, we're heading for disaster.

FB: Do you want to be the new Michel Debré?[4]

MH: Rousseau drew up a draft Constitution for Poland. This is 'my project for France'.

FB: The funny thing about you is that you're an almost Christian romantic moralist who everyone thinks of as a decadent nihilist and atheist.

MH: Yeah, it's very strange but mmm . . . it's weird. You know, if you light a cigarette while you're waiting for the TGV, you immediately get called a nihilist. The word 'nihilist' has a precise and limited historical meaning that dates from the Russian nineteenth century: nihilists were revolutionaries who said to themselves 'we don't know what we want to set up afterwards, but we must destroy everything, it's always going to be better than it was before'. But I'm no nihilist, quite the contrary, I'm a conservative, like Benoît Duteurtre.[5]

FB: It's because of him that we know each other, you know. He took me to the meetings of the magazine *L'Atelier du roman* at the Lucernaire [theatre], that must have been in 1994. Philippe Muray was there, and Lakis Proguidis, Milan Kundera and you.

MH: Yes, these writers had in common the fight against 'political correctness'. Today nobody even wants to use the expression anymore, it's become ridiculous, but it made sense, and it still does, to fight for your freedom of expression. 'Political correctness' has been making steady inroads for twenty years. People get tired of saying bad things about a thing, but the thing doesn't get tired of existing. I knew Philippe Muray: during his lifetime I disagreed with him and today I realize that he was right about everything, in fact. It's horrible what we put up with.

FB: Young people making dumplings [*quenelles*] are a consequence of the extent of 'political correctness'.

MH: Of course! Do you think I enjoyed going to trial when I was never interested in Islam? We must be able to work without being worried by censorship. Banning things is a mechanism that never stops. There's one person who's really free at the moment: Gaspard Proust. I really like him. It's one of the only shows I watch all the time, Gaspard Proust's five minutes.[6]

FB: I'll introduce you to him whenever you want! Ah! Hang on, now's the time to tackle the new subject on our list: the question of Albert Camus.

MH: Ah! I'm all ears.

FB: Can we imagine Houellebecq happy?[7]

MH: Mmmm . . . uh . . . pfffff . . . Cheerful: yeah. Happy, I'd tend to say no. In my life, I've only had odd snatches of happiness. Moments of joy.

FB: Let me remind you of the first sentence of your first book: 'The world is an unfolding suffering.'

MH: That's definitely not an optimist's phrase. Happiness, pff . . . You have to imagine Houellebecq no longer writing; I hope that's a painful prospect.

FB: You're more in favour of technological progress (for example, human cloning in *The Elementary Particles* and *The Possibility of an Island*). What do you think of Google's trans-humanist utopias?

MH: I recently lost both parents and my dog in a relatively short period of time – I wasn't happy about those deaths. If we can live three hundred and fifty years, I'm all for it: there are still so many books to read. Recently I discovered Theodor Fontane, he's great. On the other hand, I don't see the point of Google Glass, it's a bit terrifying, those cameras that can recognize people. The other day I saw an ad that scared me, on the metro, it was for a dating site and said, 'Love doesn't happen by chance.' I wanted to say, 'Oh yes it does! At least leave us the element of chance.'

FB: I can't figure out which side you're on. Are you out to protect humanity or are you in favour of an 'augmented' humanity?

MH: Let's say I don't want to be pissed off by the humanists. If we can improve humanity, why not? I remember a lecture when I was dragged through the mud and called a Nazi because I was supposedly defending eugenics, genetics and all that. There was a disabled person who spoke with difficulty into the microphone, and said: 'I . . . tend . . . to be . . . for it . . .' It was terrible, it made everyone calm down. Obviously it's no fun having a rare genetic disease. But all the same, there's a limit. You shouldn't over-normalize human beings either, because if you had to be healthy . . . neither you nor I would be alive! [*Laughs.*]

This interesting interview led to me getting slated in various articles; exceptionally, I remember two of them – no doubt because of their incongruity.

The first called me 'bobo-maurrassien'.[8] Many categories have been invented to describe me (depressive, *glauciste*, etc.), but this is certainly one of the strangest. What connection can its author have established between Charles Maurras and direct democracy? After all these years, I'm still wondering.

The second, more sober-minded piece, was actually even more bizarre. The popular initiative referendum, the author pointed out, was in fact a serious handicap for the Swiss economy; business executives constantly complained about it, due to the risk of unpredictability it entails. The Swiss economy, to my knowledge, isn't doing so badly, but that's not the point. The point is that I'd never seen someone so clearly demonstrate the impossibility of even considering a question from another angle than the economic one; the impossibility of even imagining that another angle could exist.

Unfortunately, I've forgotten the names of the authors of these two articles, and even the news outlet where they were published. It's a shame; in a way, they deserved to be preserved.

30

A remedy for the
exhaustion of being

It still happens sometimes, admittedly rarely but it does happen, that contemporary sociologists produce a relevant reflection on contemporary society. Among the absolutely new phenomena that developed in the twentieth century, the one for which no real equivalent can be found in previous centuries, one of the most ambiguous and least studied, is without any doubt *tourism*.

I was lucky enough to know Rachid Amirou, a sociologist of tourism who died prematurely a few years ago, and so I could benefit from some of his reflections, his remarks, which he didn't have time to shape into a more formal piece of work. I was particularly struck by this anecdote about a Provençal village in the hinterland, where retirees were paid a small sum by the municipality to lead *exactly their usual way of life*, as it had been popularized by, among other things, Pagnol's films: the games of pétanque, pastis on the terrace of a café shaded by plane trees; the only slightly restrictive demand made on them was that they had to adapt their schedules to the times when foreign tourist coaches came by, and to agree to be photographed by these tourists.

Our first reaction, it must be said, is distinct unease; we have the impression that these Provençal grandpas are being treated like the giraffe women of northern Thailand, or the Navajo people of New Mexico forced to perform their rain dances for the halfwits in the Greyhound bus; we have the impression of a sort of *attack on human dignity.*

This discomfort finds a particularly violent expression in the photographs of Marc Lathuillière, to the point that the lighting in all of them seems worrying (even though this lighting is actually very variable).[1] When the human face is present in a photograph, it's so essential, so central to it, that the very fact of covering it with a mask (and not even a frightening or grotesque mask, just a light, realistic mask, with no other function than to prohibit the expression of facial features) contaminates all the other elements of the photograph, introduces a doubt as to their authenticity.[2] The discomfort is, it should be noted, even more acute when the profession of the subjects being photographed is related to animal breeding, or to culinary professions (are we so worried about *what we have on our plates?*). Thus, despite the undeniably muddy feathers on its belly, the unfortunate 'farm poultry' cannot fail to be suspected of being a toy goose, the sausages of the 'garnished sauerkraut' [*choucroute garnie*] look like exhibition sausages, plastic sausages, and the 'crustaceans' look as if they come from a TV soap opera like *Plus belle la vie.*[3]

But the discomfort engendered by Marc Lathuillière's photographs seems to me even more insidious and persistent when their subject is not professional life, but touches on more intimate matters. 'Communion' bothers me deeply (and I wonder, moreover, if the priest was right to accept). The life of a family, too, isn't one of those realities that can be safely transformed into *role play.* Finally, we need to make a distinction. 'In the Lafayette salon' isn't really disturbing, as it's true that aristocrats, more or less since Louis XIV, have had no other social function than to play their role as aristocrats. But 'Bedtime' is really painful; this family (which we imagine to be middle class, Catholic, on the centre-left, readers of the newspaper *Ouest-France* engaged in humanitarian action in favour of Haiti) cannot without uneasiness be induced to *play the role of a family.*

So, at first glance, this is a body of work that will inevitably lead to a final denunciation: France has given up evolving, it has decided to stand still, to stop taking part in the evolution of the world; not only are we all tourists in our own country, but actors in tourism, the French as a whole have agreed to *play their role as French people* for the delight of international tourism.

It's possible, but is it such a disaster? A conversation with Marc Lathuillière taught me that most of the models had readily, and even gladly, accepted to go along with it all, to play their own professional (or even family) roles after donning a mask – even though most people hate being photographed, as everyone knows, and posing for a photograph is an ordeal for them. And I myself hate being photographed, I'm the worst possible model, I don't understand what the photographer wants and I have no desire to understand it, after five minutes I already feel the session's lasted for hours. But, as I realize, I'd quite easily have agreed to put on a mask, and play my own part. I suppose that, in Marc Lathuillière's project, I'd have been the Great Writer, sitting with a coffee and smoking Gitanes, at the Café du Flore. Well, I'd have done so, even with a certain pleasure (actually, it's a bit anachronistic, you're not allowed to smoke Gitanes at the Flore any more, or anywhere else, I'm not even sure that Gitanes are still openly on sale, the photo should have been taken earlier).

The difference is that the ordinary photographer asks you to *be*, and it's exhausting to *be* (with this extra annoyance that the photographer plans to capture your being, as if this were imaginable, with a lens); but Marc Lathuillière asks you to play

your own role – which is sometimes fun, sometimes exhausting, it all depends. Obviously you have to be careful before
choosing a role (because whatever role you play, you soon
become it); but it's a choice that must be carefully made, one
way or another, in life; whereas photography constantly, indis-
creetly, tends to bring you back to this painful obligation to be,
it issues an unbearable demand for profundity. And all this just
to produce, on the whole, a stupid snapshot (*un cliché*).

I never quite understood how one can 'imagine Sisyphus
happy'; Sisyphus seems to me obviously unhappy since he
performs vain, repetitive and *painful* gestures; but the being
who performs vain, repetitive and *pleasant* gestures seems to
me, obviously, to be happy. One need only compare Sisyphus
pushing his rock to a pet playing with a ball on a staircase to
understand what I mean. No doubt Camus had in mind some
obscure, nonsensical notions touching on human dignity.

No, it's not the 'literature of the absurd' that I'm initially
tempted to refer to when I think of the photographs of Marc
Lathuillière; but rather those strange sci-fi stories where the
characters, caught in a temporal rift, are made to repeat the
same gestures over and over again (I have no precise references
to provide; the memory I have of these stories is so clear that
I've probably just made them up). Anyway, these stories take
place in fine weather; under a uniform and unchangeably blue
sky. Storms and clouds are already quite dramatic; but tragedy,
like absolute happiness, invariably requires blue skies.

31

Interview with Marin De Viry and Valérie Toranian

RDDM (*Revue des Deux Mondes*): In our prep for this interview, you wanted to talk about the abolition of the Cartesian cogito, 'I think therefore I am', in *Submission*. Why?

MH: Overall, I was quite satisfied with the media treatment of this book in France. From everything that's been written about it, I'll mention just two articles. The first was by Nelly Kaprièlian, 'J'irai cracher sur votre monde' ['I will spit on your world', in *Les Inrockuptibles*], which sums up the subject of *Submission*. He points out that the book isn't primarily about Islam but is in fact, and as usual, a savage attack on the present West. The second was by Agathe Novak-Lechevalier, '*Soumission*, la littérature comme résistance' ['*Submission*, literature as resistance'], published in *Libération*, which tackles the theme of the Cartesian cogito. She comes up with the interesting idea that at one point the character (François) thinks, 'I am not. Why would I think?' The 'I am' is the problem with the formula. Indeed, the counterpart to 'I think, therefore I am' is 'I am not, therefore I do not think.'

The construction of *Submission*, although very simple, wasn't really noticed. I gradually take everything away from my character, strip him of everything: of his partner Myriam, of his parents, of a job that after all gave him some satisfaction and a certain social life, of his possible conversion too, before it fails, in Rocamadour, and finally I take Huysmans away from him (I've observed that when you think you've written in detail about an author, as my narrator has Huysmans, you can't read him anymore). When you take everything away from someone, does he still exist? With his bizarre optimism, Descartes would answer 'yes', without hesitation. I don't really agree: to be is to be related. I don't believe in the individual who is free and alone. So I reduce my character, I destroy him. Once I've done that, why would he have freedom of thought? Why not just go along with what he's offered?

RDDM: Should we see his annihilation and loneliness as the only explanations for his conversion to Islam?

MH: All his reasons for living have been destroyed, and all that's left are skin diseases and practical difficulties. Furthermore, writing manages to convince him that a God exists, that this God can weigh down on him, through more serious health problems. Resisting would therefore require real heroism. The fact that one does not really exist is present in many of my books, but *Submission* is the only one where I describe this gradual access to non-existence.

RDDM: What does 'not existing' mean? Not having anything to counter others with, not having a house, a place, an interior life or even a life in general, not having an idea of something needing to be done, to be built, not being transitive, not having any effect on the world?

MH: 'Not having any effect on the world' is a good summary. The world can't do anything for you, and you can't do anything for it.

RDDM: The narrator is a professor at the Sorbonne: is this 'non-existence' linked to his environment?

MH: It's a hugely widespread phenomenon, but much more striking in the case of someone who belongs to the elite. This was true of Huysmans himself, by the way. You have to check out the passages in *Là-bas* where he has dinner with the Carhaix couple in a tower in the church of Saint-Sulpice – for me this is what's most profound in Huysmans. We realize that his demands weren't all that considerable after all. True, he admires those women saints who greedily suck the wounds of lepers, that kind of thing. But, deep down in him, there's the ideal of the lower-middle-class man who'd like to have had a mundane household life, a few friends – not too many – and a nice little meal from time to time. Huysmans was placed on a certain social summit – he was the first president of the Goncourt academy, no small feat – but he didn't even manage to achieve that simple thing. It makes you think.

RDDM: Is it the ideal of sipping a nice glass of white wine under your pergola?

MH: It's more the ideal of the pot-au-feu ... There are two excellent descriptions of pot-au-feu in French literature, one by Huysmans and one by Proust. No other dish can boast such a literary past; there's no equivalent for the boeuf bourguignon or the blanquette.

RDDM: Is this petty-bourgeois aspiration to happiness ridiculous?

MH: I find it rather touching. But I'm on Huysmans' side against Bloy, I've said it before and I can say it again.[1] For a balanced Catholicism.

RDDM: Which of your novels best evokes the abolition en bloc of the Cartesian cogito?

MH: The first consequence of this abolition is a kind of lowering of the will. If I am not, I want less. People often mention *Rester vivant* or *Approches du désarroi*, which point to a certain loss of will in our contemporaries, a kind of dispersal. A person is no longer in a position to have an organized, constant will, pursuing a goal. She allows herself to be led by circumstances, and that's why my characters in general don't react much. People criticize me for the fact that the narrator doesn't try to hold Myriam back, but he feels that deep down there's nothing he can do about it.

RDDM: The narrator of *Submission* stopped thinking about Huysmans' work years ago. He knows it by heart but he doesn't think about it anymore . . .

MH: But he does think about it again when he writes his preface; it's not that cut and dried. Literature is still a way to escape life, even if it's not the only one. Michel, the character in *Elementary Particles,* thinks a lot about his field of activity, but not about his life. He doesn't see himself as a core of will pursuing goals, making decisions, directing his life. If my characters had to be divided into categories, on the one hand there'd be those who have an interest in life outside of their own lives, an intellectual interest, as with Michel or Jed in *La Carte et le territoire* [*The Map and the Territory*], which allows them not to live very much without this being much of a problem for them. On the other hand, there'd be those who have no interest in their lives, outside of life itself, and behave more erratically, such as Bruno or the narrator of *Platform.* François is somewhere in the middle, I'd say.

RDDM: This dissociation between the cogito and the 'I am' in everyone, is it serious, and is it new?

MH: The word 'anomie' would work here. It's serious, in the sense that it makes everyone miserable. And it's a question of age, not of background . . . Up to a certain age, when we flit from this to that, variety can be distracting. Then fatigue intervenes, along with a reduction in the possibilities of life.

RDDM: But it's a world that is ruled entirely by distraction in the Pascalian sense, by the desire to be permanently outside of oneself . . .

MH: I'd like to point out that I'm quite exceptional from this point of view, since going out less, and therefore being able to stay in my room, doesn't bother me in the slightest.

RDDM: Does it bother you, being in the outside world?

MH: Yes. But as Schopenhauer pointed out, you have to keep a minimum of social contact, just as you have to get used to the cold again when winter comes along. It's a kind of social hygiene.

RDDM: But the temptation would be to cut yourself off from everything and stay in your room with literature?

MH: Yes, it's a real temptation. As a result, I've just read Joseph de Maistre for the first time in my life. I really liked his arguments against Protestantism. But he's so eighteenth century in his tastes, in his writing even – that struck me. He must have been very unhappy, because if he'd embraced the Romantic Revolution, he'd have been more in tune with his own views. Romanticism was counter-revolutionary. So why did he stick to the classical style? He must have suffered as a result. For example, we feel that, when it came to Voltaire, he couldn't share the frank contempt of Musset: 'Do you sleep content, Voltaire, and does your revolting smile / Still flutter around over your bare bones?' Intellectually speaking, for Maistre, the eighteenth century is the height of all evil, but deep down he can't detach himself from that century. It's a shame, because for lack of an enlightened spiritual goal on the right, the romantics, who were more artists than thinkers, ended up moving to the left.

RDDM: Does the unhappiness that results from this massive anomie lead to violence?

MH: Yes, any kind of violent action can be seen as a way out of a hopeless anomie. Terrorism and activism are means of socialization. It must be very nice to have moments together, moments when you feel you're all against the police . . . The feeling of being together, against everyone. We feel more together when we have a lot of enemies. It creates real relationships, a strong friendship, even love in the case of jihadist wives.

RDDM: The lure of the hero?

MH: That's possible, but it's going to be seen as sexist if I approve of you. 'Woman goes to God through man . . .' I don't remember who said that.

RDDM: In the world of anomie, there are no more works of art?

MH: Works of art don't concern that many people as it's . . .

RDDM: The work of the craftsman, the work of the musician – the act of influencing the world through your productions . . .

MH: There's been a big decline in handicrafts . . .

RDDM: Is this world of anomie a new world or an old one?

MH: It's still recent. In the middle of the twentieth century, France was still mainly agricultural and artisanal. Things speeded up after 1945. It can be traced back to the 'Trente Glorieuses'.[2] Authors like Jean-Louis Curtis, whom I really like and who died not long ago, observed the transformation. Before the Second World War, even though Marx had already seen things starting to change, France was still overwhelmingly a rural country.

RDDM: And this submission, this frustration – can you date it?

MH: There was an enthusiasm for the industrial world that started to disintegrate at the time of the first crisis, in 1973 to be precise. So it's been forty years, after all. It's old but it's not too old. Someone old like me could almost remember what had happened before. Almost: I don't remember having lived in a world without crisis. But if I were just a bit older, I *would* remember.

RDDM: But isn't anomie related to the exhaustion of constantly being in a world in crisis? What's the point of thinking if you just discover that the objects you're thinking about are rapidly becoming obsolescent?

MH: I don't know if I'm a conservative, but I don't believe that a human being – any more than any other animal – is made to live in a constantly changing world. So the absence of balance, of a quest for balance, is in itself unlivable. The idea of permanent change makes life impossible.

RDDM: You seem to think that the man–woman couple has become unlivable since sexual liberation: too much change, too much destabilization on both sides?

MH: Let's say that we're forced to admit it isn't working. If I say that a relationship is off to a bad start because one can immediately sense that it's doomed to obsolescence – and this is often true for a male–female relationship – that makes for interesting books; it's also true for a business relationship, but that makes for more boring books.

RDDM: Is the managerial discourse of praising permanent change and the changing world a sin against the human condition, in your view?

MH: Yes, it often relies on Taoism, that kind of thing, and rightly so . . . It's a sin not against the human condition but against our civilization, which wants to build permanent entities that will be permanently valid.

RDDM: That's why Buddhism is so popular in business. They put the prospect of extinction into perspective; basically, it's a good idea for everything to come to an end . . . You have to know how to change, how to do three or four jobs, instead of just one . . .

MH: Yes, well, that's also a misunderstanding of Buddhism. I think Taoism would actually be better for business. You have to be fluid, you mustn't have a well-defined identity, you need to adapt, be polymorphous, change jobs when you're asked to do so . . .

RDDM: You've just been to Asia. Does your interpretation also work for this part of the world, or isn't Asia much more forward-looking?

MH: I wasn't in Asia for long but I guess it's the same throughout the world.

RDDM: But the collective nationalism that we see in China or Russia, for example, is a different mindset from Western anomie. The relationship between the individual and the collectivity is not a relationship of secession, disinterest, intransitivity . . .

MH: Frankly, I don't really know. In Russia, they don't produce much. They're patriots, they really love their president. It's a bit strange. In general, you stop being a patriot when your country has overstepped the mark. In France, it took a war. In Germany, it took two to stop them being patriots. In Russia, they only got one. They shed a lot of blood. Maybe it would take a second war for them to stop being patriots.

RDDM: Vladimir Putin is getting it all together, he's redrawing the national framework, to take responsibility for it himself . . .

MH: With a political base that does appear to exist, yes – but will it exist if there are too many deaths? At the moment he isn't engaged in operations that are causing too many deaths.

RDDM: In France, freedom is a matter of interest. In any case, freedom of expression, if you look at the demonstrations on 11 January . . .

MH: That demonstration was impressive and sincere. I tend to support freedom of expression.

RDDM: What do you think of the slogan 'Je suis Charlie'?

MH: It's not the best slogan of all time, but it does correspond to a reality: people are attached to some form of freedom. They want to be sure they can find a satirical newspaper on the newsstands. It's a basic freedom, one that has never been attacked so brutally and so openly. I was actually pleased about this huge reaction.

RDDM: Was it a manifestation of the desire to retain this freedom or a manifestation of identity?

MH: No, not identity, not at all. It's just that Cabu and Wolinski[3] were very well known and everyone knew at least vaguely who they were, and they did sometimes provocative things. Everyone had seen pictures of them somewhere; so that's what affected people.

RDDM: What is the balance between freedom of expression and provocation? The *Charlie Hebdo* journalists have been accused of going too far. Should freedom of expression be restricted?

MH: There are some things that go too far. I'm in favour of some censorship in certain areas but in this case, no, they weren't going too far. Anyway, let's say they were used to that freedom of tone, they were people who had known the 1960s and 1970s, and the French are used to it too. So the events shocked them, and me too. What would your character in *Submission* have done on 11 January?

MH: Probably nothing. He'd have stayed at home watching television, it's easier to watch demonstrations on television.

RDDM: You say that the demonstrations affected you. But did you say to yourself, 'Hey, something might happen, something might change', or was this demonstration just a passing moment and nothing more?

MH: What do you expect to happen? Objectively speaking, nothing. The demonstration delighted the sponsors of the attacks. They can congratulate themselves on the media stunt they achieved. What the majority of French people think isn't their problem.

RDDM: Yet it created a political base for an increase in the budget for the army, the police, the gendarmerie . . .

MH: Yes, that's true. That was an interesting practical consequence.

RDDM: Have you experienced this period as a gradual entry into a war situation?

MH: The real start was in 2001. This is like a continuation, but something interesting happened this time around. There's a discourse that has been well established since 2001, 'no lumping together, no stigmatization, Islam is a religion of peace, tolerance and love, these people are not Muslims, they're unbalanced, probably from single-parent families in great economic difficulty', and so on. In January the discourse was trotted out as usual, but for the first time there were yawns and sneers. This is where the novelty lies. There was a kind of temptation of freedom among some intellectuals, who were immediately called to order, but without success. Like Michel Onfray, who calls Manuel Valls a moron [*crétin*]. 'Moron' was the right word, and I really appreciate it when someone comes up with the right word. More generally, there's a desire for freedom among certain intellectuals.

RDDM: And a desire to name the real too?

MH: Yes, a desire not to deny the obvious.

RDDM: Was there a click, a spark, a turning point? Did you expect it?

MH: It's interesting, and came as a pleasant surprise to me. The total domination of the left over intellectuals has lasted since 1945. It's been seventy years, all the same. You'd think it would last forever, and here it completely fell apart.

RDDM: In your view, did 11 January create a bloc, a front with the desire to retain most of what constitutes France's political base?

MH: They'll form a bloc, yes. But that's not why it's going to be successful.

RDDM: When, in *Submission*, we read about the shenanigans that took place before the presidential elections, we get the impression of an irresponsible political class. François Bayrou . . .

MH: . . . François Bayrou is convinced that he has a national destiny and he's ready to do anything to have it, even if he takes the political right down with him; yes, he's irresponsible.

RDDM: A bit like Lamartine . . .

MH: Yes. But at least Lamartine had the excuse of creating beautiful sentences. Lamartine was at bottom less about personal ambition than a taste for beautiful sentences in a theatrical situation. He was first and foremost an actor, not in the least bit cruel.

RDDM: But since the enemies of Western civilization have declared war on it, might there be a resurgence among us – in the West, even in France? Or are you pessimistic even on this point?

MH: It's not clear that this resurgence would be effective. It's not an easy thing to fight a religious sect. The police are currently thwarting quite a few attacks, but a purely police response to a religious sect isn't guaranteed to win. In general, it tends to be religions that prevail over other religions.

RDDM: Is it the same to attack a religious sect and a religion?

MH: It's pretty much the same.

RDDM: Is the police response insignificant, or inadequate?

MH: No, it's not insignificant, but I don't think it's enough. When you're not afraid of death, you don't really care about the police. Even if all of France is mobilized and the police get a lot of money . . .

RDDM: Do you think that it's not so much a Muslim problem as a Catholic problem, deep down? There's no religion competing with Islam that's powerful enough to establish a balance of power.

MH: There's a Muslim problem too. There are subjects on which Muhammad didn't express an opinion, such as how to behave in secular countries; he couldn't have foreseen the emergence of secular countries. On the other hand, he spoke abundantly, on several occasions and quite clearly, about how to behave towards Christians and Jews. Daesh is clearly heretical. It's amazing, after all, that the heresy isn't being fought, that there are no anti-Daesh fatwas.

RDDM: The Wahhabi and Salafist interpretation dominates the Muslim world today.

MH: But even from a Salafist point of view, Daesh is heretical. And in any case, it's true, there's no competition with Islam: Catholicism is a bit past it.

RDDM: Do you miss Catholicism?

MH: Yes, though the masses are quite promising. There are amazing demonstrations, but the hierarchy is inactive.

RDDM: Did the *Manif pour tous* surprise you?[4]

MH: Very much. I didn't know that there were all those young Catholics that we saw on television: the '*veilleurs*' ['watchmen'], for example.[5] It was very surprising.

RDDM: And what do you think of them?

MH: I like them. But, you know, I'm too old to convert now. So I get by with a kind of nostalgia.

RDDM: There's a feeling that you're not far away . . .

MH: No, that will never work. God doesn't want me, you know. He's rejected me.

RDDM: That's pride!

MH: It's not pride at all.

RDDM: Is the conversion of Huysmans what attracts you to him?

MH: Taking Huysmans as the guideline for the narrator of *Submission* was a crucial choice. But I'm not in the same situation as my character. Huysmans wasn't someone I fell in love with at a tender age. I like him a lot, but I discovered him late, too late for me to miss him as badly as if I'd read him when I was sixteen. In my books, any judgements of works of art are mine. I take advantage of my novels to do a bit of literary criticism on the sly. *A rebours* is kind of a monolith, but I really like *En ménage* and *À vau-l'eau*. I like his naturalistic beginnings, too, and *Là-Bas* is a great success, but the three books about conversion that followed end up being a bit boring, there's a taste for enumeration that ends up weighing things down. But there's still *Les Foules de Lourdes* [*The Crowds of Lourdes*], a beautiful Catholic book.

RDDM: And the Catholic mystics, do you like them? Saint Teresa of Ávila, for example?

MH: I haven't really read all that.

RDDM: It seems like your character is incapable of love. For example, he was unable to hold onto Myriam, who leaves for Israel after trying to send him messages to which he doesn't reply because he's distraught . . .

MH: The fault is shared. It's terrible, we're supposed to be in a feminist society, but it's the man who's wrong not to hold her back, while it's the woman who actually left. After all, she simply needed not to leave. For much of the book, he keeps on screwing around. But he gets no enjoyment out of it. There's something that's broken in him. It was love, love for Myriam that means he can't have any enjoyment after her.

RDDM: Don't the women in your books have more of that core of willpower that the men lack?

MH: Yes, they have it much more than the men.

RDDM: Does this come from your observations, or something that goes beyond our era and the evolution in the status of women?

MH: It's very recent and very surprising: women decide every-thing. They decide when a relationship starts, they decide when it ends, they decide whether or not to have a child. The man is strangely inert. The male point of view sort of evaporates, and this is unsettling, after all. The male point of view, with so few opportunities to express itself, has become unknown. It's a kind of secret. It's true that this part of this book is based on a question: what does a man think about all this, deep inside himself? One guess is that he hasn't changed, not at all. The reformation of man has been a total failure, but it's a hidden failure because men have understood that they'd do better to keep quiet.

RDDM: And if he did convert, if he succeeded in his conversion when he was in front of the Virgin in Rocamadour, would he become a man? Would he exert his will, he would recalibrate his relationships with women?

FM: I think I didn't write about him converting because I was filled with dismay at the thought of describing a Christian. It's difficult.

RDDM: Isn't this inconsistency also something women blame men for?

FM: Yes it is, and women are also starting to regret the results of what feminists have unleashed. But I've already said enough bad things about feminists, I'm not going there again.

RDDM: People never talk about men's pleasure, they always talk about women's pleasure . . .

FM: It's a mysterious subject, more mysterious than women's pleasure, after all.

RDDM: Is pleasure linked to the story men tell themselves when they sleep with a woman?

FM: If I knew that, I'd tell you, seriously.

RDDM: The lack of pleasure in your hero comes after Myriam's departure . . . Should the two be linked?

FM: Every once in a while you have to admit that something remains a mystery. He experiences it as mysterious. He experiences the brief return of pleasure as mysterious as well. It does seem to have to do with feelings, in one way or another. Whereas desire isn't, not at all: desire's much simpler, at least in humans. Pleasure is stranger. Maybe we should try to understand it in relation to things that are easier to observe: giving presents, things like that. The contentment given to the recipient of the gift is a pleasure. That's the kind of thing it would be, more than an imaginary construction, a story.

RDDM: In love, too, do we submit?

MH: Yes, in love, we don't have much choice.

RDDM: The words of Saint-Just, 'Happiness is a new idea in Europe', are not part of your cultural coordinates; you've never seen the West as a world that sought to create an individual and collective happiness.

MH: It's true that I'm not a revolutionary. The very term 'collective happiness' provokes a kind of terror in me. The idea that society wants to take care of my happiness doesn't inspire me with friendly feelings. So I was never a revolutionary, I was never dangerous.

RDDM: Is civilization what protects anonymity?

MH: It's what protects us from each other.

RDDM: Is it anti-communitarianism?

MH: I live in the Chinese district in Paris, and I'm struck by the fact that the less integrated immigrants are the best liked. It's pretty much the opposite of what people usually say, but it's the truth. Things have changed but, for example, in my apartment block, not all the Chinese over fifty speak French. They'd built a completely unintegrated community, with just a few people interfacing with the rest of the world, while everyone else stayed apart. And yet everyone loved the Asian immigrants.

RDDM: Isn't that because they didn't conflict with our model?

MH: They weren't interested in our model, but they weren't violent. In fact, the whole business comes down to delinquency. It's not what people say: before, there were Catholic immigrants who were easy to integrate – Italians, Poles, etc. – and then there were Muslim immigrants who were impossible to integrate because they were Muslims. That's completely wrong. The truth of the matter is delinquency, nothing but delinquency.

RDDM: Does this mean that the question is merely social?

MH: It's probably true that there is excessive delinquency among these immigrants, and we don't like them for it. And also because of unemployment.

RDDM: So it has nothing to do with the fact that some come from former French colonies?

MH: No. Vietnam is also a former French colony. So communitarianism isn't necessarily a problem, but neither is it a solution. So much bullshit gets talked about the difference between the English, French and German formulas, and we're realizing that the result's the same. They've all failed, regardless of the path they've followed.

RDDM: You're currently promoting your book abroad. Are journalists' questions, their perception of the book, the same everywhere?

MH: Let's say things are more relaxed abroad. But all the same, it's the same things that interest people every time: it's a European book. There aren't many differences; when I think about it, it's the similarities that strike me most.

RDDM: Is the book's scenario one they could imagine in their own country?

MH: The final scenario of Muslim domination is one they can all imagine. Afterwards, in the fine detail, it varies a lot because there are countries that don't have a National Front-type political formation, for example Germany: they'd be too afraid. In Spain, Franco left bad memories. In England it wouldn't be a problem, and in Italy they forgot about fascism, which they see as a picturesque moment. Perhaps there's also no talent for guilt among the Italians, while the Germans are particularly gifted in this area.

RDDM: But the French are also very good at guilt . . .

MH: No, they were very good at forgetting. So now they pretend. I agree with Pascal Bruckner: it's all bogus.[6]

RDDM: *The Tears of the White Man* – is that bogus?[7]

MH: No, but it's become a pose on the left, a *doxa*. In actual fact, nobody feels guilty about anything, and rightly so. On the issue of slavery, it's reached an incredibly ridiculous level. I don't have an eighteenth-century ancestor who was a slave-owner . . .

RDDM: Even if you did, you wouldn't feel obliged to bear the blame for him . . .

MH: Even in the worst passages in the Bible, the curse is limited to seven generations.

RDDM: So the Europeans you meet find it easy to project themselves into this world dominated by Islam?

MH: It's true that Islam gets about an equally bad press in all European countries. Maybe it's the only thing we have in common.

RDDM: Isn't it strange living with security officers? Isn't there a disturbing 'life in the castle' aspect?

MH: The problem with life in the castle is that you need to have experienced it when young, otherwise it's very embarrassing. To go to a restaurant, for example, I'm not going to bother the elite police officers. As a result, I go out less.

RDDM: That room of yours was already looking quite attractive . . .

MH: Yes, I'm starting to think it has considerable merit.

RDDM: Is it because Europe isn't religious that your book can cross the borders so easily? If there was an extremely powerful Catholic Church, do you think your book would be so successful?

MH: No. In fact it's difficult to imagine clearly what a strong Catholic Church might be, as it's so far away. I've never seen one in working order, for example.

RDDM: In South America?

MH: No, in South America the evangelists are winning. I don't know any Catholic country, actually. I've never been to a truly Catholic country.

RDDM: Do you find a monarchy preferable? The English monarchy, for example?

MH: No, that's pretty ridiculous. And England is an even sadder country than France. With all that rather grotesque kitsch about the monarchy.

RDDM: The French are rather fond of the English monarchy. And they like Stéphane Bern![8]

MH: I like Stéphane Bern, he's a nice guy. In a monarchy, the popes keep an eye on the kings, the kings keep an eye on the aristocracy, the aristocracy keeps an eye on the bourgeoisie, the bourgeoisie keeps an eye on the people and the prelates, who are divided into aristocratic prelates and prelates of the people; everyone does their job: that's what you call a harmonious sphere.

RDDM: Balzac said that harmony is the poetry of order . . .

MH: Yes, absolutely. Let's say that a certain pessimism, which has often been noted in me, and which does exist, leads me to think that there's little chance of this structure being recreated. But I think it's a structure that I could have lived in.

RDDM: Ah, so you're a monarchist and a Catholic! Don't you also feel nostalgic for Communist patronage? For a community that seeks a form of harmony in its collective organization?

MH: Yeah, I got to know that a little bit, it was nice.

RDDM: What about cultural centres? If you take out the ideological part, and keep only their cultural aspect?

MH: The ideological part was a bit optional. Communism is less all-encompassing than Christendom, but it wasn't bad. It wasn't a form of anomie, it was quite cheerful. If I was into nostalgia, I'd miss it.

RDDM: Aren't you into nostalgia?

MH: No, but I'd prepared to imagine that Christendom, in a way, was better, although I didn't experience it at work. On the other hand, I won't accept that permanent movement is a good thing. That goes against my instincts.

RDDM: Yet even monarchy was in permanent movement.

MH: No, only the details caused any commotion. The great feudal lords had to be tamed, the country centralized – and that sums up the political history of France over several centuries. People's daily lives were remarkably harmonious. It was a time when there was no conscription, not those all-out wars that came afterwards. You just had to put up with a few soldiers from time to time ... Moreover, 1870, a war very well described by Huysmans, from the point of view of the population, was the first 'stupid' war, lying outside the monarchical tradition of limited conflict. No one understood exactly what was going on, why all of a sudden war had become a national affair. Under the monarchy, in times of war, there were certainly rapes and other atrocities of war, but it was all limited.

RDDM: Are you still interested in animal welfare?

MH: Very much so. I'm on the jury for the *30 Millions d'amis* [*30 Million Friends*] Award, so every year I read a lot of books on the subject . . .[9]

RDDM: Have you met Brigitte Bardot?

MH: Ah no, she's not all that popular with the *30 Millions d'amis*.

RDDM: Is the animal our equal, our brother?

MH: Our equal, no – nobody's ever said that. But animals must be treated with consideration, without cruelty.

RDDM: Are you against slaughterhouses?

MH: The current situation is awful. It's largely unacceptable. The conditions of breeding and slaughter are morally appalling. As for halal or kosher slaughter, it adds a little touch of exotic barbarism.

RDDM: Do you feel that the animal cause is gaining importance?

MH: Certainly. The quality of the books offered to my sagacity as a juror increases every year. Some very good authors are taking an interest in the question. Last time it was really hard to choose, there were some really great books in competition. I think it's a sign.

RDDM: Could you do a prophetic novel about animals? It's an increasingly promising subject, like a humanism for the twenty-first century . . .

MH: Yes, you're right, I've been struck by that too. You know, if I look at my books, I'd say I observe things, and then I make some projections, which aren't prophecies . . . It's pretty hard to explain, projection in science fiction. Let's take a typical case: when Orwell wrote *1984* in 1948 in England, he didn't say that was what was going to happen at all. He wanted to express a fear lurking in the unconscious of the British people of his time, namely 'We're all going to become socialized and controlled', and that fear is embedded in British culture in general. It wasn't a prediction, it was an expression of the fears of his time. In all the familiar works of science fiction, it's pretty much the same system. Science fiction isn't predictive, it expresses the fears of an era.

RDDM: Does it express a kind of clairvoyant anxiety?

MH: No, not necessarily. Sometimes, but the books aren't written for that purpose, that's not the trigger. The writer – me, Orwell, or someone else – feels an anxiety in his contemporaries and he expresses it in a book. That's what drives the process.

RDDM: And in *Submission*, the anxiety that you perceived in French society is that we could be dominated by a culture essentially foreign to the culture that founded us . . .

MH: By Islam, to be precise: let's say it clearly.

RDDM: But it's an anxiety that has no solution . . .

MH: No. It's a very pure anxiety.

32

Interview with
Agathe Novak-Lechevalier

AN-L: People are constantly talking these days about 'the return of the religious': what do you think of this expression, and would you use it yourself?

MH: Yes; I would even say *quite obviously*. I remember that when I left France at the very end of the 1990s, the most popular radio host in France among young people, Maurice, quite often did programmes about the problem of the suburbs, in which he himself had grown up. They can all be found on the Internet, and if you listen to those broadcasts, you realize that he could talk for a whole hour about the suburbs without the word 'Islam' appearing once. I came back in 2010, and people were talking about nothing *but* Islam: it was really spectacular. More recently, it seemed that there was a revival of Catholicism, and that was completely astounding, because it was really assumed that Catholicism was dying. So this phenomenon of the return of religions was at first absolutely unpredictable. If anyone says they saw it coming, they're lying: no one had foreseen it. It's a very brutal phenomenon; sometimes it's happened over the course of just a few years, and I don't think it can be denied. For example, I read Michel Onfray's latest book, which is called

Décadence. It's very strange when you think of Michel Onfray's early books; sure, he was an atheist, but it was so obvious that he didn't even need to say it: the action of the Catholic religion was over, it was slowly dying. And then – and we can salute him, because few intellectuals do so – he realized the obvious, he changed his mind, he saw that religions had once again become a major historical force.

AN-L: You have often targeted religions in your books, with a form of jubilation that is sometimes even reminiscent of the tone of *Charlie Hebdo*. Is there a particular pleasure to be had, for a writer, in attacking religions?

MH: It's become quite a dangerous pleasure – which in one way increases the pleasure, and in another decreases it. But yes, religions, for example in their incomprehensible phraseologies, are quite often ridiculous. Well, it's a lot of fun making fun of Communism too . . . but not so much. The ridiculous aspect is even more prevalent in religions: there's the feeling that you are touching on something sacred, so it's more exciting. Religion must still have some potency: I remember Chesterton, in one of his books, challenging anyone to produce a blasphemy against the god Thor. In attacking a religion, there's the idea that you're taking a risk, that it's serious, that it can be serious: so yes, there's an additional excitement in making fun of a religion.

AN-L: In *Interventions*, you criticize the person who, 'incapable of clearly discerning religions [. . .] will be even less able to judge them', because, you say, 'the examination of religions on the intellectual plane and their judgement on the moral plane are tasks imposed on every human being'. So must we judge the value of religions from a moral point of view?

MH: Yes, that's right. There aren't many autobiographical passages in *Elementary Particles*, but there is one bit that's completely autobiographical: when I was sixteen, during a class debate, a guy raised his hand to say that in his opinion what made it possible to judge the value of a religion was the quality of the morality that it could help to found. I was shaken by this: I never got over those words, in fact, they felt so true to me, I'd never thought about it. So I've never really changed my mind: there is a moral absolute that is independent of religions and that is superior to them.

AN-L: At what point in your life did you first become interested in religion? In what circumstances, and under what influence?

MH: I was brought up by people who'd been dechristianized, but who'd been so for so long that they were no longer even anticlerical – that is, religion was no longer a threat to them: religion was a kind of weird survival. Having said that, it's very difficult for me to explain to myself why I went to Sunday school when I was a child. I think it was because I lived in the countryside, and it was the only activity for kids. It was a different period: there wasn't even TV, well, at first I didn't have it, and no one in the village had it. So I went to Sunday school, and at the time I remember that I was very interested in metaphysical questions like: was there someone who created the universe? Did time have a start? Will it have an end? I found that in Sunday school people talked too much about the misfortunes of the Third World, you know, it was a little too humanitarian: it didn't answer my questions at all. Then, in high school, I went to religious instruction; this was optional, it didn't count towards anything academic. In the meantime I had discovered evil, and I was very interested in this question of evil: where it came from, whether Satan was a really powerful figure, why God had allowed evil ... But here too, they didn't really answer my questions, in fact: it was still a bit of a boy scout thing. And then – this is something I've said in my books – I discovered Pascal, a little by chance, at fifteen. And it gave me a real shock, a definitive shock, because I had never seen the power of death and emptiness expressed in this way, and Pascal's violence on these questions remains unparalleled for me in literature. There you are, there were three stages: so yes, my interest in religion does go back quite a way – to when I was eight or nine.

AN-L: And now? On several occasions in different interviews you've said that you were an atheist, then more recently, when *Submission* had been published, you defined yourself as an agnostic . . . How would you define your personal relationship to religion today?

MH: The relationship has weakened, because I feel like it's hopeless: I'll never believe, I'll always be in a state of doubt . . . so I've rather let it drop.

AN-L: You've spoken on several occasions of attempts at conversion: how did you envisage this one?

MH: Conversion acts as a revelation. In fact, every time I go to mass, I believe; sincerely and totally, I have a revelation every time. But as soon as I leave, it collapses. It's a bit like drugs: you always have to come down. I ended up telling myself that that was how I was, and there was nothing I could do about it. So I still get frissons of belief every now and then, but I know it's not going to last.

AN-L: In a 1996 interview, you asserted that 'all happiness is religious in essence'; and in *Public Enemies*, you equate atheism with 'a definitive winter': would you say the same thing today?

MH: Yes, I maintain that all happiness is religious in essence. Religion offers the feeling of being connected to the world, of not being a stranger in an indifferent world – Pascal put it better than I have. We're frightened by a world with which we feel we have nothing in common, and religion gives meaning to the world, and to your place in the world.

AN-L: Have you ever thought of yourself as a Catholic writer (a label that certain critics have sometimes imposed on you)?

MH: Not just Catholic, Jewish too! . . . [He laughs] But it's true! In Israel, during a meeting with readers, there was one who stood up to say that after reading my books he'd decided to change his life, and that now he was a rabbi. Under the influence of my books . . . So it works with Jews too! In fact, I am a writer of nihilism (nihilism in Nietzsche's sense), there's no doubt about it: I'm the writer of a nihilistic era, and of the suffering associated with nihilism. So one can imagine that people, reading me, recoil in horror and throw themselves into some faith . . . to escape this nihilism, so brilliantly described, if I may say so. So yes: I am Catholic in the sense that I express the horror of the world without God . . . but only in that sense.

AN-L: For *Submission*, you said that you first envisioned a novel about a conversion to Catholicism, then finally decided to describe a conversion to Islam: can you explain what prompted this development?

MH: Yes: it was a personal failure to convert myself, a failure in front of the Black Madonna of Rocamadour. And it's also related to Huysmans who plays a big role in the book. Because for Huysmans – what I am going to say will seem difficult to believe – aesthetic beauty is really an argument of belief; it's even the only one for him, to tell the truth: he believes because it's beautiful. But for it to work, for beauty to produce belief, it has to be with very aesthetic people, more aesthetic than I am myself: even the Black Madonna of Rocamadour, which is a great work of art – there are lots of beautiful religious statues, but this is really a major achievement of Western sculpture – didn't work with me. Admittedly, it's very old: the Romanesque era is very far away, and in a sense it's as hard to understand the people of the eighth century as the Egyptians. Their art is very strange, it gives a great impression of distance. So no: it fails. That's why I portray the character in front of the statue, and how it doesn't work, it doesn't take off.

AN-L: So why did you turn your attention to Islam? And how would you characterize the way you depict Islam in the novel?

MH: You can't really say that there's a depiction of Islam in *Submission*: that's what's so terrible about this book, most of the characters aren't actually Muslims. They declare themselves to be Muslims because it suits them, because they find advantages in it or because it satisfies their personal ambitions. Even the Muslim president – we don't feel that he's very pious: without it being explicitly expressed, we feel rather that he's an ambitious man who's used Islam as a tactic.

AN-L: So is it the political dimension of Islam that particularly interested you in *Submission*? Would you say that this is the essence of Islam for you?

MH: Not really, although it's true that Islam is much more politically precise than Christianity. The Qur'an sets out in detail the system of sharing inheritances, the question of dowries, the judicial system, the penalties for the major crimes: everything is very detailed from the point of view of social organization. But deep down, on most political issues, it's not that hard to discover what the Christian point of view is. In fact, there's recently been an explicitly Christian political party in France, a party that claims to stem directly from Christianity and that has points of view that are quite original, some close to the left, others close to the right. So there's also a Christian politics: Christianity isn't politically neutral, even if this dimension is less specified in it than in Islam.

AN-L: You've often been accused of Islamophobia. Do you want to respond to this accusation?

MH: In practice, I think I'm about as ambiguous as my characters. Having said that, ever since this all started, I've felt compelled to stand up for Islamophobia, whether I'm Islamophobic or not. Because it has to be one of those opinions that we have the right to express . . . and, well, that's it actually. Attacking a religion is a right. So, yes, I unwillingly feel compelled to stand up for freedom of expression.

AN-L: There's another religion that people talk about less in connection with you but that is found very often in your novels, and with which you're in general more lenient than with others, and that is Buddhism. What interested you about Buddhism?

MH: It's a religion that is itself more lenient than the others! . . . Contrary to what one might think, it wasn't Schopenhauer who brought me to Buddhism; rather, it was reading the *Tibetan Book of the Dead* that made quite an impression on me. You have to remember that I'm quite old, so I knew the last hippies. The *Tibetan Book of the Dead* was all the rage in those circles, and it's true that it's quite beautiful, quite astonishing: it's very visual, very baroque, and the images are very poetic.

AN-L: So you became interested in the Buddhist religion from a literary point of view?

MH: Yes. I must have read Schopenhauer soon after – Schopenhauer is an interesting case, because he himself didn't really know Buddhism, to tell the truth. He read Hindu texts; and as there were few of those in his day, in order to have more at his disposal, he tried to learn Sanskrit towards the end of his life, and he interpreted the Hindu texts after the manner of the Buddha. So in a way he retraced, on other bases, starting from Western philosophy, the path taken by the Buddha; and Schopenhauer's philosophy leads to Buddhism quite naturally.

AN-L: If I give you the names of a few authors or philosophers that you often bring up on questions of religion, would you tell me in what way they've influenced you? I'd like to start with Saint Paul . . .

MH: I owe *Rester vivant* to him. I wrote it in a state of nervous collapse, greatly inspired by him. Saint Paul is still one of the best authors I know, because he's extremely insolent, extremely edgy – you sense his nerves are on edge all the time, his sentences sting you, it's magnificent. There's a mixture of megalomania and complaint in him that is quite unmatched. And he's a great writer for this basic reason: I feel as if I can see him there, two metres away from me, when I read him; I can feel him belching. So yes, I still love all that actually. In the end, it was perhaps Saint Paul who had the most literary influence on me: it was in him that I found that aspect that we could describe as punk, sometimes, in *Rester vivant* and in *Extension du domaine de la lutte*.

AN-L: In a completely different genre, would you say that Auguste Comte was also very important to you?

MH: Comte is interesting in many respects: he's the one who expresses in the most complete and systematic way the fact that, after the French Revolution, society has lost its foundations, and won't be able to hold out for long without religion. I'm not going to get into his thought, because it's pretty complicated anyway, but let's say I found his concepts extremely compelling. His distinction, for example, between an organic age and the metaphysical age whose only function is to destroy it is very true: everything that happened between the beginning of Protestantism and the beginning of the French Revolution had a single goal, to undermine the previous society. It succeeded; the whole of society ended up in a field of ruins, without any more bases to rely on, or relatively insignificant bases such as patriotism – which isn't very serious, after all. Comte affirms all this with real intellectual force; this is someone I really admire. In addition, he tries to lay the foundations for a future religion, compatible with the progress of science, and this too strongly influenced me, since it's the basic idea behind *Elementary Particles*. The fact that science has become exactly positivist, that there is no metaphysical entity behind the laws of science, in reality reopens the possibility of a religious foundation. So yes, Comte is one of my major influences.

AN-L: What about Chesterton, whom you cite several times in *The Map and the Territory*?

MH: To read Comte for pleasure, as I do, you have to be a bit of a pervert: this man is still often close to madness, his handwriting is that of a maniac, he's a machine that sometimes goes mad, he can't stop, and this gives rise to passages of crushing boredom. Reading Chesterton, on the other hand, is a delight: he's humorous, amusing, brilliant, and he sometimes comes up with some pretty deep insights. For example, talking about Comte he remarks that the most remarkable idea of positivism is to have created a calendar; and it's true that the fact of restructuring the year, of having a time that was no longer neutral but where each moment was provided with a meaning, is fundamental – because religion, by structuring life, helps us to live. Chesterton is also the author of an idea that can't be said to have had much success – but that's a pity: an attempt at a Christian organization of the business world. It deserves to be read again: it's against big business, against industrialization, it's interesting. Chesterton is frankly Catholic, and he makes Catholicism attractive because he insists a great deal on the idea that it's a religion of the incarnation: we are made of flesh and according to him, that's rather a good thing in fact.

AN-L: Nietzsche, and Schopenhauer? What would you say about them in this connection?

MH: Nietzsche . . . If we stick to the subject of our interview, his frontal opposition to Christ was never mine.

AN-L: Is this the basis of your opposition to Nietzsche?

MH: No, because I was never very religious: my opposition is due to his refutation of morality and pity. But yes: Nietzsche competes with Christ, he wants to be the victorious rival . . . Well, it's a form of madness that's widespread in the West . . . But let's say that Dionysus, well he never convinced me as a god, and still doesn't convince me. Schopenhauer is different, he's frankly an atheist too, but it's a more intellectual atheism – he even tries, in the end, to recuperate the Catholics, a form of opportunism that I find attractive: he makes discreet invitations to them, even though he'd insulted monotheisms all his life, in the most violent terms. But he got it into his head at the end of his life that Catholicism wasn't really monotheism – and he wasn't entirely wrong: the Virgin, the saints create intermediate deities that lessen the brutality of the relationship that exists in Judaism and Protestantism.

AN-L: You've already mentioned Huysmans briefly, but would you like to come back to him?

MH: Well, other than the fact that I like him, I don't think Huysmans' aesthetic-based conversion path is suitable for many people. But of all the convert writers – and there've been quite a few – he is certainly the one who recounts his conversion best; and in any case he's the one who tells it at the greatest length, it gets almost too long at times, but overall it's captivating: I really wondered, reading *En route*, if he was really going to go to his monastery or not, whether or not he was going to convert . . . It doesn't seem like it when I say it, but Huysmans can be thrilling! A spiritual thriller, in short.

AN-L: Is there anyone that I forgot that you think is important?

MH: Chateaubriand, all the same, because *Génie du Christianisme* is an astonishing book. This book was a huge success from the outset – it seems that the elegant women of Paris were saying to each other, 'Ah, really, so this is Christianity? But it's delightful!' [He laughs]. So Chateaubriand succeeded in making Christianity fashionable, which is a tour de force, after all. This is because it's a really good book: its style works very well; the description of the death of the Christian as the most majestic spectacle there can be on earth is worth the detour; and his analysis of the same situation dealt with in the Bible and by Homer, for example, is very acute . . . He's not so good on architecture, it obviously doesn't interest him very much; but in general it's an extraordinary book. Likewise the description of the Christian bride . . .

AN-L: Do you fully subscribe to it?

MH: Oh, he exaggerates a bit, he overdoes it; but it's so good, the sentences are so good we pretty much forgive him for everything.

AN-L: At the beginning of the nineteenth century, certain poets such as Hugo or Lamartine, for example, defined themselves as lay mages, prophets. In your opinion, should literature assume certain aspects of the functions that used to belong to religion?

MH: It's still mostly Hugo . . . Lamartine a bit too, okay, but he didn't go so far as to think that Shakespeare was talking to him. He saw himself less as a prophet than as a political guide, which, given who he was, is just as comical. In any case, I'm less of a megalomaniac than them: I don't see myself as a secular prophet. Whenever I am told that I am a prophet, I say no, I point out the number of times I was wrong in my prophecies . . . Ah no, I adopt rather a low profile when it comes to the prophet thing!

AN-L: In an interview, you said that poetry is 'close to the divine'. Would you say that poetry has close links with religious language?

MH: Yes, certainly. There's one main point they share – there's no contradiction to poetry: it's an absolute discourse, which aims to pose sentences without any possibility of negation. Another thing they share is that total understanding isn't fundamental: you may not fully understand religious language, just as you don't need to understand everything when listening to poetry. And there are also texts that are used in religion that have a real poetic value: certain psalms, for example. So yes, there is a strong connection.

AN-L: The last part of your anthology of poems, *Non réconcilié* [*Unreconciled*], is titled 'La Grâce immobile' ['Motionless grace'] and it ends with a poem whose first line begins as follows: 'In the stupor that for us takes the place of grace'. What does this 'grace' represent for you? What place do you give it in your work?

MH: I don't know; but I do know that, in my life, grace is indeed not very far from stupor. Let's say I think too much, I'm too anxious – not when it comes to practicalities, but in general: so a state of stupor is a grace that has been granted.

AN-L: Is there still something religious in this form of grace, or not at all?

MH: No, not necessarily. Schopenhauer, for example, sees all of this in a framework that isn't at all religious. The only possible way, for him, is contemplation, that is, the fact of being absorbed in the object without forming any conscious thought. In fact, from this point of view again, he is frankly very close to Buddhist methods. So it's a form of grace that is related to escaping the world; contemplation is happy, but there's no thought of God behind it. Finally, let's say yes, it probably has something to do with religion, but not at all with Western religion.

AN-L: In *Platform* there's this sentence: 'What shall we compare God to? First, of course, to the female pussy.' You've very frequently associated sex and religion in your work: is this pure provocation on your part?

MH: No. This is a male point of view, but it's not a provocation. It should be remembered that the oldest representations venerated by this or that primitive tribe are male or female sexual organs (especially female, by the way, and this is probably less related to sex than to giving birth). And although it's very ancient, I don't think that because humanity is evolving that erases the previous states: those states remain there, underlying the rest. They are covered by lots of overlapping layers of civilization, but they remain potentially active. So this is not provocation: you really have to take it seriously.

AN-L: In the romantic sphere, would you say that, from *Extension* to *Submission*, your work displays an evolution in relation to its religious preoccupations?

MH: There are quite a few stages: two of my novels, after all, are marked by the basic idea found in Comte that a new religion is necessary, that in any case we need a religion compatible with the state of science. I just ended up being struck by this obvious historical fact: that Comte himself completely failed. Because he really seriously tried to found a new religion, he baptized proletarians into the positive faith, etc.; and it didn't work. So I came to what forms the raw material of *Submission*, which is that far from a new religion being formed, an old one may very well reawaken.

AN-L: For you, is the science-fiction vein, in your work and in particular in your novels, linked to a religious concern?

MH: Yes, well I think that's one of my influences; but, you know, you already have to be a great reader of science fiction to spot it, because in science fiction, the future of religions is a subject treated by very few people. But there *are* some who try to envision future religions: Lafferty does, for example. But we're not going to talk about that, because these are people that nobody knows.

AN-L: In an interview, you say that the story of Christ has 'always fascinated you, especially his planned and assumed sacrifice, the fact that he took upon himself the sins of the world'. And in *Public Enemies*, you argue that your destiny has taken a Christ-like turn. What makes you say this? Is this sacrifice the one to which the writer must consent?

MH: Yes. It's one aspect of the business – you can't call it a job. Let's say that, as I understand it anyway, writing involves taking upon oneself the negative, all the negative in the world, and depicting it, so that the reader can be relieved by having seen this negative part expressed. The author, who takes it upon himself to express it, obviously runs the risk of being identified with this negative part of the world. That's what makes writing an at times difficult activity: taking on all the negative. And indeed it has to do with Christ taking upon himself all the sins of humanity. So yes, it's true, there is a resemblance . . . That's a good conclusion, right?

33

Emmanuel Carrère and the problem of goodness

Among the many heartbreaking passages that mark *D'autres vies que la mienne* [*Other Lives Than Mine*], one of the most heartbreaking for me is that of the old English lesbian who has just lost her partner in the disaster. 'She said: "my girlfriend," and I imagine this couple of aging lesbians, living in a small English town, active in community life, their lovingly arranged house, their trips each year to faraway countries, their photo albums, all of that broken. The survivor's return, the empty house. The mugs, with each woman's name, and one of the two will never be used again, and the fat woman sitting at the kitchen table takes her head in her hands and cries and thinks to herself that now she's alone and that she'll stay alone until her death.'

Emmanuel Carrère did indeed meet this aging English lesbian, on that holiday in Ceylon, which ended so badly; but he imagined the mugs. Which places quite well, it seems to me, the margin of invention that he allows himself, in this book where 'everything is true'. It's not insignificant. Because they have their meaning, those mugs. It was exactly when the mugs appeared, I remember, that I burst into tears, and had to put the book down, unable for a few minutes to read on. It's in any case impossible to retrace the facts, even when you're doing so without any literary ambition, you're always obliged to invent, more or less. The fact remains that in all the books he writes nowadays, Emmanuel Carrère has chosen not to invent either the characters or the major events; he has chosen for the most part to behave as a *witness* (not as an exact witness, that's impossible, I just said; but as a witness). I'm obviously interested in this choice, if only because, so far, I've stuck to the opposite path. For aesthetic reasons if you will, but also for dubious reasons where laziness, insolence and megalomania are mixed (of the kind: don't bother me with the details, I have no time to waste with reality, and in any case reality is something I know better than anyone).

But anyway, let's get back to Emmanuel Carrère. I don't know exactly *when*, under what circumstances, he resolved to make this choice; but I think I have a fair idea of *why*. It comes to me, strangely, from my early work on Lovecraft. With the attractive radicalism that characterizes him, the American author takes leave of the realistic novel with these words: 'The chaos of the universe is so total that no written text can even give a glimpse of it.' It seems to me that Emmanuel Carrère, at one point, found himself confronted with a similar problem. People, to say the least, don't know how to live anymore. The chaos is so total, the disarray so generalized, that no model of behaviour inherited from ancient centuries seems applicable to the times in which we live. At one point, Emmanuel Carrère decided that it was impossible not only to use existing types, but even to create new ones. The time of the 'man without qualities', prophesied – albeit in a rough and ready way – by Musil, had come. One aggravating circumstance is that Emmanuel Carrère was close to a picturesque movement, a distant resurgence of the supporters of *art for art's sake*, who believed they were sidestepping the problem by reducing the interest of literature to the linguistic virtuosity deployed in it. In short, he found himself somewhat in the same situation as those Maoist militants who had accomplished their self-criticism, felt threatened by a formalist deviationism, and decided to return to work in the factory, in contact with the real proletariat.

(I wouldn't like this somewhat irreverent comparison to be taken badly; after all, those Maoist militants, when they decided to return to the factory, were quite simply *right*; the proof was regularly provided by the fact that, once they were *established*, they were quick to renounce Maoism, and militancy as well; theory had not stood the test of reality.)

Though he approaches the world without a preconceived theory, Emmanuel Carrère is by no means devoid of intellectual structuring; for what he possesses in the highest degree is something that is pretty much just as structuring as a theory, namely *values*. And here it's necessary to go back a little, as on this point he contrasts greatly not only with his contemporaries, but even with the two or three generations that preceded him.

For the authors of the nineteenth century, the question of good and evil doesn't arise. Neither Balzac nor Dickens, neither Dostoevsky, nor Maupassant, nor Flaubert have the slightest doubt about the moments when the behaviour of their characters seems to them estimable, admirable, slightly reprehensible or downright abject. Whether they then choose to deploy a very broad moral spectrum, to stage extreme cases, or conversely to focus their attention on average characters, is a personal aesthetic choice, where the variations are endless. But the foundations of moral judgement are with them as solid and indisputable as they have always been with the philosophers who, in previous centuries, were concerned with ethics.

Things turned a little sour at the start of the twentieth century. Under the influence of nefarious and false thinkers, who imagined they could ascribe a contingent character to moral law, a stupid, but strangely tenacious, opposition grew up between the *conservative* and *progressive* camps. In fact, this could have happened long before, under the deleterious influence of the 'philosophers of the Enlightenment'; but these so-called philosophers were intellectually too flaccid to exert any real influence on creators of a certain level, and the magnificent élan of romanticism had no difficulty in reducing them to dust. Marx and Nietzsche were, it must be admitted, of a different calibre from Voltaire and La Mettrie. Thus, a moral doubt set in, including among the best thinkers, regarding about which there can be little doubt. This doubt was mainly regarding sexual issues, and it must be admitted that the fault lies largely with the conservatives. Victorian prudery was an incomprehensible, overblown phenomenon that had never been seen before (and never will be seen again), so it's not surprising that it was in England that the confusion was greatest. It produces magnificent results in Galsworthy, an unjustly forgotten writer (I feel that an author who could create the character of Soames Forsyte is assured of immortality). But it's arguably in Somerset Maugham that these moral questions reach their highest point of tension, and culminate in the most shattering achievements. Maugham, no doubt out of modesty, had created for himself the character of a refined and cynical old queer. But, firstly, he wasn't always old, he wasn't exclusively queer (as his descendants testify), and his overt cynicism concealed very real manifestations of practical generosity. He expresses himself much more in his books. Our loved ones are not always those who deserve to be loved; this distressing and banal truth is one he absolutely cannot come to terms with. Desire is natural and healthy, it's nature that speaks through it, and he refuses to give it up; but he also wishes so much that good people were happy, that their aspiration to love could be fulfilled, and of course this isn't possible, – all of which gives us, in particular in *The Moon and Sixpence* and in *The Narrow Corner*, some of the finest pages of English literature.

The further we advance into the twentieth century, the more the confusion increases, and the more ground the moral law loses, until it's finally no longer understood at all, when it's not systematically depreciated. The adage, 'You don't make good literature with good feelings' ultimately had a huge negative impact. It even seems to me that the implausible and long-standing overestimation of the collaborationist authors stems from it. Don't get me wrong, Céline is not without merit, he's just ridiculously overrated. And Brasillach's *Poèmes de Fresnes* are very beautiful, surprisingly beautiful even in such a poor author. But all the others, Drieu, Morand, Félicien Marceau, Chardonne . . . a rather lamentable raggletaggle of mediocrities, after all. Well, it seems to me that their strange overestimation stems from a perverse emphasis on the aforementioned adage, which could be worded as: 'If he's a bastard, he's probably a good writer.'

This shows what a strange chaos we had ended up in. Which only underlines the immense merits of Emmanuel Carrère. As soon as you enter one of his books (and he is pretty much the only one of his generation of whom we can say as much), the miasma of moral doubt evaporates, the atmosphere becomes clearer, we breathe more freely. Carrère *knows* when the behaviour of his characters is estimable, admirable, odious, or morally neutral; he may have doubts about everything, but not about that. And it's this clarity of conception, this intellectual and moral uprightness that makes him and him alone (or more or less) capable of tackling certain subjects, subjects that are indeed morally delicate. We cannot praise enough, for example, his portrait of Jean-Claude Romand in *L'Adversaire*. That Jean-Claude Romand is a hateful murderer, that he deserves his punishment, is something nobody will dream of denying; but that he is very far from presenting a credible image of evil, that is no less certain, and this is where the talent of Emmanuel Carrère is made fully manifest. It's truly remarkable to see how he succeeds, little by little, in bringing Romand close to us, and even likeable, without ever allowing himself the slightest compromise on the question of evil.

(Romand is, moreover, highly significant. One of the most important qualities, and the most rarely mentioned, of the novelist is knowing how to choose his subjects. You have to think, think for a long time; then aim, aim with sufficient care, and shoot right on target. Of criminal cases there are hundreds a year, and family killings are very common in the list; but to pick a character who, in his mythomania, chose to pass himself off as a humanitarian doctor, and even for a 'big name in humanitarianism', says a lot about our society.)

Limonov is the embodiment of an older, but no less delicate problem. That Limonov was talented is almost beyond doubt; but that otherwise, in some ways, he was a downright bas- tard, is equally obvious. It's fascinating to compare Emmanuel Carrère's treatment of the Limonov case and Somerset Maugham's treatment of the Gauguin case. Maugham has boundless admiration for Gauguin, he considers him (with some exaggeration, no doubt, but never mind) to be a genius of the calibre of Michelangelo; but the brutality and selfishness he shows in his private life nauseate Maugham. The martyrdom of Dirk Stroeve, one of the people whose life was shattered by Gauguin, leads him to produce some hallucinated pages of pain; but at the same time he can't condemn Gauguin, that would be asking too much of him, and he suffers, poor Maugham, he suffers more and more, to the point that it's his suffering as an author that becomes the real subject of a superb book, but one that is an ordeal to read. Carrère, on the other hand, is not at all surprised that a talented writer can also be a bastard; he deplores it, he would prefer it to be otherwise, but for him it's not one of the *unbearable contradictions*; it's just one of those weird tricks that nature likes to engineer when it comes to shaping people. His point of view on this subject is that of Shakespeare; and; beyond that, of all the classics.

The health and clarity of Emmanuel Carrère's point of view have as a corollary a merit that, though negative, is no less considerable, and that is that *there are never any false problems*.

It's never without a pang that I see Christian thinkers (or perhaps Christian monks – anyway, Christians) pondering, with gravity and pain, the 'problem of evil'. *What* problem of evil? If there is one entity that is at home in the world, that we are not surprised to find there, whose existence is anything but problematic, it is *evil*.

And it always annoys me slightly to hear praise for the 'deep knowledge of human nature' manifested by such or such an author who, during a long career, has merely deployed an unpalatable procession of selfish and cynical characters. On the contrary, such an author, it seems to me, has exhibited only a very superficial understanding of the human heart. For some people, in a conscious and deliberate way, decide to constantly treat others with loyalty, decency and good faith; and they then conform, until death, to this maxim. Still others, quite unconstrained, boldly come to the aid of others, and do their best to help them, and to alleviate their suffering. Good exists, it absolutely exists, just as much as evil. And it's this existence, absolutely contrary to all natural law, this *counterproductive* existence from the biological viewpoint, that's really the problem. And it's this *problem of goodness*, perhaps the only problem of any value, that Emmanuel Carrère poses in the most beautiful pages of these books. Why did Étienne Rigal, the young hope of the Syndicat de la Magistrature, decide, rather than following the golden path of a ministerial post, to become a judge in Béthune. Why did he decide to come to the aid of wretched alcoholics and semi-degenerates? *Why?*

To return to the subject from a slightly different angle, it seems to me that the question of the human community, of the possibility of a human community, is the one that comes up most insistently in Emmanuel Carrère's books. Cioran briefly notes that belief in God 'was a solution', and a better one will surely never be found. There are immense benefits to this belief; I can see at least three. First, the cosmological questions about the origin of the Universe, space, time, etc., were ipso facto resolved. Second, death was conquered (one's own, and especially that of others). Third, the possibility of a human community was constituted (you will recognize them by this sign that they love one other, etc.). It has always seemed to me that, of these three points, the one that was most important to Emmanuel Carrère, the one that best explained his renewed fascination with Christianity, was the third. The most impressive illustration of this is undoubtedly the extraordinary penultimate page of *The Kingdom*, the one in which, dancing alongside Élodie the young Down's syndrome woman, in Jean Vanier's Communauté de l'Arche, overwhelmed by tears, he glimpses, he really catches a glimpse of what the Kingdom is.

On this question of the human community, I feel much less eloquent, and more contradictory. I am permeable to the greatest degree by collective emotion, and I have never felt so close to belief as when attending mass. But, also, not all masses, if I may say so, are equal, and it's when the celebration takes place on the occasion of a funeral that the Christian dream disturbs me to the utmost. The last one I attended was in honour of Bernard Maris. Emmanuel was there too (and he spoke very well of our murdered friend). I remember this certainty, this conviction that emanated from the words of the priest: no, death does not exist, it absolutely does not exist, do not cry, little children, Christ has conquered death. It throws me into pathetic nervous states, this certainty.

Perhaps also the question of the human community *in general* interests me less because I am passionately interested in the smaller community made up of a man and a woman. Emmanuel Carrère is also very interested in it, love occupies a considerable place in our books (he insists very movingly on conjugal love, on conjugal sexuality as well). But the question of the human community *in general* is one he has not abandoned. But, I must admit, I have; and what the word 'brotherhood' inspires in me is, in the first place, a certain mistrust. Far be it from me to brag about it; I'm just saying. I can see my short-comings, but I don't want to exaggerate them; my beliefs are limited, but they are violent. I believe in the possibility of the restricted kingdom. I believe in love.

This is a very modest promise compared to the promise of the Kingdom; a very limited love compared to the charity of which Saint Paul speaks; but I sometimes think that it is, perhaps, enough. I don't know what Emmanuel Carrère thinks about it, I'm not sure he knows himself; but I know that I, like all his readers, have the right to ask him (as painful as it may be, writers expose themselves to this: their readers have the right, absolutely the right to *summon* them to explain how one should live). In short, without knowing Emmanuel Carrère's answer, I believe I have read enough of it to know that he will appreciate this sentence that I borrow from Versilov (one of Dostoevsky's most enigmatic characters, enigmatic because strangely devoid of hysteria):

> As to being obliged to make the happiness of at least one crea-ture in the course of your life, but to do so practically, that is to say effectively, it's something I would set up as a command for any cultivated man, just as I would make it an obligation for every peasant to plant at least one tree in his life, given the deforestation of Russia.

34

Donald Trump is a good president

I love the American people, sincerely, I have met a lot of wonderful people in America, and I sympathize with the shame many Americans (and not just 'New York intellectuals') feel at being led by such a heartbreaking clown.

Yet I have to ask you (and I know that it's not easy for you) to look at things from a non-American point of view for a moment. I don't mean 'from a French point of view', that would be asking too much; let's say, from the point of view of the rest of the world.

Having been repeatedly asked about the election of Donald Trump, I replied that I couldn't care less. France isn't Wyoming or Arkansas. France is an independent country, more or less, and will become so again as soon as the European construction is dissolved (the sooner the better).

The United States of America is no longer the world's leading power; it was so for a long time, almost throughout the twentieth century. It is so no longer.

It remains one important power, among others.

This is not necessarily bad news for Americans.
It's great news for the rest of the world.

I exaggerated a bit in my answer. We are still obliged to take some interest in American political life. The United States of America is still the world's leading military power, and unfortunately it has not yet definitively given up on intervening outside its borders.

I'm not a historian and don't know ancient history; for example, I can't say whether it's Kennedy or Johnson who is most to blame in the sordid Vietnamese affair; but I have the impression that it has been a long time since the United States of America won a war, and that its military interventions (overt or secret) abroad have been, for at least fifty years, nothing but a succession of ignominious episodes crowned by fiascos.

Even if we go back to their last morally indisputable and militarily victorious intervention, I mean their participation in the Second World War: what would have happened if the United States of America hadn't entered the war (an unpleasant uchronia)? The fate of Asia would have been changed, no doubt about it. The fate of Europe too, but probably rather less. In any case, Hitler was already off to a bad start. Most likely, Stalin's armies would have reached Cherbourg. Various European countries that in the event were spared would have experienced the ordeal of Communism.

An unpleasant outlook, I agree; but a limited perspective. Forty years later, the Soviet Union would still have collapsed, just as actually happened. Simply because it was based on an ineffective and false ideology. In no country in the world, whatever the circumstances, whatever the culture in which it was established, has Communism managed to last for even a century.

The memory of peoples is not very long. Do the Hungarians, Poles, Czechs of today really remember being Communists? Is their way of looking at European issues so different from that found in Western Europe? One can seriously doubt it. To use centre-left jargon for a moment, the 'populist cancer' is by no means confined to the Visegrad group; but, above all, the arguments used in Austria, Poland, Italy and Sweden are exactly the same. The struggle against Islam is one of the constants in the long history of Europe; it has simply come back to centre stage.

It was mainly through the novel (the American novel, almost exclusively) that I heard about the disgusting CIA manoeuvres in Nicaragua and Chile. The first American military interventions that I really remember are those of the two Bushes, especially the son. France refused to join in its war against Iraq, a war that was as immoral as it was stupid; France was right, and I note this with all the more pleasure since France has rarely been right, since de Gaulle, let us say.

With Obama, there had already been tremendous progress. Maybe he got the Nobel Peace Prize a little early; in my view, he really deserved it the day he refused to follow François Hollande on Syria. On race reconciliation he was less successful, and I confess that I don't know your country well enough to understand exactly why; I can only deplore it. But, at least, we can congratulate him for the fact that Syria has not been added to the already long list (Afghanistan, Iraq, Libya and others I'm probably forgetting) of Western abuses in Muslim lands.

Trump is continuing and amplifying the policy of disengagement initiated by Obama; this is great news for the rest of the world.

The Americans are giving up on us.

The Americans are letting us be.

The Americans are no longer trying to spread democracy across the planet. *What* democracy, come to think of it? Voting every four years to elect your leader – is *that* democracy? In my opinion, there is one country in the world (one country, not two) that enjoys partially democratic institutions, and that country is not the United States of America: it's Switzerland. A country that stands out, moreover, for its laudable policy of neutrality.

Americans are no longer prepared to die for the freedom of the press. *What* freedom of the press, come to think of it? Since I was twelve years old, I have seen the range of opinions that can be expressed in the press constantly shrink (I am mentioning this just as a new anti-Zemmour campaign has started in France).

The Americans use drones more, which could have made it possible to reduce the number of civilian casualties if they knew how to use them (but it's true that the Americans have always been unable to carry out a proper bombardment, practically since the origins of aviation).

The most remarkable thing, however, in the new American policies, is certainly the trade policy, and here I admit that Trump has brought a salutary freshness, and that you have really done well to elect a president from 'civil society'.

President Trump tears up treaties and trade agreements when he thinks he was wrong to have signed them; he's quite right, you have to know when to indulge in buyer's remorse.

Unlike liberals (as fanatical as Communists, in their own way), President Trump does not see free global trade as the alpha and omega of human progress. When free trade is in America's best interests, President Trump is in favour of free trade; otherwise, good old protectionist measures strike him as quite appropriate.

President Trump was elected to defend the interests of American workers; he is defending the interests of American workers. We would have liked to see this kind of attitude more often in France over the past fifty years.

President Trump does not like the European construction,

he thinks that we don't have much in common, especially not 'values', and besides, that's a good thing, because *what* values . . .? 'Human rights'? Seriously? He would prefer to negotiate directly with states; I think it would indeed be preferable, as unity does not necessarily create strength (especially when we don't have the same interests). In Europe, we have neither a common language, nor common values, nor common interests; in short, Europe doesn't exist, it will never constitute a people, much less the basis for a possible democracy (cf. the etymology of the term) – above all because it *does not want* to constitute a people. The European Union, in any case, was never designed to be a democracy, its purpose was even the exact opposite. In short, a bad idea or at best a stupid one, which gradually turned into a bad dream, and from which we will eventually wake up. Victor Hugo is a good poet in places, but he is also often bombastic and stupid; his dream of a 'United States of Europe' is a case in point; it does me good, from time to time, to criticize Victor Hugo.

Logically, President Trump welcomed Brexit. Logically, so did I; I just regretted that once again the English were braver than us in the face of Empire.

President Trump doesn't view Vladimir Putin as an unworthy interlocutor; neither do I. I don't believe that Russia has any role as a universal guide, my admiration for Dostoevsky doesn't go so far; but I admire the resistance of Orthodoxy on its lands, I believe that Catholicism would do well to draw inspiration from it, that 'ecumenical dialogue' could usefully be limited to a dialogue with the Orthodox, and that the schism of 1054 was, for the Christian world, the beginning of the end (but I believe, on the other hand, that the end is never certain, not until it has actually happened).

It even seems that President Trump has managed to tame the demented North Korean; I thought this was just *really classy*.

France should get out of NATO, but maybe this will become pointless if NATO disappears for lack of an operating budget; it would be one less thing to worry about.

In short, President Trump strikes me as one of the best presidents America's ever had.

On a personal level, he is, of course, quite disgusting. That he phones for whores is no problem, who cares, but making fun of the disabled is really not good. With an equivalent program, a genuine Christian conservative, or at least an honourable and moral type, would have been better for America.

But this can still happen, maybe the next time, or the time after that if you insist on Trump. Six years from now, Ted Cruz will still be relatively young, and there are surely other great Christian conservatives. You'll be a little less competitive, but you will again experience the happiness of living, in your beautiful country, within your borders, practising decency and virtue, exporting a few products, importing a few others, well not much, the reduction of world trade is a desirable objective, and achievable in the short term.

A few violent actions could usefully speed up the process; they could easily be limited to goods. The number of sailors on those gigantic container ships, is surprisingly small; it would hardly be difficult to evacuate them in time.

Your military messianism will have entirely disappeared; the world will simply breathe all the easier for it.

Fearsome competitors will have appeared, for Silicon Valley, and to a lesser extent for Hollywood; but Silicon Valley, like Hollywood, will retain a significant market share.

China will have got over its exaggerated ambitions. This will be the most difficult; but, in the end, China will limit its ambitions

– and so will India. China has never been a global imperialist power, and neither has India – unlike the US; their military ambitions are local. Their economic ambitions, it's true, are global. They have an economic revenge to take, they're taking it right now, there is indeed cause for concern, and Donald Trump is right not to let that happen; but in the end it will settle down, their growth rate will settle down.

All of this will happen in the span of a man's lifetime.

You have to get used to the idea, esteemed American people: in the end, Donald Trump may well have been a necessary ordeal for you. Either way, you will remain welcome – as tourists.

35

Conversation with
Geoffroy Lejeune

The liturgy

MH: There is a Pentecostal movement in France; many Americans are probably unaware of it. I realized this when I lived, in Paris, near the Porte de Montreuil – then a poor neighbourhood, with many recent immigrants.[1] Drawn in by the posters, I attended several celebrations – sometimes hosted by a touring American tele-evangelist. The audience was at least ninety per cent black. I have a strange memory of it, I could almost doubt having experienced those moments. People danced, sang at the top of their lungs, 'spoke in tongues' sometimes but not too much, I never had the feeling of witnessing a collective delirium, nor of being in a sect. The 'sign of peace', reduced in Catholic masses to a brief, embarrassed and icy handshake, was here a matter of endless warm hugs. And, at the end of the celebration, we shared the copious provisions.

'If these people are saved,' Nietzsche said more or less (cruelly, but correctly), 'they should look more as if they *were* saved.' I understood from that moment that the Catholic Church had much to gain by getting closer to the atmosphere of Pentecostal celebrations.

Especially since this is not in the least impossible. It has even been attempted, with success, by communities affiliated with the 'charismatic renewal'. I spent a week in one of them, which at the time was called the Community of the Lion of Judah and the Slain Lamb, and I found exactly the same outpouring, the same warmth. There were, moreover, almost only white people there – I say that to establish, if it was necessary, that as soon as it's a question of 'matters of the heart' (and religion is one of them, to the highest degree), race is not a relevant parameter.

A scene of the same order can be found in the magnificent last pages of Emmanuel Carrère's book, *The Kingdom*, this time located in Jean Vannier's community of L'Arche: I mean that moment when he's dancing with others, opposite Élodie, the young girl with Down's syndrome, and sees the Kingdom.

Although I loved these charismatic celebrations enormously, I still felt a little uncomfortable. I only fully came to understand this thanks to the very good book by Douglas Kennedy, *In God's Country*, where he relates his investigation into the renewal of evangelical Christianity in the Bible Belt. One sometimes gets the impression, when reading it, that this renewal can only concern people who've been alcoholics, drug addicts, prostitutes or homeless; it's in no way intended for people who are normally integrated into society, having spent their childhood in a reasonably loving family. In fact, the main vocation of the L'Arche community is to take care of the mentally handicapped; and I probably wouldn't have stayed in the Lion of Judah Fellowship if I hadn't been suffering from a severe bout of depression at the time, partly related to unemployment.

In short, it seems that if the Pentecostals can pull people back from the edge of the abyss, or even sometimes those who have started to slide into it (which is already a considerable good, and hardly anyone else apart from the Jehovah's Witnesses can be compared to them in this respect), they cannot in any way do what the Catholic Church has so perfectly succeeded in doing, for many centuries: organize the functioning of society as a whole.

GL: I've been going to mass every Sunday for thirty years and I've experienced just about every liturgical style. I've frequented 'charismatics', especially within the Emmanuel Community and, like you, I've seen people dancing, singing, speaking in tongues as well, in short indulging in all the outpouring that we thought could be found only among the Americans. I must admit that in these assemblies there reigns a kind of joy, a little worrying at times, because some of the members seem possessed (their behaviour at so-called 'healing' evenings suggests that, indeed, you can't appreciate this mystery unless you're in a terrible way). But I've never felt so far from God as on those occasions: I was eighteen, I was neither sick nor depressed, and I ended up believing that, not being able to shed buckets of tears or pour my emotions out into a microphone in front of strangers, I was simply not made for the faith.

There is a wound that the Church should try to heal: the wound of not knowing God, or of not knowing how to find him. In the 1960s, when the Beatles had set the world dancing, the Church wondered how to continue to share the gospel. In 1962, it convened Vatican II. Malicious tongues noted that the cardinals arrived by boat, and left by plane: the institution had just entered modernity. By drawing closer to common mores, by speaking the language of its time, the Church believed it could maintain links with the faithful who were disturbed by the liberal and sexual revolutions. The changes concerned the liturgical aspect in particular: Latin was abandoned, the ornaments were simplified, the priest turned to the assembly.

The parishes invested in electronic synthesizers and young women began to conduct the choirs. But the drama of fashion is that it soon becomes unfashionable. Sixty years later, the synthesizers are still there, and so are the young women, but they've aged and their voices have become quavering – even the priests can't stand them anymore. Only the dynamic parishes in the city centres escape this impoverishment in the liturgy, but at best you simply get to hear a Sunday guitarist trying his hand at arpeggios and recalling this cruel truth: we can't all be Mark Knopfler.

This attempt to catch up with modernity is a glaring failure; the churches have emptied rapidly. Before Vatican II, a third of French people said they went to mass every Sunday. In 2012, this figure had fallen to six per cent, a sign of a major cultural shift.

No doubt the phenomena are related: the Church tried to conform to the world just as the world was getting uglier. This is a sufficiently serious ground for rebuke: we are entitled to expect the Church to indicate a path regardless of the upheavals of the time, to stay itself. It should point out a path, the path to God, for example. Latin was supposed to mark a difference between the language of everyday life and the language in which we address the creator. Incense rising up into the nave pointed a path for the soul to follow. The priest, with his back to the faithful, was in reality turned towards heaven. The sacred was quietly driven out of the churches, and replaced by something 'cool' and festive. Great – but also, hopelessly human. I would like to point out, just to be clear, that I've also known ultra-traditionalists for whom incense, prayers trotted out in Latin at full speed, and hours spent on their knees were the alpha and omega of faith: I consider them to be just as fanatical. What conclusions are we to draw? You have to be in the world, but not of the world, Jesus told his disciples. The Church should have taken him more seriously.

Social organization

MH: In the history of thought we can identify a strange family of spirits, who admire the Roman Catholic Church for its power to provide spiritual direction for human beings, and especially to organize human societies, without being Christians.

The first, and the most remarkable representative of this tendency, is certainly Auguste Comte. In his inimitable way, Comte describes the name 'Protestant' as a *characteristic*. Indeed, a Protestant can't do anything other than protest, it's in his nature. De Maistre, whom Comte claimed as an influence, had already noted that a Protestant would be a republican under a monarchy, and an anarchist under a republic. For de Maistre, it's even worse to be a Protestant than to be an atheist. An atheist may have lost his faith for respectable reasons, it's possible to bring him back to it, it's happened in the past; whereas Protestantism, he writes, 'is nothing but a negation'.

Intellectually the most remarkable in this strange family of 'non-Christian Catholics', Comte is also the most likeable, because of his picturesque megalomania, which leads him in the end to send out appeals to all those he deems ready to join positivism: conservatives, proletarians, women, Tsar Nicholas I. Basically he would happily have replaced the Pope in Rome, and he would have taken over the whole of the Catholic organization; it would have been enough for the Catholics to accomplish what in his view was quite a simple gesture: to convert to the positive faith.

Drawing in turn on Comte, Charles Maurras placed too much importance on political efficiency, which ultimately led him to compromises as dire as they were immoral.

The most interesting contemporary avatar of this trend is certainly, in France, Éric Zemmour. For years he reminded me of someone, but I couldn't work out who. And then, quite recently, I solved the riddle: Zemmour is exactly Naphta in *The Magic Mountain*. Leon Naphta is arguably the most fascinating

Jesuit in world literature. In the endless controversy between Settembrini and Naphta, Thomas Mann has an ambiguous position – you feel it isn't easy for him. Indisputably, Naphta is right against Settembrini, on all points; Naphta's intelligence surpasses Settembrini's, as much as Zemmour's intelligence surpasses that of his current opponents. But, equally indisputably, all Thomas Mann's sympathy (and this more and more clearly as the book progresses) goes to Settembrini, and this old Italian humanist babbler ends up making us cry, something the dazzling Naphta would be quite incapable of.

If we radically change the ambiance, leaving the shores of civilized Europe in the 1900s to transport ourselves to the heart of Russian hysteria, we can add another piece of evidence to the record: the famous scene in *The Brothers Karamazov* featuring Christ and the Grand Inquisitor, where Dostoyevsky violently attacks the Catholic Church, in particular the Pope and the Jesuits. Returning to Earth, Christ is immediately imprisoned by the ecclesiastical authorities. The Grand Inquisitor, coming to visit him in his cell, explains to him that the Church has been organized very well without him; they no longer need him – in fact, he'll just get in their way. So the Grand Inquisitor has no choice but to have him executed again. This scene, which Freud saw as 'one of the highest performances in world literature', plunges the Catholic reader into a deep and prolonged unease. For what would happen if Christ returned and wandered through the streets of Rome, preaching and performing miracles? How would the current pope react?

GL: Éric Zemmour is very fond of history but, in a few centuries, he will make the task of historians really complicated. Those who study his case to understand our time will find it very difficult to draw the right conclusions: he embodies a very powerful intellectual current in France, one that might be described as reactionary, but he finds himself almost alone in defence of these ideas, and he is fiercely fought.

The 'non-Christian Catholic' posture you describe suits him wonderfully; in fact he's one of the last of the kind. In the days of Auguste Comte, and even later, there were many of them, for a fairly simple reason: Catholicism was, in Europe anyway, in a situation of cultural hegemony, as the Italian Communists would put it. In a Christian continent, where Catholicism was often a state religion as well as a common cultural base, it was possible for great minds, believers or not, to influence the Church. In a dechristianized age, in a continent that has forgotten its roots, with legal systems aimed at erasing traces of religion, 'non-Christian Catholics' are becoming scarce – there are already hardly any Catholics as such.

In general, to feel nostalgic about the period of controversies between great thinkers on the subject of faith seems anachronistic to me. The Church itself has given up, at the same time as it withdrew from the public sphere, any attempt to play a role and to influence people's minds. In France, the law of 1905 was applied too stringently: by separating the Church from the State, the political authorities probably didn't think that they would succeed, in less than a century, in effecting this gigantic erasure. The Church has its share of the responsibility, even though it was bitterly opposed, because it submitted too easily. Now it's footing the bill.

Inter-religious dialogue

MH: The doctrine of self-examination, and the spiritual anarchy that results from it, essentially makes any dialogue with Protestants futile for lack of interlocutor. The situation is the same in the case of Islam.

Some of the problems posed by the lack of a spiritual hierarchy are clearly visible in Douglas Kennedy's book. In the small town of Enterprise (Alabama), white and black Baptists, attending different churches, never mix, while about thirty miles away, under the influence of the local pastor, they commune in the same celebrations. In a country where racial problems are as serious as in the United States, this is a real issue. (The situation is even worse in Islam, caught up almost from its origin in a war between two factions. In Islam, the bloodiest deviations are possible; if a sanction analogous to excommunication by a bishop existed in Islam, jihadism would disappear within a few weeks.)

The Orthodox Church, deeply decentralized, divided into fifteen 'autocephalous' churches (materially independent, but sharing exactly the same faith), has succeeded in avoiding any serious dissension, any schism within it. How did it achieve this? It seems to me that it was quite simply by being orthodox (I would be tempted, like Auguste Comte, to describe the name 'orthodox' as a *characteristic*). The Orthodox Church has been content, over the centuries, to keep the liturgy and doctrine unchanged; it refused to interfere in the affairs of the world.

GL: The absence of clergy in other religions no doubt explains the difficulty of dialogue with Catholics, but there is another reason, in my opinion: the absence of reciprocal will. I am struck by this ardent desire among Catholics to be reconciled with their brothers who have other beliefs, I see it as a reflex inherited from the time when they dominated the world.

Interfaith dialogue made sense from a barely concealed perspective of conquest; you could modestly call it evangelization, and it sometimes took on somewhat hostile forms. In a period of withdrawal, this dialogue is a pure delirious fantasy of Catholics, conceived by Catholics according to Catholic criteria, under the dubious eye of other religions.

It's an old fad, whose appearance could be dated to the twelfth century, when the highly influential Pierre Abelard wrote his *Dialogue Between a Philosopher, a Jew, and a*

Christian. The foundations of interreligious dialogue according to Catholics were set out: they could discuss things with all the monotheisms, they could advance together in benevolence and tolerance. Some even ended up thinking that everyone prayed to the same God, that only the rites and customs varied. Scholars, mostly Catholics, would even devote their lives to finding reasons to believe this, and all this work was carried out while Jewish and Muslim theologians worked to prove that *their* faith was the right one.

At the same time, Catholics became infatuated with Aristotle on the grounds that they had inherited his philosophy from Arab Muslims and that he had established a sort of synthesis, in Greek times, of the three monotheisms. The three 'Abrahamic' religions even worked together on translating him; in intellectual circles, there was something like a dream of 'reunification'. This optimistic current permeated the entire Christian West, through the universities, in particular.

Seven centuries later, the Church continued this enterprise, carried out systematically on her initiative and to her detriment. Paul VI created the pontifical council for interreligious dialogue (with non-Christians); then ecumenism became a cause to be defended. At mass, in the universal prayer, we have a kindly word for Protestants and Orthodox, we hope to find 'unity'. John Paul II invited all the religions to Assisi and gave them equal legitimacy – later on, he would ask forgiveness on behalf of the Church for its faults against other religions. This dialogue ends up resembling our parodies of contemporary debates, which Philippe Muray mocked in these terms: 'We debate before asking ourselves what we're debating about: the important thing is to come together.' People do not seek the truth, but consensus; this leads to confusion, which results in a form of chancy syncretism, relativism, and even in the submission of the Church.

If you talk to a Muslim, a Jew, or even a Protestant, he will always explain to you why his religion holds the truth, why Muhammad is the prophet, why Jesus is not God or why Mary is not a virgin. It's as if Catholics were the only ones to apologize for having the truth. For a non-believer, this attitude isn't very reassuring. However, if we confine ourselves to Christians alone, and if we trust Engels, according to whom 'after a certain number, quantity becomes quality', there are 1.2 billion Catholics, 900 million Protestants and 285 million Orthodox, which constitutes a favourable balance of power and a more advantageous start to negotiations than that considered in Assisi. We are obliged to believe that what Catholics have learned best from the teaching of Jesus is to turn the second cheek.

Hell

MH: Maybe people have emphasized hell too much. Without even opening the Bible again, I can see the dazzling description of the New Jerusalem, which closes the Apocalypse. There's nothing so evocative about the torments inflicted on the damned; rather, it's a question of a 'second death', of outright annihilation.

Reading the fascinating works of Philippe Ariès teaches us that a change occurred in the West at the beginning of the twelfth century. In earlier centuries, in the Roman era, the dead who belonged to the Church fell asleep, like the Seven Sleepers of Ephesus, and rested until the day of the Second Coming, when they awoke in the Heavenly Jerusalem. As for the wicked and the pagans, they were simply abandoned to non-being. In fact, having rubbed shoulders with quite a few of them, it always seemed to me that the wicked were *already* living in hell, and that some human beings were already dead – you had only to look into their eyes.

'There was no room in this conception,' writes Ariès, 'for individual responsibility, for counting good deeds and bad deeds.' The idea of the Last Judgement, of a weighing of souls, did not appear until the early Gothic era.

GL: I think many Catholics have lived for a long time with a certain idea of hell, which could be summed up by the fresco made by Michelangelo in the Sistine Chapel, *The Last Judgement*. We see the damned being conveyed in Charon's boat to a door opening onto the flames. Bodies darken the closer you get, faces twist, it's apocalyptic, it's hell.

This terrifying sight makes a lot of people smile these days. A rational person, it's true, can't stand the idea that the wicked are doomed to spend eternity roasting in the company of little devils equipped with pikes. Yet Michelangelo, who was anything but a religious caterpillar, didn't skimp on this description. He completed the fresco in 1541, in a Christian century and continent, and even took superstition so far as to slip in a self-portrait – he, the sinner who hoped to ward off fate. Why be afraid of hell? Passing under the portal of the Last Judgement in Notre-Dame Cathedral in Paris, you see an even more terrifying vision. No one is exempt, we can even distinguish eminent clerics, and we see the condemned chaining themselves, proof that it's the consciousness of sin and the rejection of God that deserve condemnation . . . Five centuries later, hell no longer exists and the whole world comes together in the idea sung by Michel Polnareff: 'We'll all go to paradise.' Let's not compare the artistic qualities of the painter and the singer; let's just say that a commonly held idea (people still believed in hell at the turn of the century) disappeared in a very short time. Fear of hell, however, long kept believers in a feverish state that impelled them to lead righteous lives on earth. I've naively interpreted Pascal's wager in this way: whether God exists or not, I have every interest in leading the life of a believer, which will make me happy on earth and save me from hell, just in case . . . We have reversed this bet. If hell doesn't exist, the devil doesn't exist, evil doesn't exist. The Church is at fault because it has stopped preaching what are called 'the last ends' and participated, at least by omission, in this enterprise of denigrating old beliefs. Where is the truth? Charles Baudelaire wrote: 'The Devil's most beautiful trick is to persuade you that he does not exist!' That's where we're at.

Christian art

MH: Which, exactly, are those centuries of Church splendour? Everyone, in my opinion, has their favourite era, and it seems to me that, more than the few written accounts, it's architecture that allows us to situate ourselves. In a Romanesque cloister I feel at peace, connected to the divinity. Gothic cathedrals are already different, beauty takes on a character that Kant later called *sublime* (beauty accompanied by the sensation of danger, such as a storm in the open sea, or a thunderstorm in high mountains). In a baroque church I really don't feel at home any more, I might as well be in a palace, at the theatre . . .

In short, it seems to me that the Church of Rome made various errors at the beginning of the twelfth century (separating itself from the Churches of the East, trying to reconcile reason and faith, trying to interfere in the affairs of temporal power, attaching too much importance to the Last Judgement and consequently to questions of morality), and that these errors made possible those civilizational catastrophes, the Greco-Latin Renaissance and, above all, Protestantism – which, by their joint action, were necessarily to lead to the Enlightenment and hence the collapse of the whole. So the problem goes back a long way.

GL: If you choose to trust architecture, there's one aspect that's striking: in the days of cathedrals, monumental places of worship were built and their construction took longer than a man's lifetime. The cathedrals of Reims, Chartres and Paris were built in seventy-five, one hundred and thirty-four and one hundred and eighty-two years, respectively: at the time, people really didn't go in for miniatures. By way of comparison, the Trump Tower in New York was designed, built and completed in two years, between 1981 and 1983. We could say that the invention of the motor engine, technical progress and new materials explain this considerable difference. That's true for business, but when we see the ugliness of modern churches, those unfortunate cubes in washed-out concrete, sometimes hideous, which hardly stand out above the horizon of the surrounding houses, we understand above all that what differentiates us from the builders of Christianity is that we 'think in terms of functionality' instead of dedicating the construction to God. It was better before, when the supernatural was seen everywhere, even in the spires of cathedrals, pointing towards the sky.

If we extend this observation to art, things are even worse. European artists, whether believers or not, found in the sacred an unlimited inspiration to irrigate centuries of Christianity with their genius. Everything was connected, homogeneous. That scandalous, whimsical and brawling character, Caravaggio, could thank his talent (and, it has to be said, a few well-placed relations) for his rehabilitation by the Pope when he was condemned to death in absentia while living in exile far from Rome. When you enter San Luigi dei Francesi, you see in his three paintings depicting the life of Saint Matthew the magnificent fruits of this cooperation between artists and the clergy. Should we compare this period to ours in terms of sacred art? Frankly, let's save time, let's skip this bogus debate.

Science

MH: The damage caused by the Galileo and Darwin affairs might have given rise to hope that the Catholic Church had calmed down in its relationship with science. This passage from the encyclical *Fides et Ratio* (1998) unfortunately seems to prove that this is not the case: 'In the context of scientific research, a positivist mentality has been imposed that has not only moved away from any reference to the Christian vision of the world, but has also and above all left aside any reference to a metaphysical and moral conception.'

Pascal (himself a talented scientist and mathematician, who knew what the scientific method was all about) writes in his *Pensées*: 'We must say roughly: it's done by figure and movement, because it's true. But to say which one, and to compose the machine, that is ridiculous, because it's useless and uncertain and painful.'

This passage, positivist *avant la lettre*, clearly establishes that science in no way leads to materialism, still less to atheism (matter, and God too, are in the eyes of the positivist just pure metaphysical hypotheses, excluded from the field of science), and consequently that science cannot constitute any danger for faith (nor for that matter any opportunity); these are two entirely separate areas of human intellectual life, and doomed by nature to remain so.

GL: Rational minds, which have become more and more numerous as the times have become more Cartesian, accept in a few rare moments in their lives that these lives conceal an element of mystery, and even sometimes feel a need for the supernatural. No one is spared, in fact: it's when he is confronted with the inexplicable that man is most inclined to turn to religion. The Church is arguably never as convincing as when it stands by a grieving family. The moment when the priest consoles people's hearts, the precise moment when he addresses a family gathered in front of a coffin – this moment is undoubtedly the moment when the Church remains truly legitimate.

I also believe that faith and reason are reconcilable, but we can only note that, especially in the face of death, reason has conquered faith. As the scientific mind could not envision life after death, this idea was simply banned. One statistic illustrates the decline in Catholic influence on this specific point: in France, in 1975, just over 2,000 people chose cremation, that was barely tolerated by the Church; now it's more than 200,000 per year, and one in two French people say they prefer this option for their own death.

If the Church is no longer a reference point at the time of death, how can we be surprised that the times are hopeless? The proclamation of eternal life is arguably the most wonderful message that Catholics can send to the world, which is in great need of it.

Political power

MH: The precept of 'rendering to Caesar' was clear; I don't think the Catholic Church applied it with sufficient rigour.

Completely devoid of any theological basis, the Anglican schism has its origins merely in the refusal of Pope Clement VII to annul the marriage of Henry VIII. Weakened by this struggle, the Anglican clergy were incapable of stemming the development of Puritanism. Without the stubbornness of Clement VII, the United States would perhaps be a Catholic country today; pretty clever! Other similar interventions have not had happier consequences. Royal weddings were a *special case*, where geopolitical considerations necessarily had their place – and any clergyman of average intelligence should have been able to understand *that*. While royal weddings nowadays are no more than a folkloric ceremony, the Catholic Church hasn't in the least stopped meddling in the government of states (intervening, for example, in their immigration policies), and eventually, it has to be said, that annoys everyone.

GL: With his 'render unto Caesar', Jesus invents secularism; the problem is that Catholics applied it a little too zealously. The history of the last century could be summed up as follows: a massive dechristianization of almost the entire West, mainly in Europe, where in a few decades they have undone what they had built up over fifteen centuries.

We can blame the Catholic Church for all sorts of things, but at the start of the twentieth century, it still played a political role, and above all, it remained in the cultural majority. In France, the drama began in 1905, with the law of separation of churches and state, which was designed to stem its influence as much as to drive it out of people's minds. The great principle of this French-style secularism is basically compatible with that decreed by Jesus: there is inner faith, and freedom is preserved from this point of view, and there is the public space, where the religious sphere can't exert any influence. According to this separation, the state is secular, of course, but at no time is it specified that society must be atheist. The problem is, the Church accepted the fact it was being kicked out, and gave up on all fronts.

Its political influence quickly subsided, but above all it abandoned what is called 'social Catholicism', which had given it a popular base. For a long time, people had lived immersed in a Catholic cultural atmosphere. Their day was punctuated by the sound of bells, they attended a few services, met at mass on Sunday. Even if, in the secrecy of their consciences, they weren't necessarily animated by an intense faith, they resorted to the services of the parish priest at the important moments of their lives: marriage, illness, death. I really like the idea of 'the faith of the coalman' sometimes described by Balzac as the fact of 'loving the Blessed Virgin the same way that you love your wife': a filial piety, an attachment devoid of theological or philosophical reflection, a fidelity to a story and to certain roots more than to a mystical revelation. I fit perfectly into that category; this simple faith provided the glue for a civilization.

After 1905, and during its vast movement of withdrawal, the Church confused 'disappearing from the public sphere' with 'disappearing altogether'. It has erased itself from the world. Formerly, it ruled souls; today, its political influence is nil, and its role in society reduced to almost nothing: you can live in France without seeing a priest all your life long. They haven't disappeared, it's just that you could see them before because they wore cassocks and organized processions on major religious festivals, while nowadays they dress in civilian clothes and hide away as in the days of the catacombs.

And the Church seems to apologize for still existing. Recently, in France, we've experienced a vast movement of insurgency on the part of those who could be called those 'left behind by globalization', the yellow vests. These people expressed an anger that went back a long way, and they were supported by a majority of the population. A social phenomenon of this order cannot fail to affect any institution claiming to have a plan for human beings. Without exerting political influence, the Church could have played its part in offering a spiritual project to those who are struggling against a global loss of meaning. There are one hundred and four dioceses in France, each with its own bishop, who are representatives of the Church in the country. One of them, only one, saw fit to go to meet the Yellow Vests. The Church can do better.

Sexuality

MH: The interest shown by the Catholic Church in the sexuality of its faithful seems to me to be clearly exaggerated. It doesn't go back to the origins of Christianity; Saint Paul was as usual blameless: 'better to marry than to burn', and sometimes sublime: 'they will be one flesh'. Things deteriorated with Saint Augustine, but this didn't have much impact for quite a few centuries. Things only really get out of hand in the modern era, again arguably through the contamination of Protestantism, and the Puritanism that stems from it. That's where we still are, and I admit to feeling real embarrassment when I hear different prelates protesting against the use of condoms, AIDS or not; in heaven's name, is it any of their fucking business?

For a long time I had the impression that the Orthodox Church was, on this point, wiser, and able to maintain the attitude of tolerance that had been that of the Catholic Church for many centuries. But it was a diffuse impression, which I struggled to justify by pointing to a text (precisely because the Orthodox are reluctant to express themselves on this question, one that in their eyes is secondary), until, in an article by Olivier Clément (we really should always go back to the best authors), I came across this quotation, a very illuminating one in my view, from Athenagoras I, Patriarch of Constantinople: 'If a man and a woman really love each other, it's not for me to go into their bedroom, everything they do is holy.'

GL: The Catholic Church does indeed have a reputation for being moralizing and puritanical – a pain in the arse, to be honest. This is both logical and unfair. In my opinion, it is following its role when it indicates a path, spiritual but also moral, and the unity that it preaches between body, mind and soul makes it absolutely normal for it to involve itself in the field of sexuality. In this regard, I prefer the Church to talk about sexuality, even if it talks too much about it, and I prefer the popes (such as Paul VI with the encyclical *Humanae vitae* or John Paul II with his theology of the body) to express themselves on this subject, rather than, as in Islam, maintaining a hypocritical and muddled relation with the subject.

The more they curl up, the more Catholics come across as moral daddy figures – their conception of love feels like a field of prohibitions, and delivering their message isolates them from the world. What we forget, and perhaps the Church doesn't insist enough on this point, is that its teaching indicates a way that's supposed to lead to heaven, and also to bring happiness on earth. Man has always been a sinner, and God forgives him; this is also what unbelievers have ceased to realize. If it could again influence people's hearts, the Church could no doubt deliver this message. We are light years away from this.

Can the Catholic Church regain its former splendour?

MH: Taking up the Orthodox label in a partisan way, I'd be tempted to call the Catholic Church the 'schism of Rome'. It was Rome that broke away, that swelled with pride, that claimed world pre-eminence – and obtained it. Closely following the movement of Western colonization (which I also condemn entirely, but that's another question), it has conquered vast dioceses. Then it allowed itself to be contaminated by Protestantism, and embarked on a long process of suicide.

Can the Catholic Church regain its former splendour? Yes, maybe, I don't know.

It would be nice if it moved away from Protestantism definitively, and moved closer to orthodoxy. Fully merging with it would be the best solution, but it won't be easy. The question of the *Filioque* can be easily resolved by competent theologians. The problem of settling Frankish barons in the Middle East no longer arises – even Donald Trump has given up. But for the Bishop of Rome to give up his universal ambition, to have only an honorary pre-eminence over the patriarchs of Constantinople or Antioch, may be difficult to swallow.

At a minimum, the Catholic Church, imitating Orthodox modesty, should limit its interventions in areas that are not directly within its purview (I have mentioned scientific research, the government of states, human love).

It should renounce the habit of organizing councils, which are mainly an opportunity to trigger schisms.

It should also renounce encyclicals, and put a brake on its doctrinal inventiveness (the Immaculate Conception, and especially papal infallibility, collide too directly with reason; reason is a big peaceful animal that uncomplainingly falls asleep during church services; but unnecessary provocations should be avoided).

It can be inspired by Pentecostalism, in the same way that pop music was inspired by gospel and blues; on the other hand, it mustn't forget a necessary dose of madness. In the Russian version it's Dostoyevsky: 'If we have to choose between Christ and the truth, I choose Christ'; in the French version we have Blaise Pascal.

It all comes down to the way the Catholic Church has, throughout its history, given too much importance to reason (and this has worsened over the centuries, no doubt, perhaps I'm insisting too much, but I don't think so, under the influence of Protestantism). Man is a being of reason – if you will; it happens, from time to time. But he is above all a being of flesh, and of emotion: it would be a good idea not to forget this.

GL: Can the Catholic Church regain its former splendour? Yes, no doubt, but it will take a long time.

If one were to sum up the last decades, one could say that the Church, after losing temporal power, tried to survive by being tolerated; with this aim, it has essentially adapted to the excesses of a world that it is supposed to save. This role reversal is indeed leading the Church to suicide, but even in the eyes of God, there is, after this tragic gesture, a possibility of salvation: the saintly Curé d'Ars once told a mother in despair over the suicide of her son that between the bridge from which he had thrown himself and the water where he had drowned, he had had plenty of time to regret his deed, and to turn to divine mercy.

To save what can be saved, we might have to break with the relativism that has been in vogue since the sixties. Perhaps the Church would regain some of its splendour if it stopped wanting to be cool, and again taught the fear of God, without which there is no love; it's exactly the same as for the education of children, parental authority has been undermined, with the same consequences.

Perhaps the Church should moderate its fascination with other religions. On the subject of Protestantism, how can we tolerate Trojan Horses such as the secretary general of the Italian Bishops' Conference, Monsignor Nunzio Galantino, who recently said that 'the Reformation launched by Martin Luther five hundred years ago was an event of the Holy Spirit'? I should point out that he's close to the Pope and is calling for a new Reformation. Pope Francis himself is sending ever more signals to Muslims, as evidenced by his recent trip to the United Arab Emirates, and he took care to define himself as a simple 'bishop of Rome' on the day of his election, a pledge of good faith, this time aimed at the Orthodox.

It might also be useful to get rid of other mafias, like the Vatican gay lobby, the Freemasons, the deconstructors of the traditional doctrine of the Church, etc.

We should put an end to the permanent quest for emotion – from this point of view, the Church cannot compete with concerts or the cinema; but if it confines itself to its mission, that of proclaiming God and leading men to eternal life, it remains absolutely essential.

Perhaps the Church would regain some credibility if it ceased to conceive of itself as a vaguely charitable NGO, albeit one that does not proclaim the source of its generosity, namely Christ. In politics, it might do well to stop casting moral discredit on certain governments (the Pope's criticism of the management of immigrants by Italian Interior Minister Matteo Salvini is a good example).

In general, since it became a minority, the Church in Europe has curled up around a few hard cores that are sociologically very homogeneous; it has almost constituted itself as a social class, and cut itself off from the majority of souls.

Its gentrification [*embourgeoisement*] is perhaps, ultimately, the greatest scourge affecting the Church at the beginning of the twenty-first century.

MH and GL: We haven't answered the second part of your question: 'Can restoring Catholicism to its former glory repair our damaged civilization?' On this point we agree, it's much simpler, almost obvious: the answer is yes.

36

A bit worse.
A response to a few friends

It has to be admitted: most of the emails exchanged in recent weeks had the primary objective of verifying that one's interlocutor was neither dead, nor dying. But, once this has been checked, people still kept trying to say interesting things, and this wasn't easy as this epidemic managed to be both scary and boring. A banal virus, unglamorously related to obscure influenza viruses, with poorly understood survival conditions and unclear characteristics, sometimes benign, sometimes fatal, not even sexually transmitted: in short, a virus without qualities. This epidemic might claim a few thousand deaths around the world every day, but it still gave the curious impression of being a non-event. Moreover, my estimable colleagues (some of them, after all, are estimable) didn't talk about it so much, they preferred to address the issue of lockdown; and here I would like to add my own contribution to some of their observations.

Frédéric Beigbeder (from Guéthary, Pyrénées-Atlantiques). A writer in any case doesn't see many people, he lives like a hermit with his books, lockdown doesn't change much. Totally okay, Frédéric, when it comes to social life there's no real difference. But there is one point that you're forgetting (probably because, living in the countryside, you suffer less from the ban): a writer needs to walk.

This lockdown seems to me an ideal opportunity to settle the old Flaubert–Nietzsche quarrel. Somewhere (I have forgotten where) Flaubert asserts that one can think and write well only when sitting down. Protests and mockery from Nietzsche (I also forget where), who goes so far as to call him a nihilist (so this happened at the time when Nietzsche had already started to use the word indiscriminately): he himself conceived all his works while walking, anything that is not conceived while walking is crap; besides, he's always been a Dionysian dancer, etc. Nobody will suspect me of exaggerated sympathy for Nietzsche, but I have to admit that, in this case, he's the one who is right. Trying to write if, during the day, you have no chance of engaging in several hours of walking at a sustained pace, is strongly discouraged: the accumulated nervous tension can't dissolve, the thoughts and the images continue to spin painfully in the poor head of the author, who quickly becomes irritable and even mad.

The only thing that really matters is the mechanical, machine-like rhythm of the walk, which is not primarily intended to bring up new ideas (although this may happen, as a side-effect), but to calm the conflicts induced by the clash of ideas born at the work table (and this is where Flaubert isn't totally wrong); when he talks to us about the ideas he came up with on the rocky slopes of the hinterland of Nice, in the meadows of the Engadine, etc., Nietzsche is rambling somewhat: except when writing a tourist guide, the landscapes one walks across are of less importance than the inner landscape.

Catherine Millet (normally tends to be in Paris, but luckily found herself in Estagel, Pyrénées-Orientales, when the lockdown came into force). The present situation reminds her annoyingly of the 'sci-fi' part of one of my books, *The Possibility of an Island*.

So at this point I said to myself that it was good, all the same, to have readers. Because I hadn't thought of making the connection, even though it's crystal clear. Besides, if I think about it, that's exactly what I had in mind at the time, regarding the extinction of humanity. Not a blockbuster film. Something pretty bleak. Individuals living isolated in their cells, without physical contact with their peers, just a few exchanges by computer, then fewer and fewer.

Emmanuel Carrère (Paris-Royan; he seems to have found a valid reason to travel). Will interesting books be born, inspired by this period? He ponders the question.

I ponder it too. I have really wondered about it, but deep down I don't think so. We have had a lot of books about the plague, over the centuries; plague has been of great interest to writers. In this case, I have my doubts. Already, I don't believe for half a second in statements like 'nothing will ever be the same again'. On the contrary, everything will remain exactly the same. The course of this epidemic is actually remarkably normal. The West is not, to all eternity, by divine right, the richest and most developed area in the world; that's all been over for some time now, it's not a scoop. Even if we examine things in detail, France is doing a little better than Spain and Italy, but less well than Germany; no big surprise here, either.

The main result of the coronavirus, on the other hand, should be to accelerate certain ongoing mutations. For quite a few years, all technological developments, whether minor (video on demand, contactless payment) or major (teleworking, Internet shopping, social networks) have mainly had the consequence (or the main objective?) of decreasing material contacts, and especially human contacts. The coronavirus epidemic offers a magnificent reason for this monotonous trend: a certain obsolescence that seems to strike at human relations. Which reminds me of an illuminating comparison that I picked up in a text written by an activist group opposed to assisted reproduction, called 'The chimpanzees of the future' (I discovered these people on the Internet; I never said that there was nothing good about the Internet). So, and I quote: 'Soon, having your own children, for free and at random, will seem as weird as hitchhiking without a web platform.' Carpooling, roommates . . . we get the utopias we deserve. Let's move on.

It would be just as wrong to say that we have rediscovered the tragic, death, finitude, etc. The trend for over half a century now, eloquently described by Philippe Ariès, has been to conceal death as much as possible; well, never has death been so discreet as in the past few weeks. People die alone in their hospital or nursing-home rooms, they are immediately buried (or cremated? Cremation is more popular these days), without asking anyone to be with them, in secret. The victims die without any evidence of it, and are reduced to one unit in the daily deaths figures, and there's something strangely abstract about the anxiety that pervades the population as the total number increases.

Another figure has become very important these last weeks: the age of the patients. Up to what age is it appropriate to resuscitate and treat them? 70, 75, 80 years old? It depends, apparently, on what part of the world you live in; but in any case, never had the fact that not everyone's life is of the same value been expressed with such calm shamelessness; the fact that, from a certain age (70, 75, 80?), it's as if we were already dead.

All of these trends, as I said, already existed before the coronavirus; they have merely become more evident. We won't wake up, after lockdown, in a new world; it will be the same world, but a bit worse.

37

The Vincent Lambert affair should not have taken place

It did take place, however, and Professor Hirsch's book, covering his chronicle of the affair from 2014 until its tragic outcome in 2019, has finally highlighted the real issues at stake.[1] There's something wrong with the way the media work: dozens of hours have been devoted to this affair, on all the airwaves, without dislodging from the minds of the general public the idea that 'the debate on the end of life was being reopened'. But this was absolutely not the point, or at least it shouldn't have been. To be convinced of this, you just need to remember that many patients in units treating persistent vegetative states or minimally conscious states (similar to that of Vincent Lambert) are there following a head trauma, generally of accidental origin. Riding a scooter without a helmet, for example, is a great way to end up in such a unit. This alone means that we're not dealing with patients 'at the end of their lives', nor even especially elderly patients (when he suffered his traffic accident, Vincent Lambert was 32 years old). We are dealing with disabled patients, victims of a very severe handicap, one of the most severe there is, and the only question that arises is whether our society has the duty to take care of them, to treat them and, in the event that it's impossible to improve their condition, to provide them with a living environment.

The answer to this question is yes, for obvious moral reasons (and, if our society were to answer no, then I would have to leave it). In this case, so far, the civil law coincides perfectly with the moral law; Professor Hirsch notes this clearly in his introduction, citing the terms of the law of 4 March 2002 relating to the rights of patients. Moreover, the Kouchner circular of 3 May 2002, specifying the application of this law, provides for the creation of units dedicated to patients in these states, and defines their distribution across the national territory.

This poses a first, nagging question that Professor Hirsch addresses in his foreword, and to which he returns throughout his book: how is it that Vincent Lambert has never been transferred to one of these dedicated units (there are about 150 in France)? At the root of this case, there is a huge error on the part of the medical institution. For seven years, Vincent Lambert was deprived of the physiotherapy and speech therapy necessary for his condition. Locked in his room, he did not have the right to those outings in a wheelchair that are not a simple 'pleasure outing' (although a pleasure outing would in itself be perfectly justified), but that may, by the multiplication of sensory stimuli, help the patient to recover his or her neurological capacities. For examples of late recovery, even after a long period in a vegetative state, exist. They are rare, very rare, but they do exist, and this hope, tenuous but real, sometimes sustains the morale of families for years. No brain imaging test, however sophisticated, can conclude with any certainty that recovery is not possible; we are here, in this field as in various others, at the limits of medical science. Therefore, it would not be appropriate to ask too much of the experts; as practitioners, they are brutally required, by the bodies that call on them, to produce a usable diagnosis; as scientists, they can (and even must, from a strictly scientific point of view) express their doubts.

Even in the event that a vegetative state is recognized with certainty as irreversible, it would still remain our duty to take care of these patients, to ensure them the best possible living conditions. No one knows the thoughts that form in their brain. They alternate between wakefulness and sleep, but no one knows if they can dream; and a life of dreams, in my eyes, is already worth living. Anyone who has tried to write a book knows this: sometimes, partially (I stress 'sometimes' and 'partially') we manage to communicate through writing things that would be impossible to communicate otherwise; and what one writes is often only a faint echo of what one imagined one might write. Finally, to put it more bluntly: the inner life of a person is not reducible to their relationships with those around them.

Friends, family ... There is no doubt that it's the 'family tragedy' aspect that explains the extraordinary media hype surrounding this affair. It had everything that the media revels in: dignity, love, tears, and even fundamentalist Catholics ... It's useful, at this stage, to underline a few principles: Vincent Lambert was a free individual, a human being, in the full sense of the term (and, incidentally, a French citizen). No one (neither his wife, nor his mother, nor any of his brothers and sisters, nor his doctors) had the right to decide on his life or his death, had the right to pronounce whether his life was 'worth living'. Absolutely no one.

However, the decision was taken for him. He hadn't left any 'advance directives', and why would he? We leave advance directives when we're aging, ill, and facing imminent death; not when we're thirty, and risk having a car accident.

Not only has the medical institution never repaired its mistake, not only will Vincent Lambert have spent the last ten years of his life in a palliative care unit where he should not have been, but in 2013 that institution decided to kill him, based at the outset on a ridiculous diagnosis, according to which he had expressed a 'desire to die'. How could a patient whose condition is characterized by enormous difficulty in communicating, even the simplest things, have made such a desire known? This is palpably absurd.

The Reims University Hospital will have found it pretty difficult killing off Vincent Lambert, in part due to his stubbornness in surviving (first stopping food: thirty-one days without eating, no less), but above all thanks to the intervention of justice. It took no less than four 'collegiate' procedures (the book suggests what the term 'collegial' means in practice), the last of which was interrupted twice, to reach the fatal outcome. The legal drama involved the administrative court of Châlons-en-Champagne (on multiple occasions), the Council of State, the European Court of Human Rights, several courts of appeal, and the Court of Cassation – all against the backdrop of repeated advice (never acted upon) from the UN Committee on the Rights of Persons with Disabilities. Its final phase provided us with the puzzling spectacle of three jurisdictions giving radically contrary opinions in the space of a few weeks, without any new element having emerged.

If I myself intervened in this debate (very late, 'at the eleventh hour'), in a column published in *Le Monde*, it was because I had been amazed to see the government appealing against the decision of the Paris Court of Appeal, which ordered the French state to resume providing Vincent Lambert with food and water.

I was at the time, I will readily agree, not very well informed; all the same, it seemed unlikely to me that giving food and drink to a sick person (even artificially) would fall within the framework of 'unreasonable therapeutic persistence'. I have since had the opportunity to see these gastrostomy bags that are used for the nourishment and hydration of patients unable to swallow; these are small, easily transportable pieces of equipment that the family can change themselves, when their relative is in their care, without needing to call in specialized medical personnel; nothing binding, nothing heavy. So, is this therapeutic persistence?

This intervention on the part of the state, without which Vincent Lambert would still be alive today, seemed to me at the time, and still seems to me, incomprehensible; it casts, and will continue to cast a shadow over Emmanuel Macron's first five-year term. Even though the French state bears some responsibility in the final phase of the drama, it's mainly, if we re-examine the facts, the murderous relentlessness of the University Hospital of Reims that is so striking in this story, when other medical units in France had declared themselves ready to welcome this patient and to offer him the care required by his condition. So it was by no means illegitimate that the hospital should be put on trial. At the first hearing, the Reims University Hospital and Doctor Sanchez were released by the Reims court. As Emmanuel Hirsch relates in his foreword, it was at the end of this trial, where he testified for the civil party, that he decided to publish this book, because he doesn't understand, he still doesn't understand why Vincent Lambert had to die.

There are more than 1,500 people, at present, in France, who live in persistent vegetative states or minimally conscious states, comparable to that of Vincent Lambert, and many are in an even more difficult situation (he could, for example, breathe naturally, without the aid of a tracheostomy, which is far from the general case). Should they henceforth be considered as corpses on borrowed time, subject to the goodwill of a court decision, when the courts have largely demonstrated their inconsistency and unpredictability (which one might be inclined to excuse, given the ambiguities, well noted by Professor Hirsch, of the Leonetti law)? And did they think of those caregivers who devote their working days, their compassion, their strength to taking care, as best they can, of these patients? What contempt has been shown for this difficult, emotionally trying job, which almost all of them have deliberately chosen! (Almost all of the caregivers who work in these units are volunteers.) Emmanuel Hirsch is not exaggerating when he speaks, in his last piece, of an 'ethical and political debacle', and he is right to fear that we are on the eve of yet more renunciations.

When I was a child, I liked Jean Rostand's popular science works. He was a somewhat 'old-fashioned' humanist, of a species that unfortunately seems extinct, but he seems to have sensed the dangers that threaten us today when he wrote in 1970, in *Le Courrier d'un biologiste* [*A Biologist's Postbag*]:

> I think there is no life, however degraded, deteriorated, humiliated, or impoverished, that does not deserve respect and is worth diligently defending.
>
> I have the weakness to think that it is the honour of a society to accept, to wish for this heavy luxury represented by the burden of the incurable, the useless, the incapable; and I would almost measure its degree of civilization by the amount of pain and vigilance it imposes on itself out of pure respect for life . . . When the habit of eliminating monsters is formed, even the smallest blemishes will appear as monstrosities. From the elimination of the horrible to that of the undesirable, there is only one step . . . This cleaned, sanitized society, this society where pity would be out of a job, this society without waste, without errors, where the normal and the strong would take advantage of the resources hitherto absorbed by the abnormal and the weak, is a society that would restore Sparta and delight the followers of Nietzsche. I am not sure that it would still deserve to be called a human society.

Sparta prided itself on efficiency 'and, for this reason, disappeared without a trace'.[2] Our society, too, likes to boast of its efficiency; it will disappear, like Sparta, and maybe all that will remain is the uncertain memory of a shame, the shadow of a certain disgust.

Sources

1. 'Jacques Prévert is a jerk', first published in *Lettres françaises* no. 22 (July 1992) and reprinted in *Interventions* (Paris: Flammarion, 1998) and *Interventions 2* (Paris: Flammarion, 2009).
2. '*The Mirage* by Jean-Claude Guiguet', first published in *Lettres françaises*, no. 27 (May 1993) and reprinted in *Interventions* (Paris: Flammarion, 1998) and *Interventions 2* (Paris: Flammarion, 2009).
3. 'Approaches to distress', first published in *Genius Loci* (Paris: La Différence, 1992), and reprinted in *Dix* (Paris: *Les Inrockuptibles/* Grasset, 1997), in *Interventions* (Paris: Flammarion, 1998), in *Rester vivant et autres textes* (Paris: Librio, 1999), and in *Interventions 2* (Paris: Flammarion, 2009).
4. 'Staring into the distance: in praise of silent cinema', first published in *Lettres françaises*, no. 32 (May 1993) and reprinted in *Interventions* (Paris: Flammarion, 1998) and *Interventions 2* (Paris: Flammarion, 2009).
5. 'Interview with Jean-Yves Jouannais and Christophe Duchâtelet', first published in *Art Press*, no. 199 (February 1995) and reprinted in *Interventions* (Paris: Flammarion, 1998) and *Interventions 2* (Paris: Flammarion, 2009).
6. 'Art as peeling', first published in the section 'La carnet à spirale'

in *Les Inrockuptibles*, no. 5 (1995) and reprinted in *Interventions* (Paris: Flammarion, 1998) and *Interventions 2* (Paris: Flammarion, 2009).

7. 'Creative absurdity', first published in *Les Inrockuptibles*, no. 13 (1995) on the occasion of this reissue, and reprinted in *Interventions* (Paris: Flammarion, 1998) and *Interventions 2* (Paris: Flammarion, 2009).

8. 'The party', first published in the magazine *20 Ans* in 1996, and reprinted in the collection *Rester vivant et autres textes* (Paris: Librio, 1999), and in *Interventions 2* (Paris: Flammarion, 2009).

9. 'Time out': these columns were published in *Les Inrockuptibles* nos. 90–7 (February–March 1997), and were reprinted in *Interventions* (Paris: Flammarion, 1998), in *Rester vivant et autres textes* (Paris: Librio, 1999), and in *Interventions 2* (Paris: Flammarion, 2009). The titles have been provided by Sylvain Bourmeau.

10. 'Opera Bianca': this was an installation by Gilles Touyard at the Centre d'Art Contemporain Georges-Pompidou, 1997; text first published in *Interventions* (Paris: Flammarion, 1998), and reprinted in *Interventions 2* (Paris: Flammarion, 2009).

11. 'Letter to Lakis Proguidis': in *L'Atelier du roman*, no. 9, Lakis Proguidis investigated the relations between poetry and the novel, focusing on Houellebecq's writings. Houellebecq's reply, the present essay, was published in *L'Atelier du roman*, no. 10 (spring 1977), and was reprinted in *Interventions* (Paris: Flammarion, 1998) and *Interventions 2* (Paris: Flammarion, 2009).

12. 'The question of paedophilia' was first published in *L'Infini*, no. 59, in 1997, and reprinted in *Interventions 2* (Paris: Flammarion, 2009).

13. 'Humanity, the second stage', first published as an afterword to Valerie Solanas' work, *S.C.U.M. Manifesto* (Paris: Mille et une nuits, 1998), and reprinted in *Interventions 2* (Paris: Flammarion, 2009).

14. 'Empty heavens', first published in the collection *Rester vivant et autres textes* (Paris: Librio, 1999) and reprinted in *Interventions 2* (Paris: Flammarion, 2009).

15. 'I have a dream': this text is the French translation by Michel Meyer of the English translation by Roel de Bie of an interview between Michel Houellebecq and the German journalist Wolfgang Farkas published on 2 November 2000 in the weekly *Die Zeit* and forming part of a series entitled 'Ich habe einen Traum' ('I have a dream'). It was published in *Interventions 2* (Paris: Flammarion, 2009).

16. 'Neil Young', first published in the *Dictionnaire du rock*, edited by Michka Assayas (Paris: Robert Laffont, 2000), and reprinted in *Interventions 2* (Paris: Flammarion, 2009).

17. 'Interview with Christian Authier', first published in *L'Opinion indépendante*, in January 2002, and reprinted in *Interventions 2* (Paris: Flammarion, 2009).

18. 'Technical consolation', first published in the collection *Lanzarote et autres textes* (Paris: Librio, 2002), and reprinted in *Interventions 2* (Paris: Flammarion, 2009).

19. 'Sky, earth, sun', first published in the collection *Contes de campagne* (Paris: Mille et une nuits, 2002), reprinted in the collection *Lanzarote et autres textes* (Paris: Librio, 2002) and in *Interventions 2* (Paris: Flammarion, 2009).

20. 'Leaving the twentieth century', first published in *La Nouvelle Revue française*, no. 561 (April 2002), reprinted in the collection *Lanzarote et autres textes* (Paris: Librio, 2002) and in *Interventions 2* (Paris: Flammarion, 2009).

21. 'Philippe Muray in 2002', first published in *Le Figaro* on 6 January 2003, under the title 'L'homme de gauche est mal parti', and reprinted in *Interventions 2* (Paris: Flammarion, 2009).

22. 'Towards a semi-rehabilitation of the hick', published online and included in *Interventions 2* (Paris: Flammarion, 2009).

23. 'Conservatism, a source of progress', first published in *Le Figaro* on 8 November 2003 and reprinted in *Houellebecq, Les Cahiers de l'Herne*, in 2017.

24. 'Prolegomena to positivism' is the preface to Michel Bourdeau, *Auguste Comte aujourdhui* (Paris: Kimé, 2003) and was reprinted in *Interventions 2* (Paris: Flammarion, 2009).

25. 'I'm normal. A normal writer': of this, Houellebecq writes 'This text, initially published in a magazine whose name I have forgotten, was included in the collection *Des nouvelles du prix de Flore* (Paris: Flammarion, 2004).'

26. 'I have read my whole life long', a text written for the fiftieth anniversary of *J'ai lu*, reprinted in *Interventions 2* (Paris: Flammarion, 2009).

27. 'Soil cutting' was published in *Artforum*, in September 2008, and reprinted in *Interventions 2* (Paris: Flammarion, 2009).

28. 'The lost text' is the preface to Rachid Amirou's book *L'Imaginaire touristique* (Paris: CNRS éditions, 2012).

29. 'Interview with Frédéric Beigbeder' was published in *Lui*, no. 7 (April 2014).

30. 'A remedy for the exhaustion of being' is the preface to Marc Lathuillière, *Musée national* (Paris: La Martinière, 2014).

31. 'Interview with Marin De Viry and Valérie Toranian' was published in the *Revue des deux mondes* in July 2015.

32. 'Interview with Agathe Novak-Lechevalier': this interview took place in Malaga in April 2017 as part of *La Noche de los libros* (online, unpublished).

33. 'Emmanuel Carrère and the problem of goodness', published in *Emmanuel Carrère. Faire effraction dans le réel,* edited by Laurent Demanze and Dominique Rabaté (Paris: P.O.L., 2018).

34. 'Donald Trump is a good president': a version of this text was published in *Harper's Magazine* in January 2019.

35. 'Conversation with Geoffroy Lejeune': a version of this text was published in *First Things* in May 2019, and reprinted in *La Revue des deux mondes*, October 2019.

36. 'A bit worse. *A response to a few friends*' was a letter read by Augustin Trapenard on France Inter on 4 May 2020.

37. 'The Vincent Lambert affair should not have taken place' is the preface to Emmanuel Hirsch's book, *Vincent Lambert, une mort exemplaire?* (Paris: Le Cerf, 2020).

Notes

All notes are by the translator unless otherwise indicated.

1 Jacques Prévert is a jerk

1 Houellebecq's summary of the reasons for Prévert's notoriety includes references to the films directed by Marcel Carné for which Prévert wrote the screenplays, including *Quai des brumes* (1938), starring Jean Gabin, *Les Enfants du paradis* (1945), and *Portes de la nuit* (1946). Antonin Artaud seems to have written fifteen screenplays for films, of which only one was made (*La Coquille et le clergyman*, Germaine Dulac, 1928). As a director, Leos Carax – whose films include *Les Amants du Pont-Neuf* (1991) and *Holy Motors* (2012) – is noted for his 'poetic' style, if not exactly for his realism. Éric Rohmer (1920–2010) was noted for his talkative films, part of the French New Wave; and Sacha Guitry (1885–1957) was active in theatre and then cinema: he decided that the advent of the talkies was a boon for film and became a prolific cinema director.

2 Emil Cioran (1911–1995), born in Romania, settled in Paris in the Second World War and became known as a French writer of pessimistic essays and aphorisms.

3 Boris Vian (1920–1959) was talented in many artistic fields, well

known as a singer and songwriter; Georges Brassens (1921–1981) was also a famed singer and songwriter.

4 Robert (known as Boby) Lapointe (1922–1972) was a humorous *chansonnier* and actor known for his word play.

5 The *Bibliothèque de la Pléiade* is a collection of (mainly French) writers deemed to be classics; to 'enter the *Pléiade*' is a mark of literary consecration.

6 Karl Marx and Friedrich Engels, *The Communist Manifesto*, available online: https://www.marxists.org/archive/marx/works/1848/communist-manifesto/ch01.htm#007.

3 Approaches to distress

1 The area to the immediate west of Paris, dominated by tall office blocks and the huge hollow cube of the Arche de la Défense.

2 Ernest Hemingway used several brands of typewriter, including the 1926 Underwood Standard Portable on which he probably wrote *A Moveable Feast*. (He actually seems to have preferred the Royal Quiet Deluxe.)

3 Pif, the dog in the cartoon strip of this name, featured (from 1948) in the French Communist daily *L'Humanité*.

4 This is an affluent small town in the eastern suburbs of Paris.

5 Interview with Jean-Yves Jouannais and Christophe Duchâtelet

1 *Whatever* is the English translation by Paul Hammond (London: Serpent's Tail, 1998) of *Extension du domaine de la lutte* (Paris: Editions Paul Nadeau, 1994), which more literally means *Extension of the Domain of Struggle*. The other works mentioned are Houellebecq's essay *Rester vivant* (Paris: La Différence, 1991) and *La Poursuite du bonheur*, a collection of poems first published as part of the same volume. His study of Lovecraft has been translated into English as *H. P. Lovecraft: Against the World, Against Life*, translated by Dorna Khazeni (London: Gollancz, 2008).

2 In a standard English translation of this work, Kant refers to

potential suicide in these terms: 'a nature whose law it would be to destroy life itself by means of the same feeling whose destination is to impel toward the furtherance of life would contradict itself and would therefore not subsist as nature' (Immanuel Kant, *Groundwork of the Metaphysics of Morals*, translated by Mary Gregor (Cambridge: Cambridge University Press, p. 32)).

7 Creative absurdity

1 Jean Cohen (1919–1994), a theorist of poetry, was the author of two works in this field: *La Structure du langage poétique* [*The Structure of Poetic Language*] (Paris: Flammarion/Champs, 1966) and *Le Haut Langage* [*Lofty Language*] (Paris: Flammarion, 1979). The second was reprinted shortly after the author's death (Paris: José Corti, 1995).

2 In his *Manifeste du surréalisme*, André Breton claimed that Paul Valéry, the poet, had told him that he (Valéry) would never condescend to writing such a banal sentence as 'The marquise went out at five o'clock' – the kind of sentence that realist novelists (as opposed to symbolist or surrealist poets) are obliged to write.

3 That is, a literary style associated with the kind of texts frequently published by Les Éditions de Minuit: often experimental, with a tendency to minimalism.

8 The party

1 The French travel company Nouvelles Frontières, founded in 1967, was originally meant to bring tourism (often to quite exotic places) within the reach of a wider public; these days, it is a branch of the German TUI group.

2 UCPA (Union des centres sportifs de plein air) is a French not-for-profit organization that provides sports holidays for younger people.

3 Lexomil is another name for bromazepam, an anti-anxiety medicine.

9 Time out

1 The *Salon de la vidéo hot* was a forum for porn videos; the Espace Champerret is an exhibition centre near the Porte de Champerret in north-west Paris.

2 Now Fnac Darty, a company selling electrical goods.

3 The first lines of Goethe's famous poem 'Der Erlkönig', which has often been set to music. The words mean: 'Who is riding so late through the night and wind? / It is the father with his child.'

4 An allusion to the 'civic wake-up call' that had featured on the front page of the previous issue of *Les Inrockuptibles* (on the controversy over illegal immigrants). [Houellebecq's note]

5 Robert Hue and Jean-Pierre Chevènement were, respectively, Communist and Socialist leaders at the time when this essay was published.

6 INSEE is the French National Institute for Statistics.

7 Bertrand Leclair (b. 1961) is a French novelist and playwright.

8 Eugénie Grandet, the heroine of Balzac's novel of the same name, is bullied by her avaricious father and betrayed by her lover.

9 Bernard Tapie (b. 1943) is a businessman and media figure embroiled in many legal difficulties – the kind of figure who greatly interested Balzac.

10 Paul-Loup Sulitzer (b. 1946) is a financier and novelist, often mocked for his commercial attitude to writing.

11 Maurice Nadeau (1911–2013) was a French writer and a critic who supported the work of contemporary avant-garde writers such as Jean Genet.

12 Valérie Taillefer works in press relations for the publishing company Calmann-Lévy.

13 Christian Bruel (b. 1948) is a French children's writer.

14 Valerie Solanas (1936–1988) published the radical feminist polemic *S.C.U.M. Manifesto* (Society for Cutting Up Men) in 1967, available online: http://kunsthallezurich.ch/sites/default/files/scum_manifesto.pdf. She shot and wounded Andy Warhol in 1968. The book by Michel Bulteau is *Flowers (d'après Warhol)* (Paris: La Différence, 1989).

10 Opera Bianca

1 Opera Bianca is a mobile sound installation designed by sculptor Gilles Touyard; the music is by Brice Pauset. This installation is made up of seven mobile objects whose shapes evoke human furnishings. During bright phases, these objects, motionless and white on a white background, store light energy. They dissipate this energy in dark phases, emitting a waning luminescence as they intersect in space – but without touching; their appearance is then similar to the ghostly spots which cross the retina when you get dazzled.

The text comes in during the dark phases. It's broken down into twelve sequences read by two invisible reciters (a male voice, a female voice). The random order of the sequences changes from one performance to another.

The first performance took place on 10 September 1997 at the Centre d'Art Contemporain Georges-Pompidou (Paris). [Houellebecq's note]

11 Letter to Lakis Proguidis

1 Lakis Proguidis (b. 1947) is a French novelist and founder of the review *L'Atelier du roman* dedicated to studies of the novel as a genre.
2 Jean-Didier Vincent (b. 1935) is a French neurobiologist and neuropsychiatrist; Trịnh Xuân Thuận (b. 1948) is a Vietnamese-American astrophysicist.
3 Oulipo, to which the novelist Georges Perec (*Life, a User's Manual* etc.) made such a contribution, is the Ouvroir de littérature potentielle (Workshop for Potential Literature), a gathering of experimental writers who produce works subject to various formal constraints; *lettrisme*, sometimes known as lettrism or letterism, is an avant-garde movement that originally focused on generating texts of a Dadaist or Surrealist kind.
4 Christian Bobin (b. 1951) is a French writer best known for novels with a religious slant (about Saint Francis of Assisi, for example).
5 Paolo Coelho (b. 1974), a Brazilian writer, is, like Bobin, best known for the spiritual themes he tackles.

6 Michel Lacroix (b. 1946) is a French philosopher who has written widely about New Age ideologies, personal development, etc.

12 The question of paedophilia

1 This essay was published following the Dutroux affair, as part of a dossier on questions raised by child protection and paedophilia, and in response to the following questionnaire:

> I – How do you explain the impact of the Dutroux affair? What do you think a child is today? What is a paedophile?
>
> II – As a minor, did you have a loving relationship with an adult and what memories have you kept of it? Do you personally have memories of infantile sexuality?
>
> III – Do you think that specialists and spokespersons for children are telling us everything? Do you have anything to add? [Houellebecq's note]

13 Humanity, the second stage

1 On Valerie Solanas, see note 14 to 'Time out', above.
2 Valerie Solanas, *S.C.U.M. Manifesto*, available online: http://kunsthallezurich.ch/sites/default/files/scum_manifesto.pdf.

17 Interview with Christian Authier

1 Pierre Assouline (b. 1953) is a French writer known largely for his biographies and his many polemical contributions to literary and cultural debates.
2 Guillaume Durand (b. 1952) is a French journalist, very active on radio and television.
3 These brands, and *Le Guide du routard* (a popular set of tourist guides), are mocked in Houellebecq's novel *Platform*.
4 Jérôme Jaffré (b. 1949) is a French academic and political analyst.
5 Julien Lepers (b. 1949) is a French radio and television presenter.
6 François Nourissier (1927–2011) was a French writer and a long-standing member of the Académie Goncourt.

7 Alain Finkielkraut (b. 1949) is a French writer, one of the 'Nouveaux philosophes'; he has written widely about current affairs.

21 Philippe Muray in 2002

1 The novel *Rose Bonbon*, by Nicolas Jones-Gorlin (b. 1972), was published in 2002 by Gallimard. The Enfant Bleu association, which protects children from maltreatment, complained that the novel might distress victims of paedophilia. After a debate about possible censorship, the then Minister of the Interior, Nicolas Sarkozy, intervened to ensure that the book could be sold, even to minors, but he advised booksellers to show 'responsibility'.

2 Taslima Nasrin (b. 1962) is a Bangladeshi-Swedish writer and activist, whose critiques of misogyny in Islam led to her life being threatened in Bangladesh, hence her flight to Sweden.

3 Edwy Plenel (b. 1952) is a French journalist. The book in question was an essay by Daniel Lindenberg (1940–2018), a historian of ideas, called *Le Rappel à l'ordre: Enquête sur les nouveaux réactionnaires* (Paris: Seuil, 2002); this short work denounced many contemporary writers as reactionary (sexist, racist, etc.) – Houellebecq was one of the authors targeted, as was Philippe Muray, and others more generally seen as liberal or even left-wing, such as Alain Badiou. Plenel defended (in qualified terms) Lindenberg's critique.

4 Pierre-André Taguieff (b. 1946) is a French writer on political themes, in particular racism and anti-Semitism.

5 Maurice Dantec (1959–2016) was a French-Canadian musician and writer, who depicted what he saw as the nihilism of much of contemporary literary culture.

6 Jean-François Revel (1924–2006) was a French writer who moved from socialism to a defence of liberal (and often American) values; Joseph de Maistre 1753–1821) was a Savoyard philosopher who rejected the French Revolution and supported monarchism and the Papacy.

22 Towards a semi-rehabilitation of the hick

1 Guy Bedos (1934–2020) was a French screenwriter and comedian, generally seen as being on the left. For the sense of 'hick' in this essay, see note 4 below.

2 Maurice Siné, known as Siné (1928–2016), was a French cartoonist, associated with *Charlie Hebdo*; he was sacked from the magazine for anti-Semitic remarks.

3 Siné expressed his dislike of Catherine Millet's explicit description of her own sex life.

4 Jean Cabut, known as Cabu (1938–2015) was a French cartoonist murdered in the attack on the offices of *Charlie Hebdo* in 2015; he used the term *'beauf'*, a slang French word for *'beau-frère'* (brother-in-law) to refer to a Frenchman who held commonplace and vulgar opinions (xenophobia, misogyny, etc.)

23 Conservatism, a source of progress

1 Taguieff developed the concept of *bougisme* (from *bouger*, to move) to refer to the way we are all now expected to keep 'moving' (i.e. be increasingly active in the globalized world of constant consumption, communication and exchange).

2 *Loft Story* was a French TV reality show (2001–2002), similar to *Big Brother* (though the French version aroused more overt hostility among the French than its UK equivalent among the British).

3 Tariq Ramadan (b. 1962) is a Swiss Muslim scholar whose views (which cannot easily be labelled as simply 'reformist', 'fundamentalist', etc.) have proved controversial.

4 Henri Queuille (1884–1970), from Corrèze (not far from Poitou, hence Houellebecq's reference to 'Poitevin'), was a distinguished politician from the Radical-Socialist Party.

25 I'm normal. A normal writer

1 Jean Ristat (b. 1943) is a French poet and publisher.

2 Frédéric Beigbeder (b. 1963) is a French writer and critic, and executive director of the magazine *Lui*. He set up the literary Prix de Flore.

3 Lydie Salvayre (b. 1948) is a French writer who also practised as a psychiatrist.

4 Marc Weitzmann (b. 1959) is a French writer and journalist; he often writes about current life in France from a sociological perspective.

5 Marie Darrieussecq (b. 1969) is a French writer and psycho-analyst whose novel *Truismes* (1969) tells the story of a female sex worker who changes into a sow. It was translated by Linda Coverdale as *Pig Tales* (London: Faber, 1997).

6 This phrase is well known to readers of H. P. Lovecraft. It is in the language of Cthulhu and means 'Ah! Ah! Cthulhu awakens!'

7 Ariel Wizman (b. 1962) is a French musician, writer and actor.

8 Vincent Ravalec (b. 1962) is a French writer.

9 BHL is the common nickname for Bernard-Henri Lévy (b. 1948), a French philosopher and writer who is often in the news.

10 Raphaël Sorin (1942–2021) was a publisher who published, among others, Houellebecq.

11 Philippe Vandel (b. 1962) is a French journalist.

26 I have read my whole life long

1 On the occasion of the fiftieth anniversary of the popular Paris-based publishing house *J'ai lu*, Michel Houellebecq sent them this text, which was reprinted in *Interventions 2* (Paris: Flammarion, 2009). The title of this essay alludes to the name of the *J'ai lu* collection (meaning 'I have read').

2 The readers of the former collection tended to be younger than the readers of the latter.

3 *Graziella* is a romantic novel by Alphonse de Lamartine (1790–1869).

4 The *Rouge et Or* collection is aimed at children.

27 Soil cutting

1 Agro: the Institut national agronomique.

28 The lost text

1 Rachid Amirou (1956–2011) was a French sociologist of Kabyle origin. His work investigated tourism from a sociological and psychoanalytical perspective.
2 Marquenterre is a nature park on the English Channel, noted for its migratory birds; *sabotiers* are clog makers.
3 *'Cantatrix sopranica L.', Scientific Papers by Georges Perec*, translated by Antony Melville et al. (London: Atlas Press, 2008).

29 Interview with Frédéric Beigbeder

1 Dominique Voynet (b. 1958) is a French Green politician.
2 Paul Léautaud (1872–1956) was a French writer, noted mainly as a drama critic and diarist. In later years his face, wizened and wrinkly, was often animated by a cheeky grin.
3 Of these three singer-songwriters, Serge Gainsbourg (1928–1991) had a rugged, raddled, unkempt face; Michel Polnareff (b. 1944) is known for his long blond-brown hair and huge dark glasses, and resembles Houellebecq around the mouth; Joseph 'Joe' Dassin (1938–1980) was rather like Liberace, except with bigger hair.
4 Michel Debré (1912–1996) was a French politician largely responsible for the current French Constitution.
5 Benoît Duteurtre (b. 1960) is a French novelist; he has criticized the French musical avant-garde (Boulez), and defended 'classical' novels (Balzac), as well as the work of Houellebecq.
6 Gaspard Proust (b. 1976) is a comedian of Slovenian-Swiss origin. His TV sketches lasted five minutes; he has a dark, mordant sense of humour.
7 Albert Camus' *The Myth of Sisyphus*, a depiction of life as an absurd and repetitive task, ends with the words 'We must imagine Sisyphus being happy.'
8 'Bobo' is slang for 'bourgeois-bohémien', i.e. someone with artistic aspirations who also enjoys a comfortable lifestyle. A 'Maurrassian' is a follower of Charles Maurras (1868–1952), notorious for his royalist, nationalist, and anti-Semitic views.

30 A remedy for the exhaustion of being

1 Marc Lathuillière is a French photographer known for his anthropological approach: as his website states, 'In 2014, he curated a double exhibition for the Month of Photography in Paris with Michel Houellebecq' (https://www.lathuilliere.com/en/about/).

2 'At the origin of this approach, his main series *Musée national*, has seen him shooting the portrait of about a thousand French people wearing the same mask for the last 15 years' (https://www.lathuilliere.com/en/about/).

3 *Plus belle la vie* is a TV series set in a fictional district of Marseille.

31 Interview with Marin De Viry and Valérie Toranian

1 Léon Bloy (1846–1917) was a French writer who moved from a youthful hatred of Catholicism to a fierce and at times dyspeptic defence of it.

2 These were the 'thirty glorious years' (1945–1975) in which France recovered from defeat in the Second World War and became a modern, prosperous country.

3 Georges Wolinski (1934–2015) was a French cartoonist, murdered in the assault on the *Charlie Hebdo* offices in 2015.

4 The *Manif pour tous* [*Demo for all*] is an umbrella group for several associations (mainly Catholic, frequently right-wing) hostile to same-sex marriage.

5 The *veilleurs* are a branch of the *Manif pour tous*; they gather at nocturnal sit-ins to protest against same-sex marriage.

6 Pascal Bruckner (b. 1948) is a French novelist and essayist. He has criticized the notion of Islamophobia.

7 *The Tears of the White Man: Compassion as Contempt*, translated by William R. Beer (New York: Free Press, 1986) is Bruckner's critique of liberal Westerners who are (in his view) too prone to self-flagellation over e.g. the history of colonialism.

8 Stéphane Bern (b. 1963) is a French journalist with a particular interest in royal families.

9 *30 Millions d'amis* is a foundation that defends the well-being of household pets.

35 Conversation with Geoffroy Lejeune

1 This conversation was published as a response to the question 'What the Catholic Church should do to restore its own splendour and repair our dilapidated civilization'.

37 The Vincent Lambert affair should not have taken place

1 Vincent Lambert (1976–2019) was a French psychiatric nurse. After a road accident in 2008, he was reduced to living in a persistent vegetative state. His widow, Rachel, wanted him to be allowed to die, apparently in accordance with wishes he had expressed before the accident. His mother, a devout Catholic, wanted him to be kept alive. After a prolonged legal battle, the courts ruled in favour of his widow; he died in July 2019.

2 I don't know to whom we owe this amusing quotation about Sparta; maybe Chesterton, it's his kind of style. [Houellebecq's note]